H. Thomas Hurt
North Texas State University

Michael D. Scott
West Virginia University

James C. McCroskey
West Virginia University

Communication in the classroom

 ADDISON-WESLEY PUBLISHING COMPANY

Reading, Massachusetts
Menlo Park, California • London • Amsterdam
Don Mills, Ontario • Sydney

ISBN 0-201-03048-9
DEFGHIJ-AL-79

This text is dedicated to the founding members of the Instructional Communication Division of the International Communication Association and to the over 3,000 public-school teachers and administrators from eleven states with whom we have worked and learned during the past four summers. Thank you for your inspiration and insight.

Morgantown, West Virginia   HTH
August 1977   MDS
                                                                    JCM

Contents

1

Introduction

What you are about to read may be one of the shortest chapters in publishing history. Nevertheless, the information presented here should provide you with some helpful clues about what you can expect from us and from this book. We hope you will find it a valuable introduction to the format and purposes of *Communication in the Classroom*.

THE PURPOSE OF THE BOOK

Several years ago we began teaching a seminar-workshop for in-service public-school teachers and administrators. We called the course "Communication in the Classroom." Our general purpose was *not* to teach communication theory to educators, but to show them how principles of communication could be applied to classroom settings, so that student learning might be facilitated and improved. We had long been convinced that the process of teaching and the process of communication were synonymous, and we were not alone in this conviction. Educational scholars have been compiling massive amounts of research on the impact of instructional technologies (e.g., forms of mass media) on learning. In addition, the federal government has been investing large sums of money in the development of instructional programming for the media—*Sesame Street* and *The Electric Company* are well-known examples.

We view all of these efforts as a highly encouraging sign of increasing interest in determining the effects of communication on learning. The focus of our class, however, was not on instructional media, but on human, inter-personal communication—face-to-face interaction between students and teachers. We wanted to synthesize research about human communication taken from several disciplines into a usable structure for professional educators.

Since it was not possible for our students to read a variety of different sources, we began to search for a textbook that would simplify life for them. We examined books in sociology, psychology, social psychology, educational psychology, and communication. While many of the books dealt with communication and learning, they did so only tangentially and sometimes by inference. To add to our problems, human communication (as opposed to speech) was a relatively new academic discipline and many of our students had not even had a basic communication course. Consequently, we needed a book which met two criteria: (1) it had to explain basic communication concepts; and (2) it had to integrate those concepts into learning environments. Since there were no texts which met both those criteria, we decided to write one. This book is the result of our efforts.

The information included in this text is taken from a variety of social-science disciplines, most predominately from the field of human communication. Much of the book is based on the results of original research generated by members of the Instructional Communication Division of the International Communication Association, whose honorary chairman for years has been the well-known researcher in the area of communication and instruction, Professor Max Black.

We have organized the text along lines suggested by the two criteria noted above. Chapter 2 provides an overview of the principles of the human communication process. The remaining chapters relate variables in that process to instruction. Chapter 3 is devoted to the general interrelationships between learning theory and communication theory, so that you can see the obvious areas of overlap. Chapters 4 and 5 deal with information acquisition (sensory communication channels) and information processing (encoding and decoding messages) in the classroom. Chapter 6 deals with nonverbal messages and learning, and Chapter 7 discusses the ways in which students perceive teachers as sources of communication and the impact of those perceptions on a variety of student behaviors. In Chapters 8 and 9 we discuss the reasons why students do and do not communicate, including an in-depth analysis of a critical but relatively unknown learning disability called communication apprehension. The remaining three chapters define the nature of interpersonal communication in the classroom, including the effects of expectancies on communication, interpersonal solidarity, and conflict and communication management.

HOW TO USE THE BOOK

All of the remaining chapters open with a list of cognitive objectives. We have included them to help direct your reading. By the time you have completed a chapter, you should be able to do the things requested by the objectives.

Nearly all of these objectives are low-level cognitive objectives. That is, they only call for acquisition of the meanings normally assigned to concepts by the people who work with them. Your instructor may wish to supplement these with higher-order objectives.

Because this is a book about the impact of communication on learning, we have provided some examples that may seem highly evaluative to you. In addition, some of our own statements may seem judgmental. Our purpose is not to criticize the teaching profession *in toto,* but rather to impress on you the powerful effect communication can have on student achievement. For this reason, we do say that certain teacher behaviors, *taken in the context of the communication process,* are good or bad. Related to this issue, you should be aware that we cannot provide you with specific rules of thumb for solving specific communication-related problems in specific classes. What we hope to do instead is increase your sensitivity to the communication process, so that you may adjust your own teaching style to your unique classroom situation.

Finally, this is *not* a book about how to teach communication skills to public-school students. Rather, it represents our belief that certification of competence in a particular subject matter is not enough to certify competence in teaching. The act of teaching is a communicative act. To communicate the subject matter of a course to a variety of different students requires an *understanding* of the process of communication, and *practice* in implementing the process. Our hope is that this book will provide you with the former in order that your experience with the latter will be more rewarding. There is, indeed, a difference between knowing and teaching, and that difference is communication in the classroom.

he Process of Human Communication

After reading this chapter, you should be able to do the following.

1. Explain the major misconceptions about human communication.

2. Explain why human communication is
   a. a process
   b. transactional
   c. symbolic
   d. multidimensional

3. Define human communication.

4. Distinguish between these two kinds of human communication:
   a. accidental
   b. intentional

5. Define these three dimensions of human communication:
   a. cultural
   b. sociological
   c. psychological

6. Explain the role of feedback in human communication.

In a day in the life of a teacher, no other activity is as pervasive as is human communication. In a day in the life of a student, no other activity is as essential to success as is human communication. But there is nothing new or unique about either of these notions. You, no doubt, have been cognizant of both for some period of time.

But the fact that you recognize the importance of human communication in the classroom environment does not necessarily mean that you fully understand the process of human communication in the classroom *environment*. If we were to assume otherwise, there would be no conceivable reason for us to advance our thinking here or in the chapters that follow. Thus, in this second chapter, we begin our analysis of human communication in the classroom by examining some of the more common misconceptions about human communication, and then move on to the nature of the process itself.

MISCONCEPTIONS ABOUT HUMAN COMMUNICATION

Misconception I: Communication Is a Universal Panacea

Throughout history people have attempted to discover some universal panacea capable of remedying the many afflictions that have plagued humankind. Examples range from the widespread practice of bloodletting during the seventeenth century to the snake-oil elixirs eagerly purchased from traveling medicine men during the "Wild West" days of the nineteenth-century American frontier.

While people are much more sophisticated today than they were in seventeenth-century Europe or nineteenth-century America, they remain susceptible to the lure of a supposed new and powerful cure-all.

As teachers, for example, we have found that a number of our students have taken to heart a notion advanced by many responsible people in responsible positions. The notion is, quite simply, that human communication is a panacea for the social and psychological maladies that currently abound. As the story goes, communication is so powerful an elixir that it can be prescribed for any of the social or psychological ailments that the modern-day individual is susceptible to—the only caveat being that the individual must understand communication and practice it within the limits of his or her understanding.

You can probably recall the student activist days of the sixties. How many times did you hear, or maybe even say, a phrase that sounded something like, "What we need is meaningful dialogue between faculty and students." In many cases, these dialogues ended in failure and the resulting frustration frequently took a more militant form.

The problems in the sixties and the problems we confront now are not necessarily caused by the failure of communication to produce some desired outcome. Rather, these problems are in many cases linked to our own failure to understand the intricacies and complexities inherent in the nature of human communication. The *act* of communicating is not sufficient grounds for saying that communication has resolved a problem. To simply tell problem students that you wish to be their friend is not always sufficient action to guarantee such an outcome.

Certainly, human communication is important—particularly with regard to teaching and the classroom. But we happen to believe what you no doubt already suspect: it is not a panacea. Rather, it is an essential human behavior that people engage in so that they can maximize rewarding experiences and minimize punishing ones.

Misconception II: We Need More Communication

Closely related to the misconception that human communication is a panacea for human ills is the assumption that the quantity of communication in a given environment is functionally related to the quality of life in that environment. For example, it is probably not atypical for us to hear our friends and colleagues say, "What we need around this place is more information," or, "Fred would certainly be a more effective administrator if he would communicate more with his faculty." But is it really wise to assume that the quality of an environment is best measured by the quantity of communication in that environment? By the same token, is it wise to assume that the quality of an environment can be improved by recommending that the people in that environment communicate more?

Before you attempt to answer either question, consider the fact that humans have limited information-processing capabilities. Information theorists tell us that while the human eye is capable of processing about *five million* bits of information per second, the human brain is capable of processing only about *five hundred* bits of information per second. In effect, this means that you can't possibly process all of the information that you might be exposed to in a given second, much less in an hour or a day. In light of this, think about the variety of communication activities that you engage in on a single day. That is, think about the several roles you assume when you process the communication of others. If you are like most people, you will quickly see that the amount of communication occurring in your environment on a single day is staggering.

Consider the case of a typical high-school student named Randi. Randi is awakened every morning by her clock radio playing the latest "Top 40" hits and providing her with the news and weather. She goes downstairs and glances at the newspaper. Her father is watching an early-morning talk show on television. Her mother is asking if she is going out with Mike again. The telephone rings and it is her friend Ellen, who says that she will be by in fifteen minutes to give Randi a ride to school. On the way to school, Randi and Ellen listen to the car radio for the results of last night's basketball games. In addition, they carry on a running conversation about Mike and Buddy, the two boys who have asked them to go to a party Friday night. At school, Randi goes to her homeroom, talks to her friends, listens to announcements, and then begins her classes—American history, algebra, biology, home economics, and art. She is assigned three papers to write, and a total of 150 pages of reading. At home that evening she talks to her parents, listens to records, and spends an hour on the telephone with Mike. The very fact that Randi is able to learn anything at all seems overwhelming. Most instructional environments operate on the assumption that our environment is "underloaded" with communication, not overloaded. Educational systems focus on the ability to skillfully generate messages. Students give speeches, write essays, and respond in class. In short, they are trained to be effective sources, and often this training is done at the exclusion of training students to be effective receivers.

The point we wish to make is that the amount of communication taking place in a majority of human environments far exceeds the information-processing capabilities of the people in the environment. Consequently, rather than improving the quality of the environment, more communication may detract from its quality. To put it simply, more is not necessarily better.

Misconception III: Communication Can Break Down

While the preceding two misconceptions are held by many, the notion that communication can break down seems to be held by a majority of the people we come into contact with. Why is that? In answer to our own question, we believe people use the word "breakdown" to avoid coming to grips with the true nature of the problems they experience when communicating with certain people.

As a case in point, consider two individuals whose transactions with one another inevitably lead to conflict and the termination of their communicating transaction. Assuming that this happens to them frequently, they both might attribute this inability to communicate to the many "breakdowns" in communication that they have had. However, the fact that they elicit each other's more irascible tendencies neither means that they can't communicate nor that communication between them has broken down. And the reasoning behind this conclusion can be simply put: Poor communication may be symptomatic of deep-seated problems existing between the individuals involved. It may be, in other words, a symptom of the disease rather than the disease itself. When we conclude that the problem is attributable to a breakdown in communication, we run the risk of ignoring the real problem in favor of attending to its symptoms.

Misconception IV: Communication Is a Good Thing

We have asked hundreds of teachers and students (probably closer to thousands) if they believe communication is a good thing. Almost universally they reply, "Yes!" This is not an uncommon response and its frequency of occurrence is probably linked to our first popular misconception: Communication is a universal panacea. Since we have listed this belief as a misconception, you may have concluded with some surprise that the authors of a text about communication in the classroom don't think communication is a good thing. So, before you get bogged down in a misconception about *us*, we would like to state our belief that communication is neither good nor bad. Communication is merely a tool that helps us adapt to and change our environment. Consider the following example. A teacher may advocate that the present educational system should be physically destroyed. On the other hand, a teacher may advocate that the educational system is the best we've got, and that any changes should be made peacefully and within the legal options available. In both cases, communication is merely a tool for adaptation and change; communication did not cause the teacher to take either position. Thus, we believe communication is a tool that can facilitate learning. But the *value* of what is learned is an issue with which teachers and students must deal.

Misconception V: Meanings Are in Words
One of the biggest misconceptions about communication is the idea that words alone convey meanings. When we subscribe to this misconception, we reduce our ability to communicate effectively, because we operate as though saying something is the same as communicating it. When we make an assignment for a term paper due on Wednesday, and then become incensed when we do not receive it until Friday, we are, in part, angry because when we say the word "Wednesday," it should mean "Wednesday." Any fool can understand *that*. Because we take communication (and words) so much for granted, our failures to communicate effectively are often blamed on others. If we consider communication (teaching) as the process whereby ideas are adapted to students in order to adapt students to ideas, we must realize that ideas are in our heads, and nowhere else. Words (and nonverbal symbols) are simply mechanisms we use to transmit and stimulate ideas. So remember: *words don't mean, people mean.*

We believe this principle to be fundamental to any understanding of the human communication process. Teaching is in large part the creation of common meanings between teachers and students. It is a process that continues throughout life, whether in the classroom or not.

Obviously, the meanings students bring to the classroom may differ from those the teacher has. Problems caused by these differences became a major area of concern for the Department of Health, Education, and Welfare during the 1960s. It occurred to somebody that it might be a good idea to match teachers with students of an ethnically similar background (reread that as: students and teachers who shared similar meanings). While this "new" idea was not bad, what frequently resulted was that teachers talked exclusively about things for which their students already had some meaning. (This has since come to be called the "tyranny of relevance.") Often, teachers were hired because they shared meanings with students, and not because of their ability to teach. We believe that real learning, in large part, involves the ability to use alternative meanings for things already known, or to acquire new meanings for new things. We will talk about this in greater detail in Chapter 5, but the process occurs by the effective use of communication, which is constantly being restructured to meet the axiom: Words don't mean, people mean.

Misconception VI: Communication Is a Natural Ability

Many people operate on the assumption that we communicate because we are born with the ability to do so. For a while, this misconception even became the focus of a theological debate, with the "natural ability" advocates arguing that if infants were never permitted contact with communicating humans, they would spontaneously develop the "natural language of God." Unfortunately for the infant subjects, most of them died as a result of this contact deprivation.

Of course, in this enlightened educational era, we no longer attempt such brutal learning experiments. On the other hand, public schools still seem to operate under the assumption that communication is a natural ability. Communication is the most ignored area of knowledge in our schools. Many schools do teach composition, public speaking, writing, and typing, but these are primarily skills-oriented courses and have very little to do with understanding the human communication process.

To communicate well is not a natural ability. It is learned, and involves at least two steps: an understanding of how communication works and an opportunity to put that understanding to work. Most teachers receive some of the latter training; very few, the first. The absence of this training is a serious obstacle to effective teaching, for teaching demands knowledge of the communication process. As a colleague once noted, "Trying to teach without understanding its relationship to the communication process is a bit like eating a chocolate sundae without the ice cream—a bit sticky, and not very satisfying."

HUMAN COMMUNICATION CONCEPTUALIZED

Human Communication Is a Process

Given the preceding framework, we would like to begin our discussion of the communication process by pointing out that people often think their communication behavior remains relatively consistent from one day to the next. Fortunately, for teachers, nothing could be further from the truth. Our communication behaviors are constantly changing as a function of the changes in our environment. If this were not the case, we would be rendered incapable of

Human communication is pervasive in the lives of all our students. Can you find a student in this photograph who you think is *not* communicating?

coping with any new or unique situation that happened to confront us. When we say that communication is a process, we are saying that communication is continuously changing—accordingly, it has no tangible beginning, middle, or end.

The important thing to remember here, and to be sensitive to, is the fact that as a teacher you initiate communication with students the moment you enter the classroom, frequently before you say a word. These initial messages to students are often the most critical in establishing subsequent classroom interaction. One high-school teacher told us that she spends as much time preparing for this "first contact" as she does for any other unit of instruction taught the entire semester. Her reason for doing this was simple: "If I create the climate in which the communication process between me and my students is triggered, then I have a better idea of how to adapt to changes in it. If I can exercise some control over the communication process, I can exercise more control over what my students are learning."

We couldn't agree more wholeheartedly. If you think of communication as a process with no tangible boundaries, you will be thinking about it correctly, but it may seem so abstract that you will be tempted to ignore its potential impact on learning. To overcome this temptation, try to do what this experienced teacher has done. Stick a somewhat artificial beginning and ending on the process (but don't forget that they're artificial). Our teacher "began" communicating the moment she came into the sensory range of her students and "ended" the moment she left the range. Within that artificial context, she believed it to be her professional obligation to create a communication environment that could directly or indirectly influence learning. Her communication boundaries forced her to constantly focus her attention on her job. The boundaries she defined may not be suitable for you. If not, try some you feel more comfortable with. The point is this: if communication is the difference between knowing and teaching, then control of the context in which the process of communication occurs will help you to become more than just an efficient storehouse of knowledge. And that's what good teaching is all about.

Human Communication Is Transactional

Assuming that communication is continuously changing, there must be a number of environmental agents that precipitate change. One such environment agent is the communication transaction itself.

When teachers communicate with students, they usually have some specific purpose in mind. They may need to know, for example, whether or not students have completed the assigned homework; or, if the students haven't completed the homework, they may need to know the reason why. But regardless of the specific purpose, a teacher operates under the assumption that students will respond in a manner that reflects the teacher's initial purpose for communicating. But what happens if students fail to respond, or respond in totally unsuitable ways? Do teachers simply shrug their shoulders in disbelief or point the way to the principal's office? In all likelihood, teachers will do neither. Rather, they will probably reassess their own communication behavior in the effort to determine whether it was inappropriate for the kind of response they desired to elicit from their students. As a function of this reassessment, many teachers will probably formulate a new set of communication behaviors and again attempt to elicit the desired student response. Thus, when we say that the process of human communication is transactional, we are simply saying that people adapt and change their own communication behavior—even as it is occurring—in response to what they perceive another person is communicating to them.

One final comment: We have been hearing a great deal about the failures of the teaching profession. In addition, we have spent a great deal of time explaining to you the complex nature of the communication (teaching) process. Both of these things may make you feel discouraged about teaching. We are not opposed to an important profession such as teaching maintaining some kind of critical standards, and we may seem critical from time to time throughout this book. But we would like to tell you now about a high-school math teacher in an Appalachian farm community who understood the complexities of the transactional nature of the communication process and used that understanding to help overcome some of the criticisms we have been hearing about public-school teachers.

The teacher told us that her first year of teaching had primarily been devoted to basic algebra. Since she knew that most of her students were "farm kids," she had used examples related to farms. Her time-motion problems involved plowing fields and driving produce to town by a certain time across a certain distance. Her students solved for such unknowns as production yield per square acre. In short, she did all the things she had been taught to make her material relevant. The problem was, it didn't seem to work. The students simply didn't do well on the final exam. She had the same problem during the beginning of the spring semester. She tried asking her students directly what the problem was. They told her they just didn't like algebra. Finally, one of the more experienced teachers told her that because she was a woman, her farm examples turned her students off. They were certain she didn't know anything about farming.

A less concerned teacher might have refused to change and adapt to students. But the teacher we spoke to was determined that her students would learn basic algebra. She began her campaign with the assumption that their perceptions of her (see Chapter 7) and their attitudes about algebra would have to be changed. She became more friendly with her students and with their parents at P.T.A. meetings and the like. When it came time for spring farming activities, she made social calls at the homes of her students. She would talk to their parents about farming problems and even participate in some strenuous physical labor. Gradually, she began to help them plan for their production year. As stories about her began to spread among her students, she found that their verbal behavior in class increased, as did their willingness to learn. By the end of that semester, her class improved by one-and-a-half grade points.

This teacher was aware of a very important point about the transactional nature of communication: relevance involves more than simply talking about topics students talk about. She knew that transaction required adjusting to the characteristics of her students, so that her communication with them was improved *without having to compromise the material she wished to teach.*

Human Communication Is Symbolic

Human communication is also the symbolic means by which we relate our realm of experience to another human being. The importance of this fact to teaching cannot be minimized—if teachers were unable to abstract and symbolize what they had learned, they would have no tangible means of relating their learning experiences to their students.

When we were discussing the misconception that words have meaning, we pointed out that meanings are learned as a result of our experiences with things, and are thus arbitrary. The same is true of symbols. We learn that certain symbols (verbal and nonverbal) stand for certain things, and we use these symbols accordingly. Thus, it is possible for two people to use the same symbol to refer to two different things, or use two different symbols to stand for the same thing. Of course, we need symbols to stand for the things about which we communicate. But failure to recognize the fact that symbols, like meanings, are arbitrary can cause a great many communication problems, particularly in the classroom.

Consider the rather humorous experience of one of the authors of this book. Shortly after moving to West Virginia from California, one of his students in an introductory course in communication asked him if there were "ramps" in California. Since the question had followed one about the traffic and smog in Los Angeles, our colleague interpreted the question to mean, "Do they have concrete ramps that enable people to enter or exit the freeway systems in California?" As a result, he replied casually, "Of course, usually about one ramp for each mile of the freeway." Much to our colleague's chagrin, the entire class broke into hysterical laughter, prompting him to inquire about what was so funny. His inquisitor, trying to control himself, pointed out that a ramp was a small, pungent, onionlike plant that, when digested, emits an odor that would drive bears from the forest.

This example serves to point out what happens when people use the same symbol to refer to different things. Our colleague and his students had fallen victims to the same mistake many of us make: we tend to think the symbol is the thing. Try to remember that communication is symbolic and that symbols are merely devices we use to convey messages. They are arbitrary and flexible and, as such, can provide us with as many problems as they do advantages.

Human Communication Is Multidimensional

Just as human communication is processual, transactional, and symbolic, it is also multidimensional. Typically, however, people are not accustomed to thinking about the dimensions of their communication transactions or distinguishing among them. In the opinion of communication scholars, people communicate on at least three dimensions: a cultural dimension, a sociological dimension, and a psychological dimension.

Cultural dimension.   When people communicate on the cultural dimension, they base their communication behaviors on characteristics of the culture—e.g., beliefs, habits, customs, and language. In other words, they base their communication activities on the norms of the culture or the culture's accepted ways of behavior. Since the characteristics of a given culture are enduring and seldom subject to radical, overnight change, we can intuit rather accurately what the acceptable communication behaviors in the culture will be from one day to the next. For example, here in the United States a number of cultural norms dictate what is acceptable communication behavior from a teacher. At the elementary level, for instance, the teacher's communication behaviors are expected to be somewhat paternalistic. At the secondary level, however, teachers are expected to exhibit a set of communication behaviors that the student can model. Thus, when we base our communication behaviors on such knowledge, we are communicating solely on a cultural dimension.

Sociological dimension. Communication on the sociological dimension occurs when we structure our communication behaviors on the basis of a person's reference groups. Examples of such groups range from social organizations like fraternities and sororities to political action groups like the now-defunct Students for a Democratic Society. Like members of a culture, members of a reference group are expected to exhibit behaviors consistent with the norms and values of the reference group. For example, members of a political party are expected to behave in a manner that reflects the party's platform, while members of a particular labor union are expected to behave in a manner that is consistent with the union's stated goals.

As a function of our exposures to the various reference groups in our culture, we develop a set of expectancies about the kinds of behaviors that are typical of the members of the reference groups. We expect "red-necks," for example, to drink beer, wear hard hats, and display bumper stickers proclaiming "America—Love It or Leave It." On the other hand, we expect freaks to smoke dope, wear head bands, and accentuate every other statement with "right on" or "far out." When we structure our communication behaviors on such expectancies, we are communicating strictly on a sociological dimension.

Psychological dimension. Communication on the psychological dimension only occurs when we are in a position to know the unique rather then stereotypic characteristics of another person. By unique characteristics we mean the unique set of identity needs that are exhibited by an individual. Needless to say, communication on a psychological dimension is only possible when we know someone intimately. Obviously, within the classroom environment, teachers rarely communicate with their students on a psychological dimension. And, whether or not this is a desirable situation is a question that we would like to put off until we have had the opportunity to present and argue our entire case.

Human Communication Is a Process in Which One Individual Stimulates Meaning in the Mind of Another Individual by Means of Verbal and Nonverbal Messages

Few issues in the discipline of human communication are as heatedly contested as the one regarding how human communication should be defined. Some scholars define human communication in a wholly deterministic manner, asserting that it is "a process in which one person intentionally engages another person for purposes of eliciting a predetermined response from that person." As a result, they would argue that communication only occurs when one person intentionally transmits a message to another person for the purpose of having the person respond in a specific manner. By contrast, a number of scholars define communication as "any process where meaning is stimulated." Consequently, they would argue that communication occurs each time we attend to some agent in our environment and the agent stimulates meaning in our minds.

Since we are interested in human communication in the classroom, we think it is important that you are aware of the effects of both intentional and accidental communication on learning. Consequently, we have defined human communication as "the stimulation of meaning." In terms of the classroom, as long as this criterion has been met (whether it was intended or not), communication has taken place.

Intentional communication.   Intentional communication takes place whenever a source consciously and deliberately encodes a message for the purpose of stimulating some specific meaning in the mind of another person. Thus, whenever a teacher makes out a specific lesson plan, orally presents a homework assignment, or even reads a poem aloud to a group of students, intentional communication has taken place. From the point of view of the student, intentional communication has taken place when the specific message encoded by the teacher is consciously and deliberately decoded so as to produce the desired meaning (learning).

Accidental communication.   Accidental communication occurs when a person stimulates meaning in the mind of another without intending to do so. Not only does this occur frequently, it sometimes occurs without the person noticing it. The teacher who comes to class with bloodshot eyes and trembling hands accidentally communicates a great deal more than the day's planned lesson. Students may also engage in accidental communication when they avoid looking at the teacher directly, flush when it is their turn to translate a German sentence, and shift around uncomfortably when the teacher asks for volunteers. In case you haven't noticed, most accidental communication is nonverbal; we will discuss nonverbal communication in more detail in Chapter 6.

Obviously, most communication between people is never totally intentional or totally accidental. To help you better understand the interactive effects of these two kinds of communication, we have divided the communication world into a two-by-two matrix, as shown in Fig. 2.1. The columns have been labeled "Teacher" and the rows "Students." We have also numbered each of the cells in the matrix for easier reference.

Cell 1 describes the ideal communication world in the classroom. Both teacher and students know exactly what they are encoding and decoding and

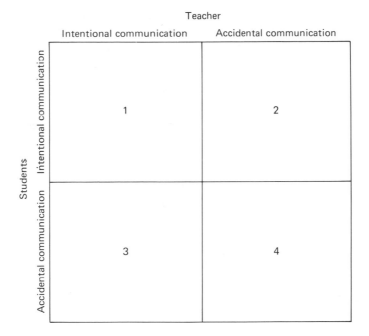

Fig. 2.1   The intentional-accidental communication matrix in the classroom.

the fidelity (accuracy) of the communication is perfect. Cell 4, on the other hand, is not such a happy place. Neither the teacher nor the students are exactly certain about everything they are encoding or decoding. In such an environment, learning is at a minimum.

   We have spent some time observing teachers and students in classrooms, and these observations coupled with interviews with members of both groups have yielded some interesting results regarding which cells teachers use and which cells students prefer in terms of describing classroom communication. Based on your own experiences, try to hypothesize which of the four cells are most representative of teachers' views and behaviors and which are most representative of students'.

   If your hypothesis for teachers predicted cell 3, you are probably wise beyond your years and experience. Most teachers we have talked to and observed think and act as though they deliberately and intentionally encode messages, but the probability that students decode correctly is only slightly better then chance.

   Students, on the other hand, frequently talk and act as though they prefer cell 2. That is, they deliberately decode and respond to messages which teachers are not even aware they are encoding. If you have ever taught at all, you've probably had the experience of walking into a classroom and feeling that the students may be snickering at you. This can be a discomfiting experience for a new teacher, especially when (s)he cannot figure out what's causing the humor.

If teachers are accustomed to cell 3, and students enjoy cell 2, then we have the makings of a serious classroom problem. When both teachers and students are attempting to gain control of the communication process at the expense of the other party, the potential for learning to be disrupted is immense. This is why we stress that it is the particular responsibility of teachers to know and understand how all of the variables in the communication process are interrelated. These variables are the subject of our next discussion. But before we go on, we would like to point out that if both of your hypotheses about students and teachers were correct, you probably ought to be in education administration.

HUMAN COMMUNICATION DESCRIBED

Human Communication Involves Encoding

Once we experience the need to communicate, we must translate the need into verbal and nonverbal symbols capable of being transmitted. This is the process of encoding and it includes at least two essential parts: (1) formulation of a message and adaptation of the message to the characteristics of the intended receiver of the message, and (2) transmission of the message to the receiver(s).

Formulation of the message.   People do not simply formulate a message and then articulate the message the best they can. People formulate messages on the basis of attending to the informational cues in their environment and their interpretation of such cues. For example, a teacher delivering a lecture on molecular biology may notice that a majority of the students look puzzled. As a result, the teacher attends to these informal cues, interprets them to mean the present message strategy is failing to stimulate the appropriate meanings in the minds of the students, and decides to formulate an entirely new message strategy—that is, one that the teacher thinks will be successful in stimulating the appropriate meanings. As you can see, then, formulating a message is both a function of attending to the informational cues in the environment and interpreting these cues.

Transmission of the message.   Typically, when people think of transmitting a message, they envision someone speaking. But, important as it is, the oral channel of communication constitutes only one of the channels open to us. Moreover, each of these additional channels has some impact on the messages we transmit—that is, in terms of how the receivers may interpret and respond to them. A teacher, for example, might orally communicate to students that a concept being dealt with is a significant one. If, however, the teacher orally communicated this with rolled eyes and raised eyebrows, this nonverbal behavior would contradict the verbal behavior. Since we deal with this topic at greater length in Chapter 6, suffice it to say that transmission of a message involves all of the channels of communication that are available to us.

Human Communication Involves Decoding

Once a message has been transmitted, the receiver must attend to the message and engage in the process of decoding. The process of decoding involves four phases.

Sensory involvement.   The process of decoding begins when our sensory mechanisms are stimulated. In most communication transaction, this means that our sense of sight, our sense of hearing, or both of these senses are stimulated. The decoding process of teachers, for example, very often begins when they see students raise their hands or when they hear students orally communicate the fact that they don't understand a point made in class or need additional information.

Interpretation.   Once our sensory mechanisms have been stimulated, neural impulses are sent to the brain for interpretation. Interpretation involves assigning meaning to the message that has been received. The meanings we attach to the message, moreover, are a function of our prior experience with sources and messages that we perceive to be similar to the source and message at hand.

Evaluation.   As a function of assigning meaning to the message, we are in a position to evaluate the message and the demands—if any—that the message makes of us. A teacher, for example, may recognize a student's question, interpret the question, evaluate the question, and then decide to answer the question. By contrast, the teacher could engage in an identical process, but, based on his or her evaluation of the question, choose to ignore it. If the teacher decides to respond, however, then he or she must transcend from the decoding to the encoding process.

Feedback.   Our abilities to accurately encode and decode messages rest on our abilities to accurately interpret the responses or feedback our encoding and decoding behaviors elicit. For example, teachers who desire to have students respond to them in a specific fashion have no idea as to whether the message they transmit is appropriate until the students do, in fact, respond. By the same token, students have no idea as to whether they have accurately decoded a teacher's message until they respond to the teacher, and, in turn, the teacher provides them with feedback pertaining to the appropriateness of the response.

Feedback serves at least three important functions in the process of human communication. First, it assists us in determining whether the messages we formulate and transmit to a receiver are appropriate. Second, it assists us in determining whether our interpretations of a source's message are accurate. Third, it serves to increase the habit strength of encoding and decoding behaviors that typically meet with success, and extinguish those encoding and decoding behaviors that have met with failure. Fourth, since it permits participants in the communication process to encode appropriate messages, it tends to increase the confidence of the persons supplying the feedback. Thus, as a general rule in the classroom, when feedback is increased, teachers' confidence that they have taught effectively increases, and students' confidence that they have learned appropriately likewise increases.

Ironically, our experience with teachers and as teachers has indicated that feedback is rarely, if ever, effectively controlled and manipulated in the classroom as a teaching strategy. We do not believe this is because teachers are insensitive to the communication needs of their students. Rather, the lack of classroom feedback may be attributed to the teacher's perception that feedback imposes certain constraints on teachers.

First, feedback tends to disrupt the *apparent* orderliness of the class. Whether we like to admit it or not, a great many schools operate under the implicit assumption that "the quiet classroom is a learning classroom" (see Chapters 8 and 9). For a teacher to deviate from that assumption can often lead to trouble for both the teacher and the students.

Second, feedback increases the time spent in communicating. It takes longer to keep checking responses from students. Thus, many teachers are stuck between choosing to teach more things with less certainty of accuracy, or fewer things with greater certainty of accuracy. It takes a great deal of skill to increase content without decreasing feedback. Whenever possible, we advocate teaching smaller amounts of material without compromising opportunities for feedback. But it is not an easy choice to make, and you will have to work at your own best method of handling the demands of your particular system without shortchanging your students.

Third, although feedback increases the confidence of the person supplying it, it can increase or decrease the confidence of the person receiving it, depending on whether the feedback is positive or negative. As a consequence, many teachers become anxious about receiving negative feedback. They may be concerned that negative feedback will somehow be used against them, if it is defined as an evaluation of their teaching. Or, they often interpret questions from students as negative feedback indicating that they have not been teaching well. When negative feedback has the potential of shaking the confidence of the person receiving it, avoidance is a natural response.

Fourth, many students are uncomfortable when they have to respond to a teacher and do not have training in how to provide feedback (see Chapter 9).

Under such circumstances, attempts to obtain student feedback may appear to be a waste of time.

It is unfortunate that feedback is often viewed negatively in the classroom. But the importance of feedback in the learning process renders it too valuable to ignore or avoid. The creation of a positive communication environment is the *prime* responsibility of any teacher. We hope this book will help provide you with some tips on how to create that environment.

Noise

Human beings do not communicate in social vacuums. They communicate in restaurants and cafeterias, in classrooms and hallways, in their places of business and in their homes. Obviously, these various arenas of communication are not devoid of extraneous influences. In a restaurant or cafeteria, for example, our transactions may be intermittently interrupted by a waitress asking for our order or the sound of dishes crashing and breaking on the floor. In a classroom, attention may be momentarily diverted from a student's question by a paper airplane of mysterious origin. Even a quiet conversation at home may be disrupted by a television newscaster's uninvited news flash.

These are, of course, all physical examples of noise and they are easy to understand. But other sources of "noise" also affect the communication process, and these are what we call the *human factors*.

Communication skills.   With the possible exception of graduate education, it is probably safe to assume that the communication skills of a teacher are head and shoulders above those of a student. While this is not necessarily a problem, it can be. If teachers, for example, overlook the dissimilarities between their communication skills and student skills, they run the risk of formulating a set of message strategies that may lead to confusion rather than understanding in the minds of their students. Perhaps you can recall—as we certainly can—a teacher in your educational experience who engaged in exactly this kind of behavior. If you can, you probably also recall the difficulties that his or her behavior caused you.

Attitudes.   No matter how hard we try to hide them, our attitudes inevitably surface as a function of our communication behaviors. Teachers of political science can seldom keep their true political beliefs secret; teachers of philosophy can seldom keep their own philosophy hidden from their students; and teachers of American literature cannot help but disclose their preference for Faulkner over Hemingway or Whitman over Dickinson. But more important to teaching and learning is the fact that our attitudes mediate our encoding as well as our decoding behaviors—that is, the way in which we formulate and interpret messages. For example, if a teacher has favorable attitudes toward the content he or she has been assigned to teach, the teacher will, in all likelihood, have a positive effect on the messages he or she formulates. If a student, however, has a negative attitude toward the same content, this will probably have a negative effect on the accuracy of the student's interpretation of the teacher's messages. Too often we forget this fact and approach teaching and learning as if our attitudes had nothing to do with either.

Knowledge. Obviously, gross differences can exist between the knowledge state of a teacher and the knowledge state of a student. Knowledge, as we are using it here, refers to the number and kinds of experiences that a person has had. Teachers can overcome these differences, however, by drawing from their students' experiences rather than from their own. For example, a high-school social-studies teacher interested in having students learn about social conformity might draw on the numerous examples existing on the high-school campus, rather than using illustrations from his or her master's thesis on the effects of social conformity in ghetto matriarchies. In any case, it is important to the fidelity of human communication transactions that conscious attempts be made to minimize the differences in knowledge state between sources and receivers. Happily, that is what teaching is all about.

Social system and culture. The communication behavior of a teacher or a student is largely the result of the social system and culture the individual grew up in. And this can be a source of tremendous problems in the classroom. Take the case of students and teachers in East Los Angeles, California. The population of East Los Angeles is predominantly Mexican-Americans. As a result, the students attending public schools in East Los Angeles are also predominantly Mexican-Americans. However, in the past, the majority of teachers in the public schools of East Los Angeles were predominantly white Anglo-Saxons. The problems that stemmed from this situation were largely the result of teachers failing to take into account the two worlds that their Mexican-American students were faced with. At home, for example, these students were expected to conform to the traditions and heritage of their Mexican ancestry—including speaking Spanish. At school, however, they were expected to conform to the cultural norms of the white Anglo-Saxon population—and were often punished for speaking Spanish. In a sense, then, the teachers in this school system were not asking their students simply to conform to a different set of cultural norms, they were asking them to reject the culture of their parents. Needless to say, this situation was hardly conducive to teaching and learning, as was reflected in the students' achievement scores and in the high rate of illiteracy among junior- and senior-high-school students.

Fortunately, this situation is now being changed as a result of the new emphasis in the East Los Angeles school system on hiring teachers of Mexican ancestry and teachers who are bilingual. Nevertheless, the example should serve as a constant reminder of the importance of social systems and cultures to communicate and the classroom environment.

You should be aware, of course, that each of these human "noise" factors influences students and teachers equally. That is why effective communication is dependent on the recognition that the entire classroom is part of the communication process.

A MODEL OF THE CLASSROOM COMMUNICATION PROCESS

By way of concluding this chapter and to help orient you to what we will be discussing throughout the remainder of this book, we have tried to put all of the communication variables we have discussed into a coherent model of the classroom communication process. This model is shown in Fig. 2.2.

As you can see in the model, we have segmented the classroom communication process into five major parts: source (teachers and students); message; channel; receiver (teachers and students); and feedback. We have combined teachers and students under the source and receiver variables in order to try and indicate the transactional nature of the communication process. In the discussion that follows, we briefly look at the role of each of these variables in the classroom. Feedback and noise have been excluded, since we discussed them in some detail earlier.

Source

There are many sources of messages for communication in the classroom. The most obvious one is, of course, the teacher. The teacher is a constant source of communicative messages in the classroom; in fact, if the teacher is present in the classroom, he or she is constantly sending messages to the students. We will look at the teacher as a source of communication in more detail in Chapter 7. But at this point, it is more important to note the existence of other sources of communicative messages in the classroom. Obviously, students are sources of communication in the classroom. All too often, teachers think of themselves as the only source in the classroom and of students as being only receivers. While this pattern of communication is very common in all classrooms, the reverse pattern is equally important. We must also not overlook other sources of messages in the classroom. In many classes, for example, the primary source of information is the textbook rather than the teacher. And, until the upper grades or college level, the person who wrote the textbook is ignored as a source. In the student's mind, the book itself is the source. In addition to books, audio-visual aids, such as films, records, or tapes, also serve as classroom sources. Thus, when we think of the source element of communication in the classroom, we must keep in mind the many and varied sources that do impinge on the classroom communication environment. All of these can have either a positive or negative impact on student learning.

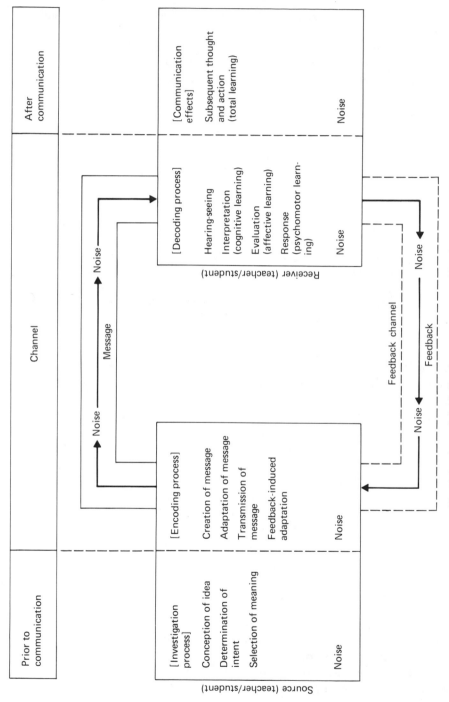

Fig. 2.2   A model of the classroom communication process.

Message

When we think of messages in the classroom environment, we frequently think of what a person is saying. But there is a lot more to the concept of "message" than just words. What the teacher *says* and what the student *says* are very often not the most important messages in the teacher-student communication. The *way* something is said often communicates much more. There are many nonverbal elements in classroom communication. Since Chapter 6 is devoted to nonverbal messages in the classroom, we will not belabor this point further here.

Channel

The most frequently employed channels of classroom communication are oral and visual channels. Most communication in the classroom is what we refer to as "interpersonal"—i.e., two-way between teachers and students. Students obtain messages in the classroom primarily by listening to the teacher and reading material from a textbook or handouts the teacher provides. But in some more modern systems of education, the communication employed to facilitate learning is not of the interpersonal type. An increasing percentage of instruction today employs mediated systems as channels for student learning. In personalized systems of instruction, particularly those that employ media learning centers, there is no direct, two-way communication between the teacher and student. Rather, the student interacts with the mediated instructional system. Of course, this does not mean that interpersonal communication between the teacher and student ceases to exist, but rather that a new form of communication has been introduced to supplement interpersonal communication. Interpersonal and mediated communication have many things in common, but they differ drastically from one another in terms of the amount of feedback available in spontaneous form. In mediated systems, feedback is much more restricted, although some can be built into the mediated system itself. While in most instances teachers have a marked preference for interpersonal communication over mediated communication, and there are good reasons for such a preference, the teacher must keep in mind the availability of these other communication channels. In some instances, mediated communication will actually be superior to interpersonal communication in producing student learning.

Receiver

Every person who is a source of communication in the classroom is also a receiver of communication in the classroom. Both students and teachers are receivers, but so are a lot of outsiders. Even the author of a textbook can be a receiver, when either the teacher or the students respond to what they have read and communicate that response to the author. Such responses are relatively infrequent, but they do occur. Numerous people outside the physical confines of the classroom also serve as receivers of communication in the classroom. The principal, the parents, and the other taxpayers all receive messages generated in the classroom. In some instances, this is a positive good; in others, teachers and/or students would prefer that it were otherwise.

You should also be aware that we have defined both decoding processes and communication effects in terms of learning. We will examine these relationships in the next chapter.

SELECTED REFERENCES

Berlo, David K. *The Process of Communication.* New York: Holt, Rinehart and Winston, 1960.

Fabun, Don. *The Dynamics of Change.* Englewood Cliffs, N.J.: Prentice-Hall, 1967.

Fotheringham, Wallace C. *Perspectives on Persuasion.* Boston: Allyn and Bacon, 1966.

Landis, J.R. *Current Perspectives on Social Problems,* 3rd ed. Belmont, Cal.: Wadsworth, 1973.

Lasswell, Harold D. "The Structure and Function of Communications in Society," in *The Communication of Ideas,* ed. by L. Bryson. New York: Harper & Row, 1948.

Lin, Nan. *The Study of Human Communication.* Indianapolis: Bobbs-Merrill, 1973.

McCroskey, James C., Carl E. Larson, and Mark L. Knapp. *An Introduction to Interpersonal Communication.* Englewood Cliffs, N.J.: Prentice-Hall, 1971.

Miller, Gerald R., and Mark Steinberg. *Between People.* Chicago: Science Research Associates, 1975.

Monroe, Alan H. *Principles and Types of Speech,* 4th ed. Chicago: Scott Foresman, 1955.

Osgood, Charles E., ed. "Psycholinguistics: A Survey of Theory and Research Problems." *Journal of Abnormal and Social Psychology* **49** (1954), Morton Prince Memorial Supplement.

Pace, Wayne R., Robert R. Boren, and Brent D. Peterson. *Communication: Behavior and Experiments: A Scientific Approach.* Belmont, Cal.: Wadsworth, 1975.

Rogers, Everett M., and Floyd F. Shoemaker. *Communication of Innovations: A Cross-Cultural Approach.* New York: The Free Press, 1971.

Ross, Raymond S. *Persuasion: Communication and Interpersonal Relations.* Englewood Cliffs, N.J.: Prentice-Hall, 1974.

Schramm, Wilbur. *The Process and Effects of Mass Communication.* Urbana: University of Illinois Press, 1954.

Sereno, Kenneth K., and C. David Mortensen, eds. *Foundations of Communication Theory.* New York: Harper & Row, 1970.

Shannon, C. E., and W. Weaver. *The Mathematical Theory of Communication.* Urbana: University of Illinois Press, 1949.

Stewart, John, ed. *Bridges Not Walls,* 2d ed. Reading, Mass.: Addison-Wesley, 1977.

Communication and Learning

After reading this chapter, you should be able to do the following.

1. Describe and provide examples of the three domains of learning.
2. Describe and provide communication examples for each of the following:
   a. reinforcement
   b. secondary reinforcers
3. Explain the role communication plays in defining the learning situation.
4. Explain the role communication plays in the process of reinforcement.
5. Explain the role communication plays in increasing student motivation.
6. Describe how communication influences the instructional sequence.

Communication and learning are truly interdependent. On the one hand, each of us had to learn to communicate. On the other hand, we each had to learn who we are, what we are, and where we stand in relationship to the world and its people. In this chapter, we take a look at the degree to which communication and learning are interdependent processes. Specifically, we look at the interdependencies between communication and the behavioral domains of learning we face in the classroom, as well as the interdependencies existing between communication and the process by which our students learn.

THE DOMAINS OF LEARNING

It is generally acknowledged that there are three broad domains of learning: a cognitive domain, an affective domain, and a psychomotor domain. While we will treat each of these domains separately here, they are by no means independent. Rather, they are like the components of a system, and a change in one is likely to affect changes in the remaining two.

The Cognitive Domain

Much of what we do in the classroom is designed to facilitate the acquisition of knowledge, and the skills corresponding to this knowledge. The cognitive domain of learning is concerned with the process of acquiring knowledge. At the lowest level of cognitive learning, knowledge refers to a specific bit of information, like the meaning of a word; a specific fact, like the date of an event; or a social convention, like shaking hands. At the middle level of cognitive learning, knowledge means methods of inquiry, such as hypothesis testing; principles and generalizations, such as "evaporation" or the laws of physics; and theories or structures, like relativity and matter. At the highest level of cognitive learning, however, knowledge means the ability to interpret or extrapolate, analyze or organize, and evaluate or synthesize the knowledge acquired at lower levels of the cognitive domain.

Some educators seem to be operating under the assumption that cognitive learning is largely rote. While this all too frequently is the case, it doesn't have to be. Ideally, the level of the cognitive domain being dealt with in a class should correspond to the learning history of the students who comprise the class. We wouldn't expect much in the way of analysis from first graders, for example, if they were just beginning to learn how to react. It probably would be quite comical to see first graders trying to analyze the deeper meanings of "See Sally run." Thus, emphasis at this level should be largely rote—beginning with things like the meaning and spelling of a single word.

Once children acquire enough meanings and demonstrate they can spell, however, we expect them to engage in a higher level of cognitive learning. We expect them to learn the basic rules of grammar, the principles outlined in simple arithmetic, or the basic structure of government. But these expectancies would never be confirmed if the children had not engaged first in the rote exercises that enabled them to learn the meanings and spellings of the words.

Finally, we expect our students to engage in the highest level of cognitive learning after they have acquired a sufficient number of rules, principles, laws, and the like. That is, we expect our students to apply the knowledge that they have acquired at each of the lower levels of the cognitive domain.

As you can see, then, it is a mistake to assume that the cognitive domain of learning concerns only the retention and recall of information. Behaviors in the cognitive domain of learning range from the simple to the complex. Try to think of the cognitive domain of learning as a hierarchy of knowledge including complex behaviors like synthesizing and evaluating, as well as elementary behaviors like simple recall. Also, remember that the level of cognitive learning demanded from students should correspond to their learning history.

The Affective Domain

Perhaps our greatest oversight in the classroom is that we do not always influence our students' attitudes, beliefs, or values as they relate to the cognitive and behavioral domains of learning. Indeed, the affective domain of learning is concerned with how a student's attitudes, beliefs, and values relate to the knowledge and skills the student has acquired.

Even the best of teachers occasionally assumes that a student has really learned if the student exits the class knowing something (s)he did not know prior to attending the class. Usually, this assumption is predicated on the student's performance on tests or other assigned work. The fact that a student correctly responds to the items on a test or completes his or her homework on time, however, does not necessarily mean that a teacher has succeeded in teaching or that the student has succeeded in learning. Success, in the sense of learning, means that the student not only behaves intelligently and responsibly with respect to schoolwork, but also has learned to generalize these behaviors to experiences unrelated to schoolwork. For example, a student may be able to respond intelligently to an examination question about the importance of good citizenship, but whether or not the student has learned to practice good citizenship is a different issue entirely. The question becomes, consequently: How can a teacher maximize the probability of a student generalizing in-class behaviors to less controlled and less contrived environments?

Basically, teachers who want their students to generalize in-class behaviors to nonclass environments must establish a link between the principles or concepts being taught and the students' attitudes, beliefs, and values. Sometimes this will require associating content with extant attitudes, beliefs, and values. With a group of athletically inclined students, for example, the teacher might attempt to associate the content being taught with some facet of sports.

If the teacher is successful in making this kind of association, the chances of the students developing a positive attitude toward the content will increase. In turn, this positive attitude will increase the likelihood of the students applying the content to their day-to-day experiences.

Whether a student develops an aptitude for a particular content area will depend largely on his or her success in the content area. By the same token, it also will depend on whether or not the student associates positive feelings with the content area. This is extremely important when a student is being exposed to a content area for the first time. As a case in point, think about a content area for which you have some aptitude. We'd be willing to wager that you have a history of success in the content area and also feel positively about the content area. Similarly, we would be willing to wager that the reverse is true about content areas in which you feel unsure about your abilities.

The point is, a student will acquire an attitude toward a content area very soon after his or her initial exposure to the content area. Whether or not this attitude will be positive or negative will depend, in part, on whether the student's initial experience elicits feelings which are pleasant.

As most teachers know all too well, even the brightest of students may achieve at a level below their potential in a particular subject matter. While there is no single explanation of this phenomenon, it seems safe to assume that student attitudes toward the subject may be a significant factor in this regard. As teachers, therefore, we cannot afford to ignore our students' attitudes, beliefs, and values as they relate to the content we teach.

The Psychomotor Domain

We can look at the psychomotor domain of learning in a couple of ways. First, we can examine it in terms of psychomotor skills, like hand, eye, and ear coordination. Depending on the subject being taught, psychomotor skills may be either terminal or mediating. Physical education teachers deal largely with terminal psychomotor skills—for example, shooting a basket, catching a football, or throwing a baseball. These terminal psychomotor skills are mediated by other psychomotor skills—for instance, hand, eye, and body coordination. The difference between terminal and mediating psychomotor skills, then, is that the former are end products, while the latter intervene and influence the attainment of the end product.

From another perspective, the psychomotor domain of learning is the observable consequence of the cognitive and affective domains interacting with each other. In discussing the affective domain, we said that learning means more than a student behaving intelligently and responsibly in the confines of the school environment. Specifically, real learning demands that students generalize their intelligence and sense of responsibility to situations outside the confines of the school environment. In such instances, we would expect *ob-*

servable behaviors that reflect the degree to which students have generalized. In a sense, then, these observable behaviors indicate that a student has learned at an optimum level.

One of the authors recalls an experience that illustrates how students may fail to learn at this optimum level. While teaching at the University of Hawaii, the author became familiar with special classes in voice and diction that were taught to Hawaiian students who spoke English primarily as a second language. They had learned a form of "pidgin English" as small children in a mixed cultural environment. At that time, students at the University of Hawaii were required to be able to speak Standard English in order to enter certain curricula. Consequently, the students took the remedial classes in English in order to develop these skills. In the classroom, most of the students demonstrated the ability to speak Standard English, but as soon as they left the classroom, they immediately reverted to their pidgin English speaking style. They knew the words, and they knew how to say them the way the teacher wanted them said. In addition, they had a positive attitude toward saying them that way in the presence of the teacher. But they did not have a positive attitude toward doing it anywhere except in the classroom. Thus, if the objective of the requirements under which these students were forced to study was to produce people who spoke "Standard English," that objective was not being met. However, if the only objective was to produce students who were *able* to speak English in that form, the objective was being met.

Ideally, we want our students to generalize what they've learned inside the classroom to their day-to-day experiences. The only way we have of knowing whether or not this actually happens, though, is through the observable behaviors exhibited by our students outside the classroom. Thus, this final perspective from which we may view the domains of learning is a crucial one.

THE LEARNING PROCESS

It would be impossible to talk about the interdependencies between the domains of learning and communication without first talking about the process by which students learn. It is not our intention to exhaust the varying theoretic descriptions of how learning occurs; we simply couldn't do justice to the thinking of Piaget, Vygotsky, and the like in a single chapter. As a result, we have decided to restrict our discussion to a single description, namely, reinforcement theory.

Over three decades of research have established that a number of the principles outlined in reinforcement theory have direct application to the classroom. We will briefly touch on each of these principles, and then move on to the interdependencies among these principles, the domains of learning and communication.

Reinforcement and Punishment

Positive reinforcement.   Positive reinforcement usually takes the form of some kind of reward which immediately follows a desirable behavior. The simple, basic tenet upon which positive reinforcement operates is the idea that behaviors that are rewarded are learned, and behaviors that are not rewarded tend not to be learned or repeated.

Negative reinforcement.   Learning by negative reinforcement involves having students behave in certain ways *in order to avoid punishment.* The only reinforcement is that which occurs because students, by behaving in some desirable way, have managed to escape some threatening consequence of failing to behave in the desired way.

Punishment.   Punishment in the classroom usually takes the form of a direct and immediate application of an unpleasant stimulus to an undesired behavior. While punishment is often assumed to be the opposite of positive reinforcement, it has also been found *not* to facilitate learning. By that we mean that punishing a student for a certain behavior does not mean that the student will stop engaging in that behavior. Rather, the student may simply learn not to engage in that behavior in the presence of the teacher. The behavioral patterns may remain with the student in all other environments.

Secondary reinforcement.   Secondary reinforcers are stimuli that retain their reward power, regardless of whether or not an organism has been deprived of them. Common secondary reinforcers are praise, affection, and certificates of achievement like a diploma. Ideally, grades also should be secondary reinforcers for the primary behavior of learning. We use the word *ideally* here because this is not always the case. Many of the students we have come into contact with view grades as a primary rather than a secondary reinforcer. In effect, this means that they engage in learning behaviors to obtain a grade rather than because of some intrinsic desire to acquire knowledge or specific skills. Needless to say, the educational system is partly responsible for this phenomenon. Entrance to graduate and professional schools, for example, largely depends on academic marks. Thus, the achievement of the mark is sometimes more important than the acquisition of knowledge or skills. What this suggests, then, is that teachers should exercise caution in using grades as a source of reward. Our goal is not to ensure that students achieve high academic marks. To the contrary, our goal is to ensure that students master the behaviors under study.

COMMUNICATION, LEARNING, AND THE CLASSROOM ENVIRONMENT

In order to clarify how communication fits in with what we have said in the preceding pages, we will begin with an examination of the relationships between communication and the learning situation itself.

Communication and the Learning Situation

In order for a learning situation to actually promote learning, teachers must do more than loosely organize a set of learning tasks and hope for the best. At a minimum, the teacher must identify to his or her own satisfaction what the learning tasks are designed to accomplish. For example: Is a set of learning tasks designed to facilitate the acquisition of knowledge at some level of the cognitive domain as it relates to whatever is being taught, or to yield observable behaviors that indicate learning has occurred? At this initial stage of the learning process, the teacher is starting to develop what we identified in Fig. 2.2 as encoding and investigation processes.

The teacher must also identify to the satisfaction of his or her students what the learning task demands in the way of individual behaviors. And herein lies the problem. While teachers may be able to identify in their own minds what a learning task is designed to accomplish, there is no guarantee they will be able to communicate this to the student. Many of the learning tasks we ask our students to engage in are unclear or characterized by a high degree of ambiguity. As a case in point, consider one of the most common learning tasks teachers employ: the term paper. A teacher, no doubt, has good reasons for assigning a lengthy essay devoted to a single subject matter. (S)he may desire to know whether the student can apply knowledge gleaned in the classroom, whether the student is creative, or a host of other things. Far too often, however, what the teacher desires to know, hopes to accomplish, or requires of the student is never understood fully by the student. This is not to say that the teacher has failed to discuss the requirements of the learning task entirely, but that the discussion is frequently unclear or ambiguous in the mind of the student. Obviously, this diminishes the probability of the student behaving in a fashion consistent with the expectations of the teacher.

Communication between teachers and students defines, in part, the learning situation. If a teacher desires to influence one or all of the domains of behavioral learning, by way of some learning task, the teacher must communicate to his or her students precisely what it is that the learning task demands of them. For example, if the learning task demands a fifteen-page evaluation with grammatical perfection and proper punctuation, then the teacher should communicate to the students precisely what (s)he means by: (1) fifteen pages, (2) evaluation, (3) grammatical perfection, and (4) proper punctuation. In other words, the teacher should clearly identify the objectives of the assignment to the students, and the behaviors the student must engage in in order to successfully complete the assignment. As a precautionary device, the teacher should also employ some measure designed to assess whether the students fully understand the stated objective, as well as the behaviors required of them. As we pointed out in Chapter 2, the only way we have of knowing whether our messages have been understood is through *feedback*.

To summarize: teachers should initially identify for themselves what a learning task is designed to accomplish, and the behavioral domain of learning at which the learning task is targeted. Following this, they should clearly identify for their students: (1) the objectives of the learning task, and (2) the behaviors the students will need to engage in to meet these objectives. Finally, we suggest that teachers devise a feedback loop—that is, a loop that will enable them to determine how well they have communicated.

In other words, the second important communication step involves the clear specification of how students should correctly decode messages, whether it be in terms of cognitive, affective, or psychomotor learning. This has three useful purposes. First, it helps to improve the fidelity of communication (and learning) by increasing redundancy. Second, it focuses teachers' attention on students and alerts them to the necessity of adapting messages to the various impositions of individual differences (see Chapter 5). Third, learning can be clearly defined in terms of the discrepancies between what was encoded by the teacher and decoded by students.

Communication and Reinforcement

While communication plays an important role in defining the learning situation, its most important function in the classroom environment is that of reinforcement. Earlier we said that students learn best when they receive positive reinforcement for their work on a learning task. You'll recall that positive reinforcement constitutes a reward. Communication between the teacher and the student is the primary means by which the student is rewarded for learning. In fact, communication with the teacher is often a reward for the student in itself.

While the following example is oversimplified, it serves to illustrate how learning most frequently occurs in the classroom. To begin with, the teacher defines some kind of learning task. The student engages in this task and emits some kind of behavior. This behavior can be a verbal response to the teacher, a paper turned in, answers to a test, or any of a variety of other kinds of behavior. A response from the teacher follows, indicating the quality of the student's behavior. This response, or feedback if you will, indicates to the student not only whether he or she has accomplished the objective of the assignment, but also how the teacher feels about the student's performance. Learning can be intrinsically rewarding; simply knowing that one has the right answer can be a reward in itself. And the way that students usually find out whether or not they have the right answer is from some communication with the teacher. In addition, the teacher can reward the student with verbal praise when the stu-

Human communication is a powerful source of reinforcement in the classroom. Both verbal and nonverbal communication can be used to induce desired behavior changes.

dent does well. Both of these forms of reward tend to reinforce the student's learning and increase the probability that the student will retain the knowledge, have a good feeling about the learning experience and the content of that experience, and/or repeat the behavior that elicted the reward.

While the illustration above describes what can happen when the teacher is in control of the situation and his or her own behavior, we must recognize that an analogous pattern occurs when the teacher is not aware of what is going on. For example, take the student who has just read some material and has acquired a certain bit of knowledge. The student attempts to communicate with the teacher to talk about that knowledge, but the teacher is busy with something else. The student therefore returns to his or her seat and goes back to work on something else. An opportunity for increased learning has just been missed, because the student did not receive rewarding communication from the teacher. In all likelihood, the teacher is not even aware that this failure has occurred. Yet, the teacher's communication behavior is the specific cause of the loss in learning. Of course, the student may retain the newly acquired knowledge long enough to talk with the teacher at a later time. But, just as likely, this will not occur.

One of the major principles that has been discovered in research on learning is that the more closely the reward is associated with the learning, the stronger will be its effect. In the learning research laboratory, of course, it is very easy to control the timing of reward; in the classroom, it is much more difficult. It is, however, absolutely essential that the teacher be in a position to recognize when a student has learned and be able to communicate that awareness with reward as quickly as possible. The uncommunicative teacher will produce much less learning than will the teacher who frequently communicates with the students. And, of course, by communication here we are not talking about lecturing to the class. When a teacher is lecturing it is not possible to know if students are learning, much less to provide reward to those students. Evidence of student learning occurs when students are talking, not when teachers are talking.

Before moving on, we need to consider student-to-student communication—a source of reward that is present in all classrooms but is frequently untapped. The traditional classroom is usually structured in such a way that communication between students is discouraged. In some extreme cases, communication between students may be a cause for punishment. This is most unfortunate, because student-to-student communication can be an invaluable facilitator of learning. Obviously, students communicate to each other on much more similar levels than do students and teachers. Therefore, the fidelity of student-to-student transactions is likely to be much higher than the fidelity of student-to-teacher transactions. Students, consequently, may be able to explain to other students something the teacher has been unable to explain. In addition, the status differences that exist between a teacher and student may cause the student to be somewhat reticent when in the presence of a teacher. While status differences also exist between students, these differences are less likely to make a student uncommunicative. Thus, students may be quicker to reveal to other students the problems or difficulties they are experiencing in the classroom.

Finally, we need to make mention of the fact that extreme attitudinal differences may exist between a teacher and student, differences that may cause the student to dislike the teacher. If the student begins to view communication with the teacher as a source of punishment rather than a source of reward, his or her progress in the classroom will obviously suffer. The teacher will have a difficult time engaging the student in the learning tasks required. This is not to say that the student will altogether refuse to participate, but that (s)he is likely simply to go through the motions instead of enthusiastically participating. What should a teacher do when confronted with this kind of situation?

First, the teacher should realize that (s)he is not perceived as a source of reward by the student. Second, the teacher should learn to accept this fact. Attempts to alter or reverse the situation may aggravate rather than help the problem. Third, the teacher should try to find out if any alternative sources of reward for the student are presently available in the classroom.

As might be expected, other students in the class are likely to be a source of reward for the student who dislikes the teacher. If the teacher can tap this alternative source of reward, and elicit the help of students in trying to communicate with the individual experiencing difficulties, the problem may be resolved or lessened.

Communication and Motivation

Although reinforcement is certainly helpful in increasing the likelihood that students will perform certain desired behaviors, it is equally important that students have a *desire* to learn, so that the act of learning itself becomes intrinsically rewarding. Communication plays a vital part in the development of such student motivation, and we have listed below some communication variables useful for increasing the desire to learn.

1. *Prelearning preparation (communication variables: information acquisition and processing).* In effect, this step simply involves ensuring that students have the basic skills necessary for correct decoding of the new subject matter to be taught. An increase in students' confidence that the knowledge base they have is adequate to begin learning increases motivation.

2. *Provide a model of terminal performance (communication variables: decoding; feedback).* The assumption operating here is that if students know what is to be done, they can better assess their own ability to do it (self-feedback), can judge the likelihood that they will be able to do it (predicting self-behavior), and can adjust their own behavior to the model of terminal performance.

3. *Active responding (communication variable: feedback).* Again, opportunity for observing one's own behavior makes it easier to adjust to the particular demands of the learning situation and increases students' confidence.

4. *Guidance (communication variables: feedback; perceptions of communication sources).* Guidance can be given in two ways: first, by providing students with a model of the desired behavior as exhibited by the teacher (source credibility); and, second, by providing verbal feedback at each stage of the learning sequence.

5. *Practice (communication variable: feedback).* This simple technique permits students to assess how closely they are able to approximate desired (future) decoding in terms of terminal skills.

6. *Knowledge of results (communication variables: feedback; information processing).* Here the student finds out rapidly the success of attempted decoding efforts. The closer the approximation to the desired outcome, the greater should be the rewards.

7. *Graduated sequence (communication variables: feedback; information processing; message preparation)*. Permitting students to progress through decoding requirements beginning with the less complex to the more difficult permits greater attention to the appropriate structuring and clarity of message content, as well as needed adaptation to individual learning differences.

8. *Classroom teaching performance (communication variables: perception of communication sources; communication skills; feedback)*. Here, the greatest motivating factor is the teacher's ability to present information in such a way as to be interesting, persuasive, stimulating, and exciting. Although we have listed this as the last step for increasing student motivation, it is in many ways the most difficult to use. Rarely are teachers *systematically* evaluated in terms of their communication skills. Recent research has indicated that many persons who have a generalized anxiety about communication (see Chapter 9) will select teaching in preference to other professions because they believe that success in public education is not dependent on success at communication. But teaching *is* communicating. And the better teachers are at communicating, the better they are at teaching.

Communication and the Instructional Sequence
To facilitate discussion of the interdependencies between communication and the instructional sequence, we have provided a representation of a typical instructional sequence (see Fig. 3.1). As you will note, the instructional processes are divided into a series of sequential steps: (1) specification of content and objectives; (2) assessment of entering behaviors; (3) determination of strategy; (4) organization of structural units; and (5) feedback. Needless to say, communication plays an important role at each step in this instructional sequence.

Specification of content and objectives (communication variables: information acquisition; encoding; decoding).   Earlier, we talked about the necessity of clearly identifying what a learning task is designed to accomplish, as well as identifying the behavioral domain of learning at which the learning task is targeted. We also emphasized the necessity of clearly identifying in the minds of students the goal of a learning task, and the behaviors students will have to engage in if they are able to attain the goal. While we do not wish to belabor the subject here, a couple of points are worthy of further comment. When we talk about something being clear in the minds of students, we are really talking about the fidelity between what a teacher communicates and the meaning the communication stimulates in the minds of the teacher's students. As most teachers know, students do not always interpret the *oral communication behaviors* of a teacher exactly as the teacher intended. One of the consequences of this phenomenon is that students sometimes fail to engage in the behaviors the teacher expects. By specifying the content and objectives of a unit of in-

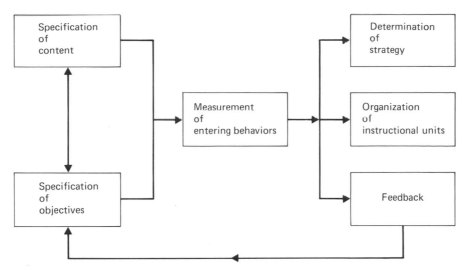

Fig. 3.1   A typical instructional sequence.

struction in writing, and by then going over this written communication orally, this misinterpretation can be overcome. If this appears to be an exercise in redundancy, you are right. But the more redundant information is to students, the more likely they are to process the information accurately. The specification of content and objectives vis-à-vis two channels of communication works to the advantage of both teachers and students.

Assessment of entering behaviors (communication variables: human factors; feedback; encoding).   Our communication behaviors toward other people are influenced by what we know about them. The more we know, the more likely it is that we will communicate to them in an appropriate fashion. And so it is with respect to our students. When we assess what a student brings to the classroom (e.g., intelligence, prior learning history, learning disabilities), we accomplish two things. First, we gain valuable information concerning the appropriateness of the content and objectives we have specified. After assessing the entering behaviors of students, for example, you may find out that the content and objectives are above or below the abilities of the students, and that you need to adjust accordingly. Second, you gain information that will assist you in communicating with a student. For instance, if your assessment indicates that a student has a potential behavior problem, this information could assist you in deciding on a set of appropriate communication behaviors when in the presence of this student.

A word of caution: The information you glean as a result of your assessment of entering behaviors only will be as valid as the measures you use to make the assessment. Thus, you must make certain these measures are not susceptible to some subjective bias.

Determination of strategy (communication variable: channel usage). Learning strategies are, in every sense of the term, communication strategies. When we make decisions about which strategy is likely to maximize learning, we are, in effect, asking, "How should I communicate with my students?" Two widely accepted communication strategies are the expository strategy and the inquiry strategy. Of the two, exposition is perhaps the most pervasive. When a teacher opts for the expository approach, (s)he or some other source of information, like a book or film, is primarily responsible for seeing that an issue or skill is adequately explained and demonstrated to students.

The inquiry, or discovery strategy as it is sometimes called, came into vogue during the 1960s. If this strategy is opted for, the teacher usually provides students with an experiential vehicle designed to assist them in reaching a conclusion or acquiring a skill on their own.

When deciding which strategy to use, teachers should first ask themselves, "Which strategy is most appropriate to the content and objectives being taught?" Second, teachers should ask, "Which strategy is most likely to work for me and my students?" The final decision about which strategy to use should be made only after the teacher feels these two questions have been answered satisfactorily.

Organization of instructional units (communication variables: messages; encoding; decoding).   How the instructional units are organized in a class will depend largely on the content being taught. Even so, in organizing instructional units, a few things need to be kept in mind. First, there is the notion of successive approximation. Theory and research strongly suggest that students learn to retain and generalize information at an optimum rate when the information is divided into small, successive chunks. Second, there is the notion of hierarchical learning. Theory and research also suggest that students learn best when they begin with relatively easy learning tasks and then move on to successively more difficult learning tasks. Finally, there is the notion of serial communication. It is a well-established fact that forgetting and distortion increase proportionally with the amount of information a person is exposed to. Collectively, these three notions lead to these inescapable conclusions: the units of instruction in a class should contain relatively small amounts of information, should be linked successively, and should be structured hierarchically.

Feedback.   The last and perhaps most important step in the instructional sequence is feedback. While we can't show it in the linear model depicted in Fig. 3.1, feedback should be present at each step of the instructional sequence.

Feedback from previous semesters or contact with students and teachers should be taken into account when a teacher specifies the content and objectives. In addition, the assessment of entering behaviors is a form of feedback.

Feedback becomes most prominent, though, when students are actually attempting to master the units of instruction. The behaviors of students as they make attempts at mastery provide feedback information to the teacher. For example, student behaviors communicate about their abilities, the level of difficulty of a particular unit of instruction, and the overall success of the learning strategy. At the same time, of course, the teacher's behaviors feed back information to the students about their performance. A couple of things need to be said in this regard. First, it is absolutely essential that a teacher provide his or her students with *continuous* feedback about their performance. Second, it is just as crucial that the teacher provide the students with feedback that is *reinforcing*. Both of these practices will minimize the frustration students commonly experience in a class, as well as maximize the probability of the students attaining the objectives of the course.

SELECTED REFERENCES

Anglin, J.M., ed. *Jerome S. Bruner: Beyond the Information Given.* New York: Norton, 1973.

Ausubel, D.P. "Cognitive Structure and the Facilitation of Meaningful Verbal Learning." *Journal of Teacher Education* **14** (1973a): 217–230.

Ausubel, D.P. *The Psychology of Meaningful Verbal Learning.* New York: Greene and Stratton, 1963b.

Ausubel, D.P. *Educational Psychology: A Cognitive View.* New York: Holt, Rinehart and Winston, 1968.

Banduar, A. "Behavioral Modifications through Modeling Procedures." In L. Knasner and L.P. Ullman, eds., *Research in Behavior Modification.* New York: Holt, Rinehart and Winston, 1965.

Bandura, A. *Principles of Behavior Modification.* New York: Holt, Rinehart and Winston, 1969.

Bandura, A. *Psychological Modeling: Conflicting Theories.* Chicago: Aldine, 1971.

Bijou, S.W. "What Psychology Has to Offer Education Now." In P.B. Dews, ed., *Festschrift for B.F. Skinner.* New York: Appleton-Century-Crofts, 1970, pp. 401–407.

Bloom, B.S., ed. *Taxonomy of Educational Objectives.* (Handbook I: Cognitive Domain). New York: McKay, 1956.

Bruner, J.S. *Toward a Theory of Instruction.* New York: Norton, 1966.

Ferster, C.B., and B.F. Skinner. *Schedules of Reinforcement.* New York: Appleton-Century-Crofts, 1957.

Gagne, R.M. *The Conditions of Learning.* New York: Holt, Rinehart and Winston, 1965.

Homme, L., and D. Tosti. *Behavior Technology: Motivations and Contingency Management* (Units one and two). San Rafael: Individual Learning Systems, 1971a.

Homme, L., and D. Tosti. *Behavior Technology: Motivation and Contingency Management* (Units three and four). San Rafael: Individual Learning Systems, 1971b.

Krathwohl, D.R., B.S. Bloom, and B.B. Masia. *Taxonomy of Educational Objectives* (Handbook II: Affective Domain). New York: McKay, 1964.

MacMillan, D. *Behavior Modification in Education*. New York: MacMillan, 1973.

Mager, R.F. *Preparing Instructional Objectives*. Belmont, Calif: Lear Siegler, 1962.

Shulman, L.S. "Psychological Controversies in the Teaching of Science and Mathematics," Science Teacher **35** (1968): 34–38, 89–90.

Skinner, B.F. *The Behavior of Organisms*. New York: Appleton-Century-Crofts, 1938.

Skinner, B.F. *Science and Human Behavior*. New York: Free Press, 1953.

Skinner, B.F. *Verbal Behavior*. Englewood Cliffs: Prentice-Hall, 1957.

Skinner, B.F. *The Technology of Teaching*. New York: Appleton-Century-Crofts, 1968.

Skinner, B.F. *Contingencies of Reinforcement: A Theoretical Analysis*. New York: Appleton-Century-Crofts, 1969.

Skinner, B.F. *Cumulative Record: A Selection of Papers*. New York: Appleton-Century-Crofts, 1972.

Skinner, B.F. *About Behaviorism*. New York: Knopf, 1974.

Snelbecker, G.E. *Learning Theory, Instructional Theory, and Psycho-Educational Design*. New York: McGraw-Hill, 1974.

Thorndike, E.L. *The Psychology of Learning*. Educational Psychology, vol. 2. New York: Teachers College, Columbia University, 1913.

Vargas, J.S. *Writing Worthwhile Behavioral Objectives*. New York: Harper & Row, 1972.

4

Information Acquisition in the Classroom

After reading this chapter, you should be able to do the following.

1. Define the following concepts:
   a. information
   b. understanding
   c. selectivity
2. Define and distinguish among the following types of selectivity:
   a. exposure
   b. attention
   c. perception
   d. retention
3. Identify the best predictors of exposure.
4. Describe the factors affecting selective attention.

As teachers, and as students, we would probably all agree that one of the most important communication variables in the classroom relates to our ability to select the appropriate messages (information) to facilitate learning and adaptability. Yet the ability to select useful messages—those which will best meet our needs—is a complex behavior which frequently appears to be deceptively simple. As a consequence, we make many selection errors.

Tom emphasizes the wrong material in a textbook and flunks an important exam. Mary is sitting in class, looking directly at the teacher, and does not catch a critical point of a homework assignment. Mike's teacher does not like him and consequently "overlooks" many of the positive things that he does in class. Mike ends up with a negative evaluation of his social behavior in the classroom. All of the above examples are probably familiar to us. They are instances of information-acquisition errors. In the first case, Tom *selected* inappropriate information. In the second instance, Mary was *attending to* inappropriate information. In the last example, the teacher was *distorting* information received to suit his or her own needs and biases and was *not perceiving (decoding) it accurately*. In this chapter, we examine some of the reasons why these errors occur, and what we as teachers can do to try and minimize the frequency of their occurrence. But before we begin, let us try to arrive at some common meanings for some critical terms in the process of information acquisition. These are *information, understanding,* and *selectivity*.

BASIC CONCEPTS OF INFORMATION ACQUISITION

Information Defined

It is unfortunate, but true, that we often use the word "information"—much as we do the word "communication"—without having any real comprehension of what we mean by it. At a very simple level, information is what we derive from the verbal and nonverbal messages in our environment. This is probably very close to the "folk meaning" many of us have for information. A better, but slightly more technical definition views information as *the meaning that we assign to some stimulus that reduces our uncertainty about something*.

The second definition of information is the one we prefer and will be using throughout this book. It has two important implications for classroom communication. First, since information is defined partly as the "meaning assigned" to certain stimuli, then the information present in a message, like meaning, is partially determined by the receiver of the message and is somewhat arbitrary and susceptible to individual differences. Thus, what is informative to us may not be informative to you, and vice versa. Even more serious, what is informative to you as a teacher may not be informative to your students; thus, they may miss critical aspects of the content you are trying to communicate to them.

Secondly, messages are only synonymous with information *to the extent that they have the potential for reducing uncertainty.* In other words, if you are teaching a unit in an algebra class dealing with time-motion problems, only *some* of the messages you encode will have any information potential at all, and of those that do, the potential may vary considerably. Although any given message may reduce uncertainty about a number of things, we would consider it to be informative only to the extent that, for the student, it reduces uncertainty about the specific referent of the message you intended to communicate. Thus, a message may be unintentionally informative about something you had not intended to teach. For example, the way in which you talk about time-motion problems may generate a message that reduces the students' uncertainty about you as a teacher, but does nothing to reduce their uncertainty about time-motion problems. It may be helpful to think of the teacher as a sign maker. In the classroom, every message intentionally encoded should be a carefully constructed sign designed to keep your students from getting lost on an unfamiliar path.

Understanding

We define understanding as *the reduction of uncertainty within individuals (and groups of individuals) brought about through the accurate decoding and encoding of messages.* This definition is very close to another folk meaning for understanding—that is, the accuracy or fidelity with which we comprehend verbal and nonverbal messages.

In the classroom, we use many indicants for assessing understanding. Unfortunately, one commonly used indicant is recognition and recall of information. While it is not necessarily wrong to think of recognition and recall as prerequisites to understanding, there is a great deal wrong with treating them as synonyms for understanding. Think of the exams you have been asked to take as a student, and may have given as a teacher. How many times was the only skill required by the test an ability to recall certain messages? How many times as a teacher have you heard the complaint, "I understand the material, but I can never remember it when I am taking a test"? These instances point to a critical distinction about understanding. While recognition and recall may be *necessary* for understanding to occur, they may not be *sufficient* to say that it has. As teachers, we must be concerned with not only helping students to remember information, but also with communicating it in such a way that the accuracy or fidelity of our meaning is maximized for them. It is only when we have attempted to do both of these things that we can say with some confidence that we have begun to teach.

Selectivity

Selectivity refers to *the degree to which we receive or reject stimuli.* More specifically, it is *the degree to which we choose to expose ourselves to, attend to, perceive, share, and retrieve messages from others.* Selection may be a conscious act, or it may occur below our level of immediate awareness. Let us examine some of these selection processes in more detail.

Selective exposure.   In our brief examples at the beginning of this chapter, Tom's decision to emphasize certain aspects of the material in the textbook he was reading is an instance of a person making a decision to expose himself to certain kinds of informational stimuli. In this case, Tom's decision was not an appropriate one, since he failed the examination.

Selective attention.   Mary's failure to process information about certain aspects of a homework assignment represents a common instance of selective attention. Even though Mary appeared to be paying attention to the teacher (she was looking directly at the teacher), it is quite possible that she had chosen to attend to stimuli other than what the teacher was saying. Often, these choices are a function of certain internal factors in receivers, such as attitudes or needs. If Mary had had a fight with her boyfriend the night before, it is possible that she was thinking about what time the class would be over so she could see him again in order to make up. Other times, however, choices to attend to certain stimuli are a function of external factors related to the stimuli themselves, such as the intensity of the stimulus. If the teacher was droning along in a monotonous manner, those messages may simply have been "lost" to Mary, since their intensity was not sufficient to compete with the intensity of her feelings about her boyfriend.

Selective perception.   The teacher's failure to process information about the more positive aspects of Mike's behavior represents an example of selective perception. The teacher had selectively screened out all of Mike's successes and screened in all of his failures. Thus, selective perception differs from selective exposure in that once we have been exposed to information, we may choose to screen, or process, only certain aspects of it.

Selective intention.   Another reason why the teacher may have failed to positively evaluate Mike's behavior is because (s)he was selectively retaining only certain aspects of the information being received. While it may have been possible for the teacher to perceive certain good things about Mike, when it came time to evaluate him, (s)he chose to forget most of that positive information.

Since selective perception and retention are considered to be subsidiary effects of exposure and attention, the remainder of this chapter will deal primarily with selective exposure and selective attention. Now let us see how these processes affect the acquisition of information in the classroom.

THE PROCESS OF ACQUIRING INFORMATION IN THE CLASSROOM

Selective Exposure

Selective exposure options.   Selective exposure refers to a decision made by an individual to place himself or herself in a position of proximity to certain communication sources, so that it will be possible to receive messages containing potential information. This decision refers literally to physical proximity to a source. Once we are in proximity to a source, we have four options regarding our exposure behavior: we may choose to select some information; we may choose to reject some information; we may choose not to select some information; or, we may choose not to reject some information. Although some of these options appear to be different ways of stating the same process, they do represent different aspects of the selective-exposure phenomenon. In order to examine these differences, let us create a fictional student, Brad, and see how each of these decision options may operate.

In the first case, Brad may decide to read a homework assignment, or not read the assignment. His choice is one of selecting or not selecting to expose himself to the assigned information. There is a critical aspect of this decision which teachers, in particular, should be aware of. Brad's (or any student's) failure to select to expose himself to information does not necessarily mean he has rejected it. Brad may have had to choose between two competing reading assignments about which he was equally interested. Consequently, his choice to read one and not read the other does not represent rejection of the assignment he did not read. In this case, Brad's choice is most clearly described as a choice between selection and nonselection of information. In fact, Brad will probably read the nonselected assignment at a later time. Thus, his nonselction of a reading cannot be inferred to mean that he does not like the class or the material. In most cases, selection and nonselection decisions are made as a function of not being able to process competing stimuli at the same time, or at approximately the same time. As teachers, we may tend to forget that students often must juggle competing priorities.

On the other hand, let us assume that Brad has to make a choice betweeen going to a drive-in movie with a girl he has been trying to date for a long time, and doing a homework assignment in which he is not particularly interested. If Brad chooses to go to the drive-in and not do his assignment, he is clearly selecting one type of informative experience and rejecting another. In this case, a reading assignment in a book tightly bound in a colorful cover has lost out to a girl tightly bound in a colorful sweater. (Do not selectively perceive that last comment as being representative of a chauvinistic attitude. Rather, it is an attempt at an accurate representation of our own experiences as adolescent boys. If you wish, you may reverse the sexes.)

Finally, Brad may have to choose to read one assignment from among several, none of which he is interested in. Here, his selective-exposure option is best described as a not-reject versus reject decision. Although Brad may not like any of his assignments and would never select one of them if he had that choice, he has clearly made a decision not to reject one of them. And, of course, if Brad is not at all interested or concerned about learning, he may reject all of them and worry about the consequences later.

Thus, selection versus nonselection of information represents a choice between or among two or more informational stimuli that are positively valued. A selection-rejection choice represents a choice made between or among stimuli, some of which are positively valued and some of which are not. Finally, a nonrejection-rejection choice represents a choice between or among stimuli that are all negatively valued.

As teachers, we would all prefer to have our students select the information we try to communicate to them in our classes. At worst, we would like to create a situation where students are making selection versus nonselection choices. Situations where students feel they are making only rejection versus nonrejection decisions are not desirable outcomes of our efforts in the classroom. Thus, the obvious solution seems to be to attempt to create such positive attitudes toward school that students are always choosing positively valued information. But sometimes the obvious solution is not always the best or most accurate solution. Remember, defining selective-exposure options is not the same as explaining them or predicting what choices our students will make.

Explaining and predicting selective exposure. Being able to explain the selective-exposure behavior of people and to predict what information they will expose themselves to has been a major concern of researchers in the social sciences for several years. To help us examine some of that research, we are going to create another fictional student, Velma, and try to relate her behavior to the selective-exposure research.

One intriguing explanation of selective-exposure behavior has nothing to do with the potential information content of a message. Rather, it relates to our perceptions and knowledge about the *source* of a message. Let us imagine, for example, that Velma has decided to enroll in a class that is not required for graduation by her high school. In other words, for this semester she has been allowed to choose a free elective. She has little or no information about any of the courses among which she has to choose, but she has gotten some critical information from some of her friends. She has been told that one of the course instructors is very good and relates well to students. After hearing this, Velma decides to enroll in the course taught by that instructor. Her behavior demonstrates a significant principle in selective exposure: people's perceptions of the *similarity* between themselves and the source and the *competence* of the source significantly affect their decision to expose or not expose themselves to information. As teachers, we should remember that initial perceptions of who we are as sources is frequently a major predictor of subsequent learning. We will discuss students' perceptions of teachers in more detail in Chapter 7.

Now let us suppose that Velma is an ardent supporter and advocate of the American Way of Life—someone whom we might refer to as a "super-patriot." Velma is trying to decide between two courses: "The Structure of the American Republic" and "The Structure of Communism in the Soviet Union." She has no further information about either course, and so on the basis of their titles she chooses the first. Velma's behavior is consistent with the findings of a large body of selective-exposure research: people who exposed themselves to certain messages or sources of messages were in agreement with those messages and sources. Here, the person's choice is dependent on whether or not the information is perceived as being *reinforcing* to the person's existing perceptions of reality. Velma *selected* a course about the American government because she expected it to be reinforcing to her attitudes about the United States. She probably *rejected* the course on communism because she imagined it would not be reinforcing to her attitude about communism. By the same token, she might not attend certain classes in a "Modern Governments" course on days when the assignment was to discuss the values of communism, whereas she would not miss discussions about the values of the American democracy.

Imagine now that Velma has to make a decision based on several fairly attractive (to her) course offerings. In this case, the important variables are not the courses themselves, but rather *what happens to Velma once she has made a decision to enroll in one of them*. Situations of the sort described here fall under a theoretical explanation of selective exposure called *dissonance theory*. Dissonance theory states that, once a choice among several fairly attractive alternatives has been made, dissonance or anxiety occurs relating to whether or not the choice made was a correct one. People attempt to reduce this dissonance by selectively exposing themselves to information that reinforces the decision they made, and by avoiding information that would not. Velma, having made her decision about which course to take, would then probably seek out other members of the class who were enthusiastic about it and expose herself to information from fellow students who already had had the class and liked it. She would avoid exposing herself to information from unhappy class members. If the dissonance was intense enough, she might increase her exposure to positive information and, by the end of the semester, might be convinced that it was the greatest learning experience she had ever had (and all of this is possible without any undo effort on the part of the instructor)!

There is a critical variable operating in the dissonance-theory approach to selective exposure which you may have already noticed. Obviously, the dissonance occurs *after* a decision has been made among all the possible alternatives. But what if Velma's decision had not been a voluntary one? Suppose she had been required to enroll in the course? In terms of dissonance theory, when the occasion to make a voluntary choice is minimized, the amount of dissonance experienced is also minimized. In Velma's case, she could have rationalized her enrollment in the course by saying that the choice had not been up to her. In addition, her selective-exposure behavior would probably not have been greatly affected and the teacher might have had a much more difficult task in creating a positive attitude toward the course. While we cannot discuss dissonance theory in detail here, the question of voluntary versus involuntary decision making has some interesting implications for issues regarding required courses and work assignments, and for the way in which students will expose themselves to information about such courses and their content. You may wish to explore some of these issues with your students or your instructor. They are certainly well worth the time.

Another approach to explaining and predicting selective-exposure behavior is *involvement theory* (sometimes called social-judgment theory). This theory argues that we become involved in issues that we perceive as being directly relevant to our own self interests. We use our perceptions of those issues as "anchors" to judge whether or not we will accept the information in certain messages. In other words, we have a range or latitude for messages containing acceptable information and a latitude for messages containing unacceptable information. If our latitude of acceptance is wide, we will accept more messages containing information that deviates from our anchor judgment. Fewer messages will be considered unacceptable. If our latitude of acceptance is narrow, then our latitude of unacceptance will be wider, and we will consider fewer messages to be acceptable to us. Usually, the greater our involvement with an issue, the narrower our latitude of acceptance relating to it.

Back to Velma. Suppose she wishes to be a truck driver when she graduates from high school. Her friends all laugh at her, but she is adamant. She wants to be a truck driver! It is her life. She is so involved in the issue that she even subscribes to a monthly magazine called *Ms. Trucker*. As a consequence, Velma's latitude of messages containing acceptable information about women truck drivers is quite narrow. She refuses to consult with her advisor who thinks she is being silly, and only takes courses in auto mechanics, which the magazine has informed her will increase her chances of employment following graduation. Velma's behavior is indicative of two important selective-exposure principles relating to involvement theory. Not only will we expose ourselves to messages containing acceptable latitudes of information about an issue, we also place *sources* of information (Velma's guidance counselor) into our latitudes of acceptance or rejection.

A final attempt at explaining and predicting selective-exposure behavior is worth mentioning. *Utility theory* views information in terms of a cost/benefit ratio. The time and energy necessary to obtain information is its cost; the ability of that information to reduce our uncertainty about something is its benefit. Thus, if Velma has a great deal of information about analytic chemistry, she is not going to be very happy about exposing herself to further information on the subject, since (from her point of view) the amount of uncertainty reduced by any new information would probably not justify the cost in terms of the time and energy required to obtain it. One of our teachers told us a story about a fifth-grade boy who was required to read a book about penguins and report to the class. When the time came for his report he said, "This book told me more about penguins than I needed to know."

This "penguin problem" is a severe one for teachers. Students will often make cost/benefit decisions about selective exposure based on inadequate information. We are sure that you have heard students complain about certain courses being nothing more than "painful extensions of the obvious." They may not feel any need to expose themselves to the information presented in class because they think it is redundant and they already know more than they want or need to about the topic. We know of no totally successful way to keep students from making cost/benefit decisions. But certain variables relating to selective attention to information can be useful, and we will examine these later in this chapter.

In terms of predicting selective-exposure behavior, the episodes involving Velma provide a useful summary.

1. Students (and teachers) will expose themselves to sources they perceive as being competent or similar to them. Unfortunately for the careless teacher, this might turn out to be the peers of their students.

2. When confronted with forced choices of selection or rejection of information, simple reinforcement theory may be the best predictor of students' (and teachers') behavior.

3. Dissonance theory is a useful predictor of selective exposure behavior when important voluntary decisions about exposure to messages and message sources have been made.

4. Involvement theory is a useful predictor when students (and teachers) are highly involved in certain issues.

5. Finally, the utility-theory approach is a useful predictor when we are concerned with predicting exposure behavior over a long period of time in relation to other issues which also demand attention. This is the norm among students enrolled in several different classes with different assignments.

In general, each of these approaches to selective exposure gives us a sense of the significance these variables should have for people concerned with class-

Not all students attend carefully to the same messages. What can teachers do to increase students' levels of attention?

room communication. Ideally, an educational environment requires and teaches flexibility and adaptability to a world filled with complex information. To the extent that both teachers and students tend to seek out only information they perceive as being useful or reinforcing to their attitudes and the decisions they have made, then to that extent their flexibility and adaptability are reduced and an important mission of instruction is diminished. Perhaps along with reading, writing, and arithmetic, children should be taught early the ability to adapt to the needs and demands of their information environment. Some of the teachers with whom we have worked argue that this is more important than any specific content their students may acquire. Perhaps so. This is certainly an issue with which all of us must soon come to grips.

Selective Attention

Selective attention defined.   Selective attention may be defined as *a selective physiological set to receive a stimulus* (message). What this means is that attention may be thought of as the act of tuning your senses (message channels) to selectively receive part of your information environment. In other words, we "tune in" on some stimuli to facilitate reception of them and to facilitate the nonselection and nonreception of other stimuli.

In effect, all of our sense organs have variable thresholds of information receptivity; a person can "raise" or "lower" the stimulation threshold of a sense organ in order to make it more or less sensitive to information. By the same token, your students can tune you in or out while you talk to them in the classroom. This ability to tune in sensitivity to some informational stimuli while simultaneously tuning out others is a complex process which is usually achieved in one of the following ways: (1) by shifting attention rapidly from one stimulus to another (watching a number of things happening on a movie screen in class); or (2) by widening the focus of attention (reading words rather than individual letters). Our ability to attend to a single stimulus at one time ranges from two to twenty-four seconds. The most common attention span to a single stimulus is five to eight seconds and, in general, younger children fall in the lower limits of that range. Thus, unless there is a considerable variety of related stimuli in the classroom, students' attention will tend to become unfocused and their information-acquisition skills will be impaired. In the following section, we examine some of the other factors that influence students' attention.

Factors influencing students' attention. A variety of factors affect a student's ability to pay attention in the classroom. Some of these, fortunately, can be controlled by the teacher; others are not so easily manipulated. In general, however, two things affect attention. The first is the *internal* state of the receiver—i.e., a student's physiological abilities, mental set (predisposition), and anticipatory adjustments (vicariously adapting to your class). Undoubtedly, physical health, sensory capacities, anxieties, and the like also will affect attention. Unfortunately, the teacher cannot easily exercise control over these internal factors. For example, if a student is hungry, he or she may very well be more interested in thinking about food than attending to a discussion of social problems in Latin America which is scheduled to begin forty-five minutes prior to lunch.

    External characteristics of the stimulus also affect attention. These characteristics are frequently linked to involuntary attention—that over which students have little control. Fortunately, skillful communication sources can manipulate these factors and increase the selective attention of their receivers. We have listed these external factors below:

    1. *The background or setting in which the object of attention is embedded.* Any stimulus (or message) is attended to in relation to the other stimuli surrounding it. To the extent that these stimuli are more attention demanding, a person will pay more attention to them. To the extent that they are equally attention demanding as the embedded stimulus, a person will have difficulty focusing attention. You have probably all had some experience with what we call the "sloppy blackboard" phenomenon. Blackboards have become useful teaching aids, but many teachers overuse them. Messages and diagrams often overlap or are crammed into tiny sections of the blackboard. When that occurs, selective attention to the intended information is often

reduced and, in fact, students may simply shift their attention to something altogether different. To the extent that a teacher's style of delivery is less demanding than a game of softball going on outside the classroom window, students' attention will also be misdirected. Recall the case of Mary mentioned at the beginning of this chapter. She was more interested in selectively attending to problems relating to her boyfriend (an internal factor) than to her homework assignment. These are all instances of stimuli losing their attention value by virtue of the setting in which they are embedded. As teachers, it is painful to think that we are no more "interesting" than other things in our students' lives. As a result, we all too often take our "attention value" for granted, a dangerous assumption to make.

2. *The intensity of the stimulus.*   Intensity refers to how loud, or bright, or vivid a stimulus may be. We always notice the loud and frequent talkers in class. Sometimes they are the only students whose names we know! As a teacher, the intensity of your message (the extent to which it deviates from a neutral position) can have a significant attention value. But a word of caution is in order. Although the intensity of your message can enchance your credibility and your ability to influence student attitudes, it may well reach a point where your audience can no longer tolerate it. If your students are highly involved in an issue, for example, highly intense messages advocating a position opposite from theirs may result in a negative attitude toward you as a teacher. On the other hand, if they are not very involved in your class or the issue you are discussing, highly intense messages can be a useful tool to insure that you have their attention.

3. *The extensity of the stimulus.*   Extensity refers, literally, to the size or amount of the stimulus. We tend to pay more attention to larger stimuli. Communication research has indicated that people pay more attention and assign more credibility to larger (taller!) male sources. These individuals are also perceived as being more attractive. Whether you are a male or female teacher (or student) you know how difficult it can be when you are vying for attention with a 7'2" high-school basketball star. Of course, you can increase selective attention to your messages using easily visible teachings aids (which also have a high level of intensity).

4. *The concreteness or complexity of the stimulus.*   Concreteness refers to the degree to which a stimulus has a definite physical structure. Students will pay more attention to a discussion of interior design when they can work with a model rather than simply listen to an explanatory lecture. Complexity, on the other hand, refers to the ease with which a stimulus can be recognized. It is difficult to talk about "love" in a family-relations class, since love is such a difficult concept to define and make recognizable.

Communication research has provided us with some useful tips for dealing with problems of concreteness and complexity of stimuli. First, when you are dealing with abstract concepts, try to find concrete verbal analogies for them; connect them to the physical world. The reason students have difficulty paying attention to more abstract stimuli is because the number of sensory channels that are useful to them is reduced. For younger children in particular, it is important that they be allowed to feel or touch or taste or smell or see what you are talking about. When dealing with complex stimuli, a great deal of time should be spent in organizing your messages carefully, so that the simpler structures of the stimuli are made easily recognizable. This, coupled with concrete examples, should help to increase the attention span of your students.

5. *The contrast and velocity of the stimulus.* Contrast and velocity refer to the striking quality, variety, novelty, change, movement, and activity that a stimulus, message, or source possesses. In general, the more activity you engage in with your students, the more likely they are to pay attention to you. Just be careful not to overdo this—you may wind up competing with your own message for their attention. Moderate extroversion has been found to be a desirable characteristic of communication sources.

6. *The impressivity of the stimulus.* Impressivity refers to the duration and repetition of the stimulus. Research has indicated that repetition of a message can increase the accuracy of its reception and helps to overcome the effects of competing stimuli. With respect to duration, you know how long a pause can be when you are waiting for someone to respond to a question. Often we will pay more attention to that than to the answer.

These, then, are the six external factors that influence selective attention and can be manipulated by a careful teacher. The significance of selective attention to learning cannot be overlooked. One of our most important planning activities is to determine the *conditions* and *techniques* we will use to present messages in our classes. Remember: that which is best attended to is also best understood and remembered—and that means it is most likely to be learned.

SELECTED REFERENCES

Bach, S., and G. S. Klein. "Conscious Effects of Prolonged Subliminal Exposures of Words." *American Psychologist* 12 (1957): 397.

Baker, L. L. "The Influence of Subliminal Stimuli upon Verbal Behavior." *The Journal of Experimental Psychology* 20 (1957): 84–99.

Broadbent, D.E. "A Mechanical Model for Human Attention and Immediate Memory." *Psychological Review* 64 (1957): 205–215.

Broadbent, D. E. *Perception and Communication.* (London: Pergamon Press, 1958).

Brock, T.C., S.M. Albert, and L.A. Becker. "Familiarity, Utility, and Supportiveness as Determinants of Information Receptivity." *Journal of Personality and Social Psychology* 14 (1970): 292–301.

Canon, L. K. "Self-Confidence and Selective Exposure to Information." In *Conflict, Decision, and Dissonance,* L. Festinger, ed. Stanford: Stanford University Press, 1964, pp. 83–96.

Chapanis, N.P., and A. Chapanis. "Cognitive Dissonance Five Years Later." *Psychology Bulletin* **61,** no. 1 (1964): 22.

Crane, L. D., R. J. Dieker, and C. T. Brown. "The Physiological Response to the Communication Mode: Reading, Listening, Writing, Speaking, and Evaluating." *The Journal of Communication* **20** (1970): 231–240.

Davis, W. L., and E. J. Phares. "Internal-External Control as a Determinant of Information-Seeking in a Social Influence Situation." *Journal of Personality* **36** (1967): 547–561.

Deaux, K. "Variations in Warning, Information Preference, and Anticipating Attitude Change." *Journal of Personality and Social Psychology* **9** (1968): 157–161.

Dieter, J. "The Nature of Subception." Ph.D Dissertation, University of Kansas, 1953.

Deutsch, J., and D. Deutsch. "Attention: Some Theoretical Considerations." *Psychological Review* **70** (1963): 80–90.

Donohew, L. et al. "A Conceptual Model of Seeking, Avoiding, and Processing." In *New Models for Mass Communication Research,* P. Clarke, ed. Beverly Hills, Cal.: Sage, 1973.

Donohew, L., and P. Palmgreen. "An Investigation of Mechanisms of Information Selection." *Journalism Quarterly* **48** (1971): 412–420.

Donohew, L., and P. Palmgreen. "A Reappraisal of Dissonance and the Selective Exposure Hypothesis." *Journalism Quarterly* **48** (1971)

Donohew, L., J.M. Parker, and V. McDermott. "Psychological and Physiological Measurement of Information Selection: Two Studies." *Journal of Communication* **22** (1972): 54–63.

Eagle, M. "The Effects of Subliminal Stimuli of Aggressive Content Upon Conscious Cognition." *Journal of Personality* **27** (1957): 578–600.

Egeth, H. "Selective Attention." *Psychological Bulletin* (1967): 41–57.

Fox, M. "Differential Effects of Subliminal Stimuli and Supraliminal Stimulation." Ph.D. dissertion, New York University, 1960.

Freedman, J. L. "Confidence, Utility, and Selective Exposure." *Journal of Personality and Social Psychology* **2** (1965): 778–780.

Freedman, J. L. "Preference for Dissonant Information." *Journal of Personality and Social Psychology* **2** (1965): 287–289.

Gaito, J. "Stages of Perception, Unconscious Processes, and Information Extraction." *Journal of General Psychology* **70** (1964): 183–197.

Garner, W. R. "The Stimulus in Information Processing." *American Psychologist* **25** (1970): 350–358.

Gibb, J. D. "Experimental Study of the Effects of Subthreshold Prestige Symbol in Informative and Persuasive Communication." Ph.D dissertation, Wayne State University, 1966.

Hendrick, C. "Preference for Inconsistent Information in Impression Formation." *Perceptual and Motor Skills* (1969): 459–466.

Hills, J. W., and W. D. Crano. "Additive Effects of Utility and Attitudinal Supportiveness in the Selection of Information." *Journal of Social Psychology* **89** (1973): 257–269

Hovland, C. I., and M. Sherif. *Social Judgment.* New Haven: Yale University Press, 1961.

Jecker, J. D. "Selective Exposure to New Information." In *Conflict, Decision and Dissonance,* L. Festinger, ed. Stanford, Cal.: Stanford University Press, 1964.

Johnson, J. R. "Psychology in Advertising: What Research Says about Subliminal Stimulation." *The Journal of Business Education* **36** (February 1961): 205–207.

Katz, E. "On Reopening the Question of Selectivity in Exposure to Mass Communication." In *Theories of Cognitive Consistency,* R. P. Abelson et al., eds. Chicago: Rand McNally, 1968, pp. 788–796.

Kendler, H. H., and T. S. Kendler. "Selective Attention Versus Mediation: Some Comments on Machintoch's Analyses of Two Stage Models of Discrimination Learning." *Psychological Bulletin* **66** (October 1966): 4.

LaVoie, A. L., and S. K. Thompson. "Selective Exposure in a Field Setting." *Psychology Reports* **31** (October 1972): 2.

Lubrosky, L., R. Rice, D. Phoenix, and C. Fisher. "Eye Fixation Behavior as a Function of Awareness." *Journal of Personality* **36** (1968): 1–20.

McCarthy, M. V. "Commitment, Utility, Relevance, and Supportiveness as Determinants of Information Receptivity." *Dissertation Abstracts* **33A,** no. 5 (1972): 2495–2496

McCleary, R. A., and R. S. Lazarus. "Autonomic Discrimination Without Awareness: An Interim Report." *The Journal of Personality* **18** (1949): 171–179.

McConnell, J. V. "Subliminal Stimulation: An Overview." *American Psychologist* **13,** no. 5 (1958): 229–239.

McGuire, W. J. "Selective Exposure: A Summing Up." In *Theories of Cognitive Consistency: A Sourcebook,* R. P. Abelson, E. Aronson, W. J. McGuire, T. M. Newcomb, M. J. Rosenberg, and P. H. Tannenbaum. Chicago: Rand McNally, 1968, pp. 797–800.

Miller, J. C. "Discrimination without Awareness." *American Journal of Psychology* **52** (1939): 562–578.

Mills, J. "Effect of Certainty about a Decision upon Post-Decision Exposure to Consonant and Dissonant Information." *Journal of Personality and Social Psychology* **2** (1965): 749–752.

Mills, J., and A. Ross. "Effects of Commitment and Certainty upon Interest in Supportive Information." *Journal of Abnormal and Social Psychology* **68** (1964): 552–555.

Norman, D. A. "Toward a Theory of Memory and Attention." *Psychological Review* **75,** no. 6 (1968): 522–536.

Paletz, D. L., J. Koon, E. Whitehead, and R. B. Hagens. "Selective Exposure: The Potential Boomerang Effect." *Journal of Communication* **22** (1972): 48–53.

Paschal, F. G. "The Trend in Theories of Attention." *Psychological Review* **48** (1948): 383–403.

"Paranormal Communication: A Symposium." *Journal of Communication* **25** (1975): 96–194.

Plax, T. G., and E. R. Hays. "A Systems Approach to the Study of Information-Seeking Behavior: A Valuable Area for Communication Research." Paper presented at the International Communication Association Convention, Montreal, April 1973.

Raleigh, K. K. "Children's Selective Listening to Stories: Familiarity Effects Involving Vocabulary, Syntax and Intonation." *Psychology Reports* **33** (1973): 255–266.

Rhine, R. J. "Some Problems in Dissonance Theory Research on Information Selectivity." *Psychological Bulletin* **68** (1967): 21–28.

Robinson, D. O. "The Limits of Selective Attention in DAF Shadowing." *Physionomic Science* **21**, no. 6 (1970): 325–327.

Rosen, S. "Post-Decision Affinity for Incompatable Information." *Journal of Abnormal and Social Psychology* **63** (1961): 188–190.

Saegert, S., W. Swap, and R. B. Zajonc. "Exposure, Context, and Interpersonal Attraction." *Journal of Personality and Social Psychology* **25** (1973): 234–242.

Schramm, W., and D.F. Roberts, eds. *Process and Effects of Mass Communication.* Rev. ed. Urbana: University of Illinois Press, 1971.

Sears, D. O., and J. L. Freedman. "Commitment, Information Utility, and Selective Exposure." *USN Technical Reports,* ONR, Nonr-233 (54) NR 171-350, no. 12 (August 1963).

Sears, D. O., and J. L. Freedman. "Selective Exposure to Information: A Critical Review." *Public Opinion Quarterly* **31** (1967): 66–97.

Sears, D. O., and J. L. Freedman. "The Effects of Expected Familiarity with Arguments upon Opinion Change and Selective Exposure." *Journal of Personality and Social Psychology* **2** (1965): 420–426.

Sherif, M., C. Sherif, and R. Nebergall. *Attitude and Attitude Change.* Philadelphia: Saunders, 1965.

Singer, J. E. "Motivation for Consistency." In *Motivational Antecedents and Behavioral Consequences,* S. Feldman, ed. New York: Academic Press, 1966, pp. 47–73.

Smith, G. J., D. P. Spence, and G. S. Klein. "Subliminal Effects of Verbal Stimuli." *Journal of Abnormal Social Psychology* **59** (1959): 167–176.

Stanek, F. J. "The Effect of Stimulus Complexity on Selective Attention." *Dissertation Abstracts* **31** (11-B) (1971): 6959.

Triesman, A. M. "Contextual Cues in Selective Attention." *Quarterly Journal of Experimental Psychology* **12** (1960): 242–248.

Triesman, A. M. "Strategies and Models of Selective Attention." *Psychological Review* **75**, no. 3 (1969): 282–299.

Vernon, J. A., and D. H. Badger. "Subliminal Stimulation and Human Learning." *The American Journal of Psychology* **72** (1959): 265–266.

Vernon, M.   "Perception, Attention, and Consciousness." In *Foundations of Communication Theory,* K. K. Sereno and C. D. Mortensen, eds. New York: Harper & Row, 1970.

Vidman, N., and M. Rokeach.   "Archie Bunker and Bigotry: A Study in Selective Perception and Exposure." *Journal of Communication* 24 (Winter 1974): 36–47.

Vohs, J. L.   "An Empirical Approach to the Concept of Attention." *Speech Monographs* 31 (1964): 355–360.

Voor, J. H.   "Subliminal Perception and Subception." *Journal of Psychology* 41 (1956): 437–458.

Wheeless, L. R.   "The Effects of Attitude, Credibility, and Homophily on Selective Exposure to Information." *Speech Monographs* 41 (1974): 329–338.

Wheeless, L. R.   "The Relationship of Attitude and Credibility to Comprehension and Selective Exposure." *Western Speech* 38 (1974): 88–97.

Zajonc, R. B.   "Attitudinal Effects of Mere Exposure." *Journal of Personality and Social Psychology,* Monograph Supplement 9 (1968): 1–24.

5

Communication and Information Processing in the Classroom

After reading this chapter, you should be able to do the following.

1. Define "concept."
2. Define each of the following concept rules:
   a. single attribute
   b. conjunctive
   c. disjunctive
   d. relational
3. Explain what is meant by "conceptual hierarchy."
4. Explain the relationship between concepts and language.
5. Explain the relationship between concepts and meaning.
6. Describe and explain the variables that affect perception.
7. Describe and explain language variables that affect information processing.
8. Discuss the effects of concrete information processing styles on:
   a. formal classroom communication behavior.
   b. interpersonal interaction.
9. Describe techniques for establishing appropriate learning environments for students whose conceptual systems range from concrete to abstract.

In the preceding chapter, we discussed the ways students acquire information in the classroom. We are now going to begin to explore the mechanisms students use to process information they receive *via* communication.

For years, many people concerned with the study of communication and human interaction—sociologists, psychologists, anthropologists, and communication researchers—assumed that communication outcomes could be explained in terms of a simple stimulus-response model. They said, in effect, that the outcomes of communication events were responses we had learned, through the process of socialization, to associate with certain communicative stimuli (messages). This S ⟶ R model, as it is sometimes called, can be diagrammed as follows: stimulus (message input) ⟶ response (behavioral output) ⟶ reinforcing stimulus. As discussed in Chapter 3, this model implies that if any given response emitted in the presence of some stimulus is reinforced (rewarded), that response will, across time, tend to become associated with that stimulus. Although there are many kinds of conditioning, or learning, models, the type of learning described in this model is called stimulus-response learning. It is one of the most popular and widely used explanations for how we learn to communicate. Even though we used this model in Chapter 3 as the basic framework for the learning process (because we are convinced that it is, at least in part, basic to all learning), it nevertheless leaves unanswered some very fundamental questions regarding what happens to the informational stimuli students acquire. We would like now to briefly explore some of those questions with you and discuss some of the issues relating to what goes on between the "S" and the "R" when we begin the process of instruction.

If you have ever communicated with anyone (and we assume that you have) you have probably noticed that the same person does not necessarily respond the same way to the same communicative behavior all the time. That variability refutes a very basic assumption of the stimulus-response model: that there is a one-to-one, or linear relationship between stimulus and response. This model may explain the behavior of rats very well, but until rats learn to talk, it is a gross oversimplification of a very complex process. But even if we do accept this simplified explanation, some very bothersome questions still remain. What do we mean by stimulus? What is a response? It is probably possible to find a response to any communicative stimulus if we define response at a molecular level, that is, in terms of very small response units. For example, we can talk about changes in neural states, or gross muscle twitches, and so forth. But does knowing about these kinds of responses help us to know about the effects of our communication? Do you pay attention (indeed can you even attend to) those kinds of responses when you interact with someone? We doubt it. Consequently, defining what a stimulus and what a response is can be very troublesome and perhaps not even very useful. Although we are not ready to completely abandon all of learning theory, we would like to extend it beyond the psychology lab to human communication behavior in the classroom.

How can we explain that your students do not respond in any noticeable and useful way to some of the communicative stimuli that they receive? For example, they may not appear to be making any response at all to a book you are reading to them. How are you (as an instructor) to reinforce them if you cannot perceive their responses? On the other hand, how are you to explain the variability of the responses that they do make to communicative stimuli? Are you to assume that their conditioning has not been appropriate, or that you have not communicated, or that communicative behavior cannot be predicted? As communicators and teachers, we cannot accept the latter, since unless we could do so we could not adapt to our environment. Equally, we cannot do much about the first, since we will never be able to know *exactly* what a given student's conditioning history is and, in any case, we probably could not do much about it if we did know. And it is especially difficult to tell in some cases if we have communicated with students at all, since many of their responses are either not immediate or not observable. Instead of answering these questions, we are going to offer an alternative explanation as an "out." We are going to assume the existence of variables that "mediate" the communicative stimuli your students receive and affect the responses they make. These mediators can affect the rapidity of their responses or the variability of the responses they make to similar stimuli. These mediators, in other words, are the mechanisms they use to process information. We are going to call these mediators "concepts." Before we begin to consider how concepts affect information processing, however, we need to learn a few basic things about concepts themselves.

THE PROCESS OF CONCEPT ATTAINMENT

Concepts Defined

Quite possibly, you may think you already have a meaning for the commonly used word "concept." You have probably heard people say, or you may have said, something like, "That is an interesting concept," or, "I can't quite seem to get that concept." These statements illustrate fairly well what we mean by the word "concept," but they do not help us to explain how we get and use concepts. As an example, try to imagine how you would define "concept" to someone who has never learned the word. In other words, imagine that you are teaching it to a naive student. Was your explanation clear, could it be communicated accurately? Did you succeed in teaching your student a concept for "concept"? Hopefully, this little exercise will help to convince you that although "concept" is a fairly commonplace word, it is not easily definable. We also suspect that, even though you may use the word a great deal, you do not understand it and are probably not aware of the significance of the thing to which it refers. In order to try to make things a little clearer, we offer the following definition of concept: *a learned technique for grouping incoming stimuli into psychological classes, such that it is possible to discriminate stimuli*

that are members of a class from stimuli that are not members of that class.
This is the formal definition generally used by the people who study concepts.
Before we develop this definition, however, we would like to demonstrate the
process by which we acquire the concepts we have—the process of concept
attainment.

Imagine for a moment that you have volunteered to participate in an
experiment. You do not know what the experiment involves, except that it has
something to do with human learning. Consequently, you are probably experiencing some anxiety as you approach the learning lab. When you arrive at the
lab, however, you find that the experimenter is a kindly gentleman with gray
hair, a gray beard, and a white lab coat. He asks you to be seated at a small
rectangular table. On the table is a strange-looking device called a memory
drum. The experimenter tells you that he is doing research on the way in which
people memorize lists of words. The words, he says, are nonsense syllables. He
informs you that as you look into the memory drum you will be shown one picture at a time using one of the nonsense syllables. The full array of pictures
you might see is shown in Fig. 5.1. As a subject, you would not see all of them,
but only one at a time. For example, the picture in the top left column might
appear first. The experimenter pronounces the word "Ling." Then comes the
picture just below and the experimenter pronounces the word "Fard." The
experimenter tells you that you are to learn the name of each picture and as
soon as you are able to do so, you are to anticipate the experimenter, saying
the word before he does. He then names all of the pictures in the first row as
they appear to you. The first two, of course, are "LING" and "FARD." The
remaining pictures are named by him for you and they are called "RELK,"
"PRAN," "LETH," "DILT," "STOD," "MANK," and "MULP." The
second row is the second series of pictures, although no temporal break between series marks the beginning of a new cycle. Also, the first picture in the
second series is now called "PRAN," the second picture is now called
"RELK," and the third, "DILT." Somewhere in this series you begin to realize that you know the names of the pictures before the experimenter tells you.
Before you continue reading, try and see if you can correctly name all of the
pictures in Fig. 5.1. Remember, we have named all of the pictures in the first
row, and part of the second.

At the risk of sounding like the people who construct those tests published
in the supplementary sections of your Sunday newspaper, we are going to suggest that if you named all of the pictures correctly, you have developed the
appropriate concept for each of the nonsense syllables and can now correctly
identify instances of each of the stimulus pictures that belong in the classes
named by those nonsense syllables. Now, try to think about the process you
used to form those concepts. The first thing you had to do was discover the
characteristics or attributes common to stimuli belonging to a single class. For
example, the attribute common to all stimuli you classified as being "RELK"
was a *human* face—not monkey faces or giraffe faces or cow faces. Similarly,

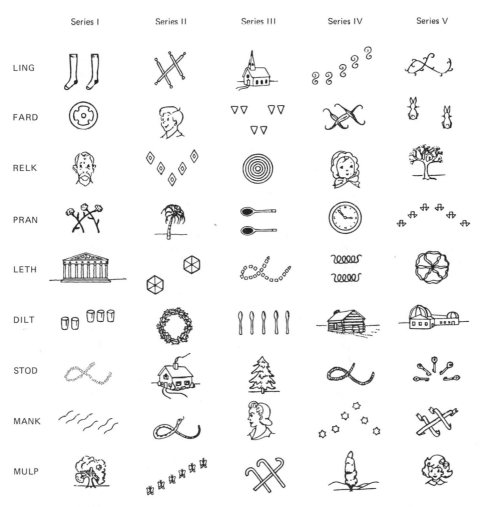

	Series I	Series II	Series III	Series IV	Series V
LING					
FARD					
RELK					
PRAN					
LETH					
DILT					
STOD					
MANK					
MULP					

Fig. 5.1 A concept learning task. (From Edna Heidbreder, "The Attainment of Concepts: Terminology and Methodology," *The Journal of General Psychology* 35: 173–189. Reprinted by permission.)

the attribute that defined instances of the concept called "FARD" was circularity. In this case, it does not matter if the circle is a clock, a gear, or a wreath; only the circularity of the stimulus matters. Therefore, the first principle of concept formation is that we must *learn* to *abstract* those attributes of a stimulus which are useful for identifying it as being a member of a particular class of stimuli. Learning, of course, implies that we are *taught* these attributes and that they are not genetically transmitted to us. The second principle of concept formation is that we must be able to *generalize* our ability to abstract these attributes to new instances of stimuli which are to be classified together in a concept. In addition, you will notice that not all of the stimuli called "FARD" possess exactly the same attributes. Since these stimuli varied in terms of certain characteristics, you had not only to abstract and generalize attributes, you also had to learn which attributes were *criterial*—that is, useful for identifying members of a concept. Other attributes of those stimuli were *noisy*—they appeared to be criterial, when, in fact, they were not.

We assume that you now have a concept for each of the stimuli named by the nonsense syllable. But we cannot see your concept, we can only infer it from your overt behavior—your ability to name new instances of the concept before they were named for you. Yet this process of inferring the existence of concepts can cause some trouble. For example, it has been argued that if we consider concept formation to be only the ability to perceive common attributes in stimuli, we could not distinguish between concept formation and all learning in general. Considering the example of a rat trained to jump toward a particular triangular form, one psychologist wondered if we should conclude that rats understand the abstract concept of triangularity.

It seems rather silly to think of rats *understanding* an abstract concept. Yet this point is a good one and should be considered. How do we know when a concept has been learned? Is it when we have learned to make a common response to a group of stimuli? Other psychologists have argued that a concept is considered to have been attained only when a subject is able to identify new instances of it without further training.

You know by having gone through the pictures in Fig. 5.1 that not all of the concepts are equally easy to learn; some are much more diffficult than others. For example, the concept "DILT" was probably much harder for you to learn than the concept "RELK." Yet suppose the experimenter had had to train you to make the appropriate response to each of those stimuli. You would have had to go through at least one training period for each of those forty-five stimuli. Imagine how long it would take if you had to go through similar training for all of the stimuli you encounter in a single day! An even better example of the difference between simple S ────▶ R learning and concept formation is found in the complaint teachers commonly hear from their students following a test. The students say, in effect, that although they learned to memorize the correct answers (responses), they didn't learn the material (form a concept). The implication, of course, is that there is more to learning a concept than just learning a common response to a particular array of stimuli. It is the ability to generalize new instances of a concept without further training that is the criterial attribute we use to determine if students have mastered a concept. *It is this ability which frees them from control of specific stimuli.* To determine if your students have learned any concepts in class, try this simple experiment: have them generalize concepts from the classroom to the "real world." We are willing to bet they won't be able to do so with a high degree of success. But, if you can help them to acquire this ability, it may be one of the most valuable and rewarding teaching experiences you will ever have.

Concept Rules

The single-attribute rule.   As you were trying to learn the concepts for the pictures presented in Fig. 5.1, you not only had to discover which attribute of each stimulus was criterial, but also, if there were more than one criterial attribute, you had to determine if their particular relationship helped to define conceptual membership. When we talk about conceptual rules, we are talking about *the perceived relationship(s) among criterial attributes within a given class of stimuli.* As far as we can tell now, four rules govern attribute relationships which are psychologically useful to us. The first, and simplest, of these rules is called *the single-attribute concept* (these rules, incidentally, name the kinds of concepts we use). The stimulus members of such a concept share a common criterial attribute not found outside that concept. All of the pictures in Fig. 5.1 belong to *single-attribute* concepts. The only attribute which defined "RELK," for example, was human face. Although single-attribute concepts are the easiest to use because they do not tax our memories very greatly, once we get beyond the laboratory and into the real world, it is difficult to think of very many concepts governed by the single-attribute rule. Perhaps you can think of some. As an exercise, see if you now have a concept for "single-attribute concept."

The conjunctive rule.   The second kind of conceptual rule is a very common one, although fairly complex. It is called the conjunctive concept. Stimuli which are members of this kind of concept have several appropriate criterial attributes which may be present in variable amounts. The rule governing the relationship among these attributes is expressed by the semantic rule "and," which for most of us has the general meaning "in addition to." If we have a conjunctive concept "X," with stimuli having the criterial attributes "P," "Q," "R," the conjunctive concept rule would be expressed as "X = P *and* Q *and* R." "Science fiction," for example, is the name of a concept of stories that are fictional *and* have plots revolving about some hypothesized scientific advances *and* examine the social effects of those advances.

The disjunctive rule.   A disjunctive concept is defined by any one of a set of alternative attributes. If we have a disjunctive concept called "X," with attributes "P," "Q," "R" criterial for the stimuli that are to be assigned to "X," the semantic expression of the relationship among those attributes would be expressed as "or." Thus, our disjunctive concept might be written as "X = P *or* Q *or* R, *or* P *and* Q *and* R." The "strike" in baseball is the name of a clearly disjunctive concept. A strike is a pitch that is between the batter's knees and shoulders and is across the plate, *or* it is a pitch that the batter swings at and misses, *or* it is a pitch the batter hits into foul territory. We will say more about this type of concept later in the book.

The relational rule.   The fourth type of rule identifies classes of stimuli called relational concepts. The rules governing the association between attributes in relational concepts are usually expressed in such phrases as "greater than," "less than," or "equal to." Of course, the same relational rule is not needed to express the relationships among the attributes criterial; stimuli classified in relational concept "X" might be shown as "X = P which is *less than* Q which *equals* R." Or, it might be given as "X = P which is *greater than* Q which is *less than* R." Relational concepts are most often used in systems of inquiry which employ formalized logical rules as the method of analysis. Such systems would be areas of study like physics, math, and logic. You may recall learning relational concepts in your high school or college geometry courses. For example, "equilateral triangle" is the name of a relational concept which classifies stimuli as being geometric figures consisting of three enclosed sides, with each side being of equal length.

At this point, you should be able to specify the minimal conditions necessary to say that students have formed a concept. These are:

1. the ability to abstract criterial attributes in the stimuli to be classified;
2. knowledge of the rules which associate those criterial attributes; and,
3. the ability to generalize to new instances of the concept without further training.

The Structure of Conceptual Systems

The conceptual hierarchy.   As we noted above, all of us have concepts for the things we "know." But concepts, to have their greatest functional utility for us, do not necessarily exist independently of one another. Let us use as an example a concept from the field of biology. Suppose, as the teacher, you had just completed teaching a unit on marsupials (e.g., kangaroos or an Appalachian favorite, the opossum). You have tested all of your students and now assume that they have attained the concept. For your students, however, the single concept of marsupial is not very useful. In order for them to use the concept appropriately, they must first integrate into it the concepts they have for kangaroos and opossums. This integration may, in turn, produce a new integration of those two concepts. Finally, your students will probably have to integrate marsupial into all of the concepts they have about animals, and that, of course, is integrated into the concept they have about biology. Thus, all of the concepts people use to decode information are arranged into appropriate hierarchies, starting with the most general concepts (macro) down to the small-

One of the ways teachers can tell when students have learned a concept is when they can correctly identify an instance of the concept. This is basic to all accurate decoding of information.

est, most specific concepts (micro). We call these hierarchical orderings of concepts "conceptual systems"; all of the concepts in a system are interrelated, and a change in any one of the concepts will produce a change in the others. Of course, any one of these conceptual systems may be related in varying degrees to any of the other conceptual systems we have. And, while some of our conceptual systems are more closely linked than others, all of them help us to define who we are in relation to what we perceive. Thus, for us and our students, the total of our conceptual systems represent "reality." They help us to adapt to our environment by providing decoding systems for the information we receive. They affect the variety of ways in which we behave.

Concepts and language.   The concepts we form and change throughout our lives would not be of much use to us as human beings if we could not communicate them to other members of our social environment. Indeed, the word "communication" has its historical root in an ancient Greek word which we translate as meaning "to make common." The things, of course, which we are trying to make common when we communicate are the concepts we have attained. Without the commonality of concepts across people it is very likely that there would be no such thing as culture. We need some system for communicating the rich variety of concepts within a given individual. Simple whistles, grunts, and gestures do not permit enough variation to communicate unique concepts. The system that we use to communicate is called *language*, which can be simply defined as *the systematic ordering of symbols into meaningful units*. The systematic rules for ordering symbols are called *syntax* rules; you receive formal training in these rules when you study grammar. You receive less formal training when you go through the process of acquiring language throughout your life. Syntax helps us to process language into discrete conceptual segments. If you have ever tried to learn a second language you know that when you initially hear a sentence in that language it sounds like a continuous stream of vocalization. That perception of continuity between symbols is a function of the fact that you have not yet learned the concepts that will help you to segment these sounds into their appropriate discrete units.

The basic elements we use to form very elementary language concepts are called *phonemes*. Phonemes are, for the most part, vowels and consonants, and they correspond roughly to the letters of our written alphabet. Phonemes are not meaningful; they have no semantic content. We shall return later to the problem of how symbols acquire semantic content—i.e., the study of meaning.

We also learn to form concepts that are combinations of phonemes, or *morphemes*. Morphemes are the smallest unit of meaningful sounds in a language. All of the words that we use in a language consist of one or more morphemes.

Whether we are talking about phonemes or morphemes, it is obvious that we must form concepts of sounds (phonemes) and combinations of sounds (morphemes) before we can begin to communicate in a given language. So not only must we develop concepts for segments of a language—defined partly by syntactical rules—we must develop concepts for the *suprasegmental* parts of a language, the variations in pitch and stress and tone that also help us to conceptualize discrete language segments. When we write, we use a variety of symbols to represent the attributes of language segments. Try to make sense of a sentence lacking these attributes: "Mary where Jane had had had had had had had had had the teacher's approval." This sentence will probably make more sense to you if we add commas and semicolons to indicate pauses, and if we italicize words to indicate stress. "Mary, where Jane had had *had,* had *had* had; had had, had the teacher's approval." If you have not yet figured out that sentence, keep trying. We are not going to give you any further information. Perhaps the difficulty you may be having in translation will help to reinforce the notion of the importance of the segmental and suprasegmental concepts we must learn before we have any agility at all with a language.

Concepts and Meaning

Thus far, we have been discussing the relationship of concepts and the syntactic, or structural rules of language. But an important part of language and usage is the semantic content of symbols. The concepts we have and the se-

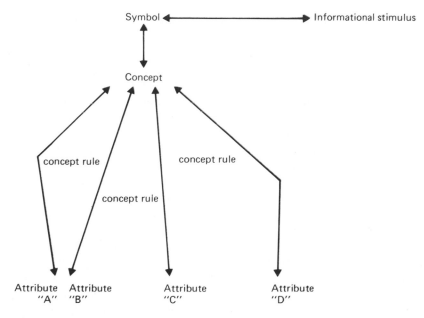

Fig. 5.2 The relation of concepts to meaning.

mantic content of what we communicate are related in a very complex way. We have tried to simplify this somewhat and have diagrammed this relationship in Fig. 5.2.

The relationships of concepts and meaning.   As you recall from doing the little concept-attainment exercise earlier in this chapter, while you were learning the concepts you were also learning a name for each concept (in this case a nonsense symbol). While the symbols we learn may be either verbal or nonverbal, for the present we are only going to deal with verbal symbols. (We will discuss nonverbal communication in Chapter 6.) These verbal symbols name, or stand for, the concept and are called *concept-referents*. The informational stimulus which is assigned to a psychological concept is called an *object-referent*. In Fig. 5.2, the arrows we have used to associate concept- and object-referents and attributes with the concept point in both directions. We have done this to imply that saying a word, perceiving a stimulus, or thinking of a concept are all acts which are equally capable of evoking each other. Thus, when we use the word "student," we are able to evoke your concept for "student" without having to show you one. Or, if we were to show you a student, it would also evoke in you the concept and the symbol "student." Of course, when the "student" concept is evoked, so also are the attributes you have in that concept. By the same token, when you are teaching and use a word such as "marsupial" for which a student does not have a concept, the word functions as a guidepost or cue that a concept should follow. Whenever we hear an unfamiliar word for which we have no concept, the flow of our information processing feels disrupted.

The concepts we use to decode information function to define reality for us. Because the critical variables we use to classify informational stimuli are the criterial attributes we have learned to associate with those stimuli, we also use those attributes to define the object-referents of concepts. For example, if you were to ask your students to define "water," or "cats," or "trees," they would probably give you a list of descriptive adjectives, such as bubbly, or retractable claws, or leafy. Consequently, we define meaning or the semantic content of symbols as a partial function of the attributes of a concept associated with its concept-referents and object-referents.

Whenever we use a word in isolation, there may, however, be a great deal of confusion about its meaning. By itself, the word "cat" can evoke concepts ranging from a furry animal to a type of heavy-construction equipment. But because we seldom are exposed to words in isolation, we have come to expect them to occur in certain *linguistic contexts*. Thus, if we are talking about pets when we say "cat," our listeners are not apt to think of a piece of heavy-construction equipment. By the same token, whenever we do hear a word in isolation, we have certain expectations regarding its meaning. For example, when we hear the word "help," we expect that the source of the word—i.e., the person calling "help"—is in need of some immediate assistance. Thus, the meanings that we associate with symbols are also derived from the context in which they occur.

Finally, and we cannot stress this point too strongly, even though there is a commonality of concepts and meanings across people in similar cultural and social groups, a great deal of variability exists from one individual to the next in terms of the meanings they assign to symbols and to object-referents. This is what we mean when we say that *meanings are in people, not in symbols*. For example, the American flag, as a symbol, has no meaning; the meaning is given by the people who perceive the flag. This principle has important implications for classroom teachers. Language changes across time. Many of our students speak a language that often seems to exclude those outside their peer group. It gives them cohesion and makes it more difficult for adults to intrude. Accompanying this change in language has been a change in what is permitted to be said. The use of what we may think of as obscenity is now commonplace, even in male-female interactions. Consequently, we are more likely to hear these words in our classes. Frequently, many teachers respond to an obscene word as though it was the thing it stood for. Of course, students and their parents do this as well. This can result in nonproductive, time-consuming confusion, as the following example illustrates. One of the authors of this book, as a graduate student teaching an introductory course in human communication, was teaching a unit on the effects of obscene language. We will relate the story to you as he told it, leaving in the "obscene" word which caused the problem.

> While I was teaching the unit on obscene language, I said to my students that if I were to use the word "shit" many of them would be more offended than if I had brought in a bucket of it. Nothing much happened, the class ended, and I went home. One of the students, however, was a commuter and when she went home she told her parents what I had said in class. About two days later the chairman of my department gave me a letter which he had received from the girl's mother, objecting to the so-called obscenity, and demanding my immediate removal from the classroom. A copy of the letter had also been sent to the dean of the graduate college and the president of the university. Well, after days of administrative shuffling and substitute teachers taking over my classes, I finally ended up in the president's office. He asked me what happened to cause all of this and I repeated the incident. He looked at me for a long time and said, "I guess this proves your point." Then he tore up the letter.

We can probably all think of many examples similar to this one. There is no ideal language style and, consequently, words can evoke a variety of meanings for people. Therefore, we should not make any attempt to change a student's language, for that can be very damaging to the student. At most, we should try to impress on our students that there may be occasions when a certain language style may not be perceived as appropriate and to assist them in developing alternative language styles.

VARIABLES AFFECTING
INFORMATION PROCESSING IN THE CLASSROOM

Now that we have examined the mechanisms students use to process information (concepts), we would like to further explore variables that facilitate or inhibit their ability to accurately process the messages you attempt to communicate in your classroom. These "human factors," which we discussed in Chapter 2, should help you to better understand the need for assessing the entering behaviors of your students before you plan how to communicate with them.

Sensory Limitations

When we think of students who have sensory limitations relating to processing information, we tend to think of those who may be deaf, or mute, or blind. Clearly, their encoding and decoding capacities are, initially at least, limited. But what we tend to forget is that all human beings have sensory limitations, for humans have only a limited number of sensory mechanisms (channels) through which to receive information about the world. Thus, any teaching strategy that reduces the number of senses used by students to receive messages reduces their ability to accurately process information. The standard one-to-many lecture format (which we do *not* advocate), for example, restricts students to using visual and auditory channels as the primary means of receiving information. You are probably all familiar with the now commonplace use of "multisensory" teaching strategies, employed in special education or primary grades with considerable success. It is unfortunate that such techniques are not systematically utilized in the higher grades as well.

Perception Levels

As we pointed out in Chapter 4, the attention levels of students may vary considerably. In addition, their levels of perception may vary a great deal as well. In fact, a great many perceptual processes occur below the level of conscious awareness. Considerable evidence suggests that different potential information is "routed" to different areas of the brain for processing. Words that people perceive as obscene do not appear to go through the normal information-processing centers of the brain; rather, these words are "short-circuited" to more emotional response areas. (Remember the story of the response to the obscene word we shared with you earlier.) In addition, some information to which we are negatively oriented may be processed below the level of awareness and also routed to some highly emotional information-processing areas.

Learned Habits

The environment in which students learn concepts and the extent to which those concepts have been reinforced affect their interpretation and understanding of the information received. As a result, students build up "patterning tendencies" in the ways they process information about stimuli:

1. *Similarity*.   Items of the same shape, size, or quality are more likely to be perceived as a group or pattern than are dissimilar elements (even if those attributes are "noisy"). Students, for example, may assign to all teachers the same stereotypical characteristics.

2. *Proximity*.   Items that are close together physically may be grouped together psychologically. Teachers may think of students from an inner-city area as being a group, and thus essentially alike.

3. *Continuity and closure*.   There is a tendency to avoid breaking the continuous flow of a live design or pattern, whether the stimuli be visual or a spoken message. As a result, missing information is "filled in," often at the expense of accuracy.

Expectancy

Clearly, the ways in which students and teachers expect each other to behave and communicate affect the ways in which they process information. We think this is a serious problem, and have devoted Chapter 10 to a more in-depth discussion of it. At this point, however, a simple example will serve to illustrate the effects of expectancy on information processing.

One of our colleagues used to play a simple trick on his students. He would uncork a small bottle, smell the liquid inside, and grimace. Then he would pass the bottle around the class and ask students to raise their hands when they could smell something in the bottle. Soon, the "confederates" he had planted in the class would raise their hands and, after a while, the other unsuspecting students would also begin to smell odors ranging from ammonia to perfume. The bottle, of course, contained nothing but clear, odorless water. What his students expected to perceive, they perceived.

Anxiety and Conflict
People have much more difficulty processing information under conditions of high anxiety, stress, or tension. You have probably taken exams where you were so tense that it was difficult to read the questions. This is why we stressed in Chapter 3 that it is very important to clearly specify the decoding objectives you have for students. While this technique will not overcome all processing difficulties due to anxiety, it will help to alleviate some tension before it can become a problem.

Social and Physiological Needs
When social and physiological needs become intense enough, they will affect information-processing capabilities. In one set of now-famous experiments, hungry students saw food through translucent glass, even though none was present. This is, of course, one of the reasons why the government has been advocating hot-breakfast and lunch programs in public schools. It is hard for students to understand the causes of the Civil War or to learn set theory while they are thinking of steak and eggs!

You have probably also had the experience of students seeming concerned only with how much an exercise counts toward their final grades, how long a term paper should be, or what they should study for an exam. Here, information processing is affected by social needs—the need to do well, to please parents, or to "look good" to their peers. Once again, learning takes second place to evaluation.

Attitudes, Beliefs, and Values
As we pointed out in Chapter 4, our internal states (attitudes, beliefs, and values) affect information acquisition. These same variables also affect information processing. For example, our fictional student Velma selected a particular course because she was more favorably disposed to the teacher. Similarly, students will also interpret information and process it according to their perceptions of the teacher. If a student does not like you, then it is not likely

that (s)he will respond very favorably to the information you provide. We will look more closely at the problem of source perceptions and attitudes on information processing in Chapter 7.

Message Variables

In general, verbal and nonverbal messages that contain those elements which increase attention (see Chapter 4) are more likely to be accurately processed. We would like now to briefly examine some of the more common elements relating to message content and arrangement which teachers must deal with when determining the content to be taught and the size and order of instructional units.

Organization.   Most of us would expect that the organization of a message affects its comprehension and processing. Research, however, indicates that this is not always the case. If a message is moderately well organized, it usually produces the same level of comprehension as an extremely well organized message. Only when a message is extremely disorganized does detrimental information-processing occur. The order in which important points are placed in a message does, however, affect processing and recall. In general, material presented first or last in a message is better remembered and understood.

Message sidedness.   Research has shown that two-sided messages are more persuasive than one-sided messages. A two-sided message presents opposing views and sometimes refutes them. This produces greater retention and comprehension, because attention and perceptions are increased by the contrast, change, and novelty introduced by the message strategy. This type of message structure is particularly important when a teacher is concerned with affective learning.

Language intensity.   Language intensity refers to the extent to which a source's position deviates from neutrality. Many teachers feel that intense language facilitates learning; and, to a certain extent, it does in that it increases students' attention levels. If students' anxiety levels are increased by the intensity of the language, however, then it becomes difficult for them to discriminate among critical aspects of the message. After a while, information processing of the message will be terminated.

Concreteness and ambiguity.   As teachers, we usually expect that the more concrete (or specific) our language and examples are, the better they will be remembered and processed. For the most part, this is correct. The difficulty in accurately processing ambiguous language cues comes from the fact that lack of specificity in a message will often cause students to distort the message to fit their own past experiences, attitudes, and needs. We will look further at the effects of an orientation for processing concrete information later in this chapter.

Suggestions for Teaching Concepts in the Classroom

In this chapter, we have been trying to demonstrate to you the complexities of information processing by having you attain some concepts of your own. We have attempted to facilitate this by giving you visual stimuli to work with (e.g., Fig. 5.1). Most of the formal teaching we do in a classroom, however, is done linguistically. Consequently, our students learn concepts vicariously, without having a great deal of direct commerce with the object-referents of those concepts. This makes learning concepts very difficult. Therefore, we must be doubly careful that our students have, in fact, attained the concepts we are teaching. We recommend that the following communication strategies be employed when preparing for any teaching experience.

1. Carefully describe the concept verbally and, when possible, provide a physical example of the concept. We call this starting with a "positive instance."

2. Make sure you have defined the criterial attribute of the concept.

3. Always define the concept rule. It may be single-attribute, conjunctive, disjunctive, relational, or some combination of these. People attain concepts faster and with fewer errors when concepts rules are explained to them. Disjunctive concepts may be particularly troublesome, because one cannot always tell which attributes are criterial, even though one has the concept. Remember that a disjunctive concept rule is expressed as "P or Q" *or* "P and Q." Thus, if we preccive some stimulus as possessing "P" or "Q" we may be able to classify it as an instance of the concept "X" and decode it appropriately. On the other hand, if we ask our students to pick out instances of "X" and we start with the concept first, they may not be able to tell if "P" or "Q" or maybe both of them are going to be criterial. Therefore, whenever we are teaching disjunctive concepts, we must provide our students with as many examples as possible of things that are *not* examples of the concept. We should also explain why they are not.

4. Provide as much feedback as possible for students' attempts at classifying instances of the concept you are teaching. They need to know promptly if they have selected appropriate criterial attributes of the object-referent. Through feedback, they are able to eliminate some assumptions about the criteriality of attributes and retain others.

5. Provide them with ample opportunities to encounter the concept on their own, without any assistance from you. Try to use instances that you have not specifically taught in class.

6. Now you can test them.

INDIVIDUAL DIFFERENCES IN INFORMATION PROCESSING

As we noted earlier, information-processing capabilities are a function of the richness of the conceptual structure the student has developed. These capabilities are then *inferred* by the teacher on the basis of certain verbal or nonverbal behaviors the student exhibits in the classroom. The extent to which those behaviors lead to inferences about concepts similar to those the teacher wished to communicate will determine how favorably the student is evaluated. Thus, testing becomes the primary means of affording the teacher some relatively objective criteria for making those inferences.

Most of us, as teachers, have encountered or will encounter students who seem either highly resistant to processing new information or readily adaptable to all sorts of information. No matter how hard we try to structure messages to facilitate learning for the resistant group of students, they remain recalcitrant and rigid in their ability to adopt to new information in the classroom. All too often, we tend to equate this with a lack of intelligence; yet, in many of these instances, the problem runs much deeper. All students exhibit some degree of consistency in the ways in which they process types of information, even when these types are quite diverse. This consistency is referred to as a "cognitive style." Some students' cognitive styles are more useful and adaptable to classroom information than are others. The remainder of this chapter will be devoted to examining variations of one cognitive style that we believe to be of critical importance in classroom information processing: *concreteness-abstractness.*

Concreteness-Abstractness

Although the information-processing capabilities of students (and teachers) may differ in many ways, the continuum of concreteness and abstractness represents one of the most significant dimensions of information-processing behavior the occurs in the classroom. This continuum refers to the richness of the conceptual system the student utilizes. More specifically, it refers to the degree of differentiation the student's conceptual system permits, the extent to which the student is able to modify existing informational structures to generate new and useful solutions to problems, and the extent to which the student is "open" to new information.

As with all conceptual systems, concreteness-abstractness may be inferred from behavioral components exhibited in the classroom. At the extreme level, concreteness as a cognitive style is represented by behaviors that demonstrate high stimulus-response connections. For example, the student who consistently makes correct responses to test items that tap concepts which have been *specifically* explained in class, but who is unable to make a correct response to items that require the *student* to make the item-concept connection, is exhibiting a *concrete* conceptual system. As teachers, we often use this type of behavior as an attribute for classifying those students who have memorized correct responses without demonstrating any understanding of the concepts being taught. Conversely, students whose conceptual systems place them on the more abstract end of this continuum indicate less stimulus-bound types of behavior, and often behave in ways we think of as being more creative and less rigid.

There has been a great deal of empirical research related to the impact of concreteness as a cognitive style on subsequent information-processing outcomes. We have summarized the major findings of these studies, and have grouped them into two categories: (I) those studies related to information processing of the formal content of a class; and (II) those related to interpersonal relationships with other students and teachers. Students with more abstract conceptual systems tend to exhibit reversed behaviors in terms of each of these findings.

**Concreteness Category I: Information-Processing
Outcomes in Terms of Formal Classroom Content**
Students demonstrating concreteness as a cognitive style may exhibit:

1. a greater inability to change information-processing styles and try different approaches and, thus, a greater rigidity in solving new and complex problems;

2. a greater tendency toward trite and normative behavior and, thus, a lower level of creativity;

3. a greater intolerance and difficulty in processing ambiguous information;

4. a greater tendency to confuse means with ends and to concentrate on details, resulting in a longer time to complete class projects and assignments.

**Concreteness Category II: Information-Processing
Outcomes Affecting Interpersonal Relationships in the Classroom**
Students demonstrating concreteness as a cognitive style may exhibit:

1. a greater tendency to form and generalize impressions of other people from incomplete information, often resulting in stereotypic responses;

2. a reduced capacity to role play, to "put oneself in another's boots," resulting in a low degree of empathy and tolerance for individual differences in the classroom;

3. a greater reliance on information relating to role, status, and formal authority for use as guidelines to judgments and behaviors, resulting in excessive dependency on the teacher to provide rules for appropriate ways of interacting and making decisions;

4. a greater insensitivity to interpersonal feedback, which results in a tendency to persevere in old, if inappropriate, ways of interacting with others in the classroom;

5. a greater tendency to make more evaluative, polarized, and extreme judgments of others in the classroom.

The nine information-processing outcomes (and their opposites) described above are associated with several conceptual systems occurring along the concreteness-abstractness continuum. In the sections that follow, we discuss four of these conceptual systems and offer some suggestions for structuring messages to help ensure that students representative of these types may successfully decode information and learn more efficiently.

It should be noted that we are not concerned with *changing* the conceptual systems or cognitive styles of students. If such change is believed necessary, a trained, competent professional is called for. Rather, we are presenting simple descriptive statements regarding the behavioral correlates of these conceptual systems, so that the teacher may begin to gather information which will at least minimally facilitate classroom planning around these individual differences. The systems, as they are described below, are ordered from "most concrete" to "most abstract." In addition, we have attempted to avoid using evaluative terminology when labeling them. Instead, we have called them "CS1," "CS2," "CS3," and "CS4." If this seems less than elegant to you, consider the dangers involved in linking certain expectations about students to certain assigned categories.

Communication Correlates of CS1 Students
Students who are most representative of this system tend to behave in a high stimulus-response fashion, similar to the "concrete" student described above. Because of this, their responses to certain informational stimuli in the classroom are very rigid and stereotypic. Many of the statements they make about their peers and teachers are highly evaluative and absolutist. For example, we often hear students making statements such as: "Teachers can't be trusted," "Anyone over thirty is a drag," or "English is worthless." While many students have probably said similar things at one time or another, it is the frequency and repetitiveness of such statements, even in the face of continuously contradictory information, which is characteristic of the CS1 student. Because they are not easily adaptable to information that runs counter to their own conceptual systems, they tend to become overcommitted to a single solution—"the right way." In addition, their nonadaptive behaviors lead them into blind adherence to formal rules, and to high levels of dependency on persons whom they perceive as being in positions of authority, such as teachers, school administrators, and parents. Since they often need to rely on others for guidance and direction, they are highly fatalistic, believing that what happens

to them is often not under their control. Very frequently, these students will make comments such as, "There is no point in me studying, since whatever happens to me in school is all up to the teachers anyhow."

Establishing appropriate learning environments for CS1 students. Conceptual System 1 students do not function well in an environment which rewards responses to unstructured and ambiguous information. They will tend to do less well on problem-solving tasks, have a lower level of satisfaction with the overall classroom environment and materials. For such students, it is important that the instructor make all of the criteria for receiving a particular evaluation clear and easy to understand, that the behaviors the student must perform to receive such an evaluation be equally clear and easily understood, and that there is a great deal of redundancy in the presentation of these criteria and behaviors. In cases such as these, the use of good behavioral objectives incorporated into a syllabus is especially recommended. We believe, and much of the communication research has indicated, that it is unreasonable to evaluate CS1 students largely on the basis of creative or original thinking. Rather, they have a better opportunity of attaining classroom concepts in a highly structured information environment. Perhaps more importantly, they will develop more positive attitudes toward the total learning environment if they are given some structure, which may encourage them to seek out further information and "learn on their own." Such independence is one of the most desirable outcomes of the effective use of communication in the classroom.

Communication Correlates of CS2 Students
One of the most frequently observed communication behaviors of the CS2 student is negativism and an antiauthority orientation. They rebel against the formal guidelines of behavior used by the CS1 student, and perceive themselves as highly alienated and not well integrated into the communication systems used by their peers. They are often suspicious and distrustful of their peers and authority and thus attempt to avoid any social contact through interpersonal communication. They are highly unwilling to disclose important aspects of themselves, particularly those which may be useful to teachers, since they often believe that such disclosure has the potential of being used to manipulate and control them. Thus, they tend to be, as one teacher described, "very distrustful loners." Although they have a somewhat richer conceptual system then do CS1 students, they associate unstructuredness and ambiguity with distrust. While they may often rebel against power and authority when they do not have it, they will use it tyrannically against others when they gain such means of control.

Establishing appropriate learning environments for CS2 students. CS2 students are not easy students to deal with in the classroom. Although they have a richer conceptual system than do CS1 students, they nevertheless require a highly structured information environment. Thus, as with the CS1 student, they will probably learn best when the behavioral criteria for attaining classroom rewards are clearly stated. At this point, however, a word of caution is in order. Empirical research has indicated that CS2 students learn best in a structured environment in which *the teacher is perceived as not being highly authoritarian*. When CS2 students believe their teacher is exercising a great deal of control over their behavior, they tend to rebel, oftentimes becoming disruptive influences in a classroom.

Many CS2 students also exhibit behaviors reminiscent of those of the communication-apprehensive students (to be described in Chapter 9). To the extent that many of these students are apprehensive, or appear to be apprehensive, we must reinforce the point that frequent and forced interactions with other students and teachers can potentially be damaging to CS2 students. Since interpersonal communication may be such an anxiety-producing situation for them, it is likely to increase their feelings of distrust of, and alienation from, others. Many teachers report to us that they believe that increased interaction with CS2 students, plus attempting to create a "warm, human climate" for such students, is the best approach. As we point out in Chapter 9, in the absence of any systematic technique employed to overcome communication anxiety, we could not *disagree* more, particularly in the case of CS2 students. Our concern here is with the creation of information environments in the classroom that maximize each student's learning potential. While we as teachers may not prefer certain of these environments, these "undesirable" ones may provide necessary adjustments for some students.

Communication Correlates of CS3 Students

CS3 students have a conceptual system which is next to the highest level of abstraction we will deal with. CS3 students are characterized by communication behaviors that imply a desire to be liked, and which attempt to establish interpersonal relationships that encourage mutual dependency and will permit them to manipulate others. In fact, this type of manipulation through interpersonal communication is often the primary method used by CS3 students to control their environment. Thus, CS3 students tend to see themselves as causal agents, particularly among their peers, which gives rise to a more differentiated conceptual system and a greater tolerance for ambiguous and unstructured information. Ironically, however, they tend to have a less well-developed sense of personal values and must rely heavily on interpersonal feedback from peers and other socially significant persons in their reference group. As a consequence, they are highly adaptive and well liked by their peers, often emerging as opinion leaders in the classroom. As one teacher told us, "These are the kids who are always voted 'best liked' by their senior class." On the other hand, CS3 students are especially sensitive to threats of rejection and social isolation, and are particularly vulnerable to situations where classroom performance is evaluated on the basis of individual performance.

Establishing appropriate learning environments for CS3 students.   CS3 students do not need a highly structured information environment. They do, however, need a great deal of feedback, particularly from the teacher, regarding the quality of their work. Perhaps of all of the students we will discuss, CS3 students have the highest need for communication with their teacher. Thus, teachers should make some plans for frequent interaction with such students.

In addition, CS3 students should not be heavily evaluated on work they have done by themselves. It is not so much a function of the fact that their own work is inferior, as it is the fact that working in isolation under high evaluation conditions is so anxiety producing to them. In fact, these students often make very good task and social leaders in classroom work groups and can provide a great deal of assistance to the teacher. Our teachers have reported a great deal of success and student satisfaction when these students are used as group leaders for teaching such a diverse variety of subjects as reading, history, and mathematics, ranging from the sixth-grade level through college.

Communication Correlates of CS4 Students

CS4 students represent the highest level of abstract conceptual systems we will discuss. Their communication behavior indicates a high task orientation, independent information seeking and exploratory behavior without inappropriate negative attitudes toward teachers or peers, and well-developed personal criteria for evaluation of their work. Because they have a highly developed conceptual system, they are tolerant of new information and are well able to integrate it into existing psychological frameworks. Because they have a tendency to avoid rigid behaviors, they are often able to articulate several alternative ways of obtaining a solution or a goal. As a consequence, it is often CS4 students who are perceived by peers and teachers alike as being competent task leaders.

Establishing appropriate learning environments for CS4 students.   Because CS4 students seem so highly adaptable to a variety of information environments, there is the risk that teachers will ignore them when it comes time to prepare syllabi for classes. Although these students do learn well across a range of environments, they are probably happiest and have a higher level of satisfaction with courses where they are permitted to learn on their own, with a minimum of external influences. Thus, it becomes paramount that CS4 students are given opportunities to explore alternative solutions to problems, to test the utility of these problems, and perhaps to discover new problems on their own. In short, these are the students who are likely to perform best and be happiest in an unstructured environment, in an environment many educators now refer to as "the open classroom."

There is a second, and equally significant, risk teachers must be aware of when dealing with CS4 students. Because these students appear to be so well adjusted, teachers will frequently spend a great deal of their time interacting with these students, perhaps even to the exclusion of other students. While it is always important to communicate with students, our positive expectations about students may lead to increased interaction with those students who will, in turn, show substantial improvement gains in learning. In sum, some CS4 students may do well in a class because certain behaviors lead a teacher to *believe* they will do well and, as a consequence, the teacher increases interaction with those students. While this is not detrimental to CS4 students, it puts other students in a situation where their behavior is evaluated in terms of CS4 students' behavior. We are opposed to evaluating students in terms of their *different* responses to what a teacher believes to be the *one* ideal learning environment, or *one* ideal "type" of student. Rather, students should be evaluated only in terms of their learning achievement in the environment that is best suited to their information-processing styles.

Some of you may now be wondering (and reasonably so) how in the world you could implement all, or even some, of these various recommended strategies in a single classroom without generating utter chaos for both you and your students. The suggestions that follow have come to us from several of the teachers with whom we have worked. We are not recommending specific teaching methods; rather, we are recommending the creation of learning environments within which the teaching methods you have learned may be employed.

Suggestion 1:   Spend as much time as possible during the first two weeks of class interacting with all of your students and observing their interactions with other students. Within this period, you may wish to assess their responses to a variety of informational stimuli, ranging from completely structured to unstructured. If possible, avoid grading these responses. You may wish to use the nine information-processing outcomes listed above to "sort" students' behaviors.

Suggestion 2:   Given this information, try to assess the predominate conceptual styles of each of your students, using the four categories we have provided. You may wish to add some of your own, given the particular nature of the classes you teach. *Remember, however, that these are gross judgments which you should be willing to modify as the classroom progresses and you acquire new information.* (These judgments are also absolutely confidential. Sharing them with others would be highly unfair to your students.)

Suggestion 3:   Using the recommendations following the description of each of the four conceptual systems, create several learning environments (in terms of the ways in which information is structured and obtained) in which all of the students participate. Equal participation ensures that all students have an equal amount of input into the learning process, and that any judgmental errors you may have made about the students can be corrected.

Suggestion 4:   Weigh the evaluations of such student's work in a particular learning environment given the suitability of that environment to each student's conceptual system. In this way, students who do well across a variety of environments can be appropriately rewarded, whereas others will not be unfairly punished for performing poorly in an environment to which they cannot as easily adapt.

SELECTED REFERENCES

Andersen, P.   "An Experimental Study to Assess the Effects of Source Credibility on Comprehension." Paper presented at the Speech Communication Association Convention, New York, November 1973.

Ashby, W. R.   *Design for a Brain.* New York: Wiley, 1960.

Atkin, C.   "Instrumental Utilities and Information Seeking." In *New Models for Mass Communication Research*, Peter Clarke, ed. Volume II of Sage Annual Reviews of Communication Research. Beverly Hills: Sage, 1973, pp. 205–242.

Ayres, H. J.   "An Overview of Theory and Research in Feedback." Paper presented at the ICA Convention, Phoenix, Arizona, April 1971.

Beighley, K. C.   "An Experimental Study of Three Speech Variables on Listener Comprehension." *Speech Monographs* 21 (1954): 248–253.

Bersheid, E., and E. Walster.   "Interpersonal Attraction." Reading, Mass.: Addison-Wesley, 1969.

Bierei, J.   "Cognitive Complexity-Simplicity and Predictive Behavior." *Journal of Abnormal and Social Psychology* 51 (1955): 263–268.

Block, J., and J. Block.   "An Investigation of the Relationship Between Intolerance of Ambiguity and Ethnocentrism." *Journal of Personality* 19 (1951): 303–311.

Bowers, J. W., and M. Osborn.   "Attitudinal Effects of Selected Types of Concluding Metaphors in Persuasive Speeches." *Speech Monographs* 33 (June 1966): 147–155.

Broadbent, D. E.   *Decision and Stress.* London: Academic Press, 1973.

Broadbent, D. E.   "Information Processing in the Nervous System." *Science* 150 (1965): 457–462.

Brown, R.   *Words and Things.* New York: The Free Press, 1957.

Bruner, J. S., J. J. Goodnow, and G. A. Austin.   *A Study of Thinking.* New York: Wiley, 1956.

Carter, R. R.   "Stereotyping as a Process." *Public Opinion Quarterly* 26 (1962): 77–91.

Chall, J. S.   *Readability*. Columbus: The Ohio State University Press, 1958.

Cherry, C.   *On Human Communication*. New York: Wiley, 1957.

Claunch, N. C.   "Cognitive and Motivational Characteristics Associated with Concrete and Abstract Levels of Conceptual Complexity." Joint ONR and NIMH Report, Princeton University, 1964.

Cohen, A. R.   *Attitude Change and Social Influence*. New York: Basic Books, 1964.

Darnell, D. K.   "The Relation Between Sentence Order and Comprehension." *Speech Monographs* **30** (1963): 97–100.

Deese, J., and S. H. Hulse.   *The Psychology of Learning*. New York: McGraw-Hill, 1967.

DeFleur, M. L.   *Theories of Mass Communication*. New York: McKay, 1970.

DeVito, J. A.   "Comprehension Factors in Oral and Written Discourse of Skilled Communicators." *Speech Monographs* **32** (1965): 124–129.

Driver, M. J.   "The Relationship Between Abstractness of Conceptual Functioning and Group Performance in a Complex Decision Making Environment." M.A. thesis, Princeton University, 1960.

Ehrensberger, R.   "An Experimental Study of the Relative Effectiveness of Certain Forms of Emphasis in Public Speaking." *Speech Monographs* **12** (1945): 94–111.

Gange, R. M.   *The Conditions of Learning*. New York: Holt, Rinehart and Winston, 1965.

Gardiner, J. C.   "A Synthesis of Experimental Studies of Speech Communication Feedback." *Journal of Communication* **21** (1971): 17–35.

Gillie, P. J.   "A Simplified Formula for Measuring Abstraction in Writing." *Journal of Applied Psychology* **41** (1957): 214–217.

Goldstein, K., and M. Scheerer.   "Abstract and Concrete Behavior: An Experimental Study with Special Tests." *Psychological Monographs* **53** (1941): 86–94.

Goss, B.   "The Effect of Sentence Context on Associations to Ambiguous, Vague, and Clear Nouns." *Speech Monographs* **39** (1972): 286–289.

Gurwitsch, A.   *The Field of Consciousness*. Pittsburgh: Duquesne University Press, 1964.

Guthrie, M. L.   "Effects of Credibility, Metaphor, and Intensity on Comprehension, Credibility, and Attitude Change." M.A. thesis, Illinois State University, 1972.

Haney, W. V.   "A Comparative Study of Unilateral and Bilateral Communication." *Academy of Management Journal* **7** (1964): 128–136.

Harrell, M., J. W. Bowers, and J. P. Bacal.   "Another Stab at 'Meaning': Concreteness, Iconicity and Conventionality." *Speech Monographs* **40** (1973): 199–207.

Harvey, O. J., D. E. Hunt, and H. M. Schroder.   "Conceptual Systems and Personality Organization." New York: Wiley, 1961.

Hastorf, A. H., D. J. Schneider, and Polefka.   *Person Perception*. Reading, Mass.: Addison-Wesley, 1970.

Hayakawa, S. I.   *Language in Thought and Action*. New York: Harcourt, Brace, 1949.

Henneman, R. H. "Vision and Audition as Sensory Channels for Communication." *Quarterly Journal of Speech* **38** (April 1952).

Hill, W. F. *Learning.* Scranton: Chandler, 1971.

Hovland, C. I. "A Communication Analysis of Concept Learning." *Psychological Review* **59** (1952): 461–472.

Hovland, C. I., O. J. Harvey, and M. Sherif. "Assimilation and Contrast Effects in Reactions to Communication and Attitude Change." *Journal of Abnormal and Social Psychology* **55** (1957): 244–252.

Hovland, C. I., and W. Mandell. "An Experimental Comparison of Conclusion-Drawing by the Communicator and by the Audience." *Journal of Abnormal and Social Psychology* **47** (1952): 581–588.

Hovland, C. I., and M. Sherif. *Social Judgment.* New Haven: Yale University Press, 1961.

Hovland, C. I., and W. Weiss. "Transmission of Information Concerning Concepts Through Positive and Negative Instances." *Journal of Experimental Psychology* **45** (1953): 175–182.

Janis, I. L., and W. Milholland. "The Influence of Threat Appeals on Selective Learning of the Content of a Persuasive Communication." *Journal of Psychology* **37** (1954): 75–80.

Jersild, A. T. "Models of Emphasis in Public Speaking." *Journal of Applied Psychology* **12** (1928): 611–612.

Jones, R. W., and J. S. Gray. "Systems Theory and Physiological Processes." *Science* **140** (1963): 461–466.

Jordan, W. J., L. L. Flanagan, and R. W. Wineinger. "Novelty and Recall Effects of Animate and Inanimate Metaphorical Discourse." *Central States Speech Journal* **26** (1975): 29–33.

Kamin, L. J. "Predictability, Surprise, Attention, and Conditioning." In *Punishment and Adversive Behavior*, B. A. Campbell and R. M. Church, eds. New York: Appleton-Century-Crofts, 1969.

Knapp, M. L. *Nonverbal Communication in Human Interaction.* New York: Holt, Rinehart and Winston, 1972.

Kibler, R. J., L. L. Barker, and D. J. Cagala. "Effect of Sex on Comprehension and Retention." *Speech Monographs* **37** (1970): 287–292.

Korzybaski, A. *Science and Sanity: An Introduction to Non-Artistotelian Systems and General Semantics.* 3d ed., rev. Lakeville, Ct.: The International Non-Aristotelian Library Publishing Co., 1948.

Kurtz, K. H., and C. I. Hovland. "The Effect of Verbalization During Observation of Stimulus Objects Upon Accuracy of Recognition and Recall." *Journal of Experimental Psychology* **45** (1953): 157–164.

Lashbrook, W. B., P. Hamilton, and W. Todd. "A Theoretical Consideration of the Assessment of Source Credibility as a Function of Information Seeking Behavior." Paper presented at the Western Speech Communication Association Convention, Honolulu, November 1972.

Livingston, H. M.   "An Experimental Study of Effects of Interest and Authority Upon Understanding of Broadcast Information." Ph.D. dissertation, University of Southern California, 1961.

Luria, A. R.   *Higher Cortical Functions in Man*. New York: Basic Books, 1966.

Mabry, E. A.   "A Multivariate Investigation of Profane Languages." *Central States Speech Journal* 26 (1975): 39–44.

Mackay, D. J., and T. Bever.   "In Search of Ambiguity." *Perception and Psychophysics* 2 (1967): 193–200.

Mackay, D. M.   "Information Theory in the Study of Man." in *Readings in Psychology*, J. Cohen, ed. London: Allen and Unwin, 1964.

McCroskey, J. C.   "Measures of Communication Bound Anxiety." *Speech Monographs* 37 (1970): 269–277.

McCroskey, J. C., and W. H. Combs.   "The Effects of the Use of Analogy on Attitude Change and Source Credibility." *Journal of Communication* 19 (1969): 333–339.

McLaughlin, B.   "Effects of Similarity and Likableness on Attraction and Recall." *Journal of Personality and Social Psychology* 85 (1971): 51–64.

Miller, G. A.   *Language and Communication*. New York: McGraw-Hill, 1951.

Miller, G. A.   "The Magical Number Seven, Plus or Minus Two: Some Limits on Our Capacity for Processing Information." *Psychology Review* 63 (1956): 81–97.

Miller, G. R.   "Human Information Processing: Some Research Guidelines." In *Conceptual Frontiers in Speech Communication*, Kibler and Barker, eds. New York: SCA, 1969, pp. 51–67.

Mills, R. G.   "A Relative Frequency Principle in Processing Contingent Information." *Psychonomic Science* 18 (1970): 215–217.

Minsky, M.,   ed. *Semantic Information Processing*. Cambridge, Mass.: MIT Press, 1968.

Nichols, A. C.   "Effects of Three Aspects of Sentence Structure on Immediate Recall." *Speech Monographs* 32 (1965): 164–168.

Nichols, R. G.   "Factors in Listening Comprehension." *Speech Monographs* 15 (1948): 154–163.

Osgood, C. E.   *Method and Theory in Experimental Psychology*. New York: Oxford University Press, 1953.

Osgood, C. E., G. J. Suci, and P. Tannenbaum.   *The Measurement of Meaning*. Urbana: University of Illinois Press, 1957.

Pagano, D. F.   "Information Processing Differences in Repressors and Sensitizers." *Journal of Personality and Social Psychology* 26 (1973): 105–109.

Paivio, A., J. C. Yullie, and S. A. Madigan.   "Concreteness, Imagery, and Meaningfulness Values for 925 Nouns." *Journal of Experimental Psychology, Monograph Supplement* 76 (1968): 1–25.

Paschal, F. G.   "The Trends in Theories of Attention." *Psychological Review* 48 (1948): 383–403.

Paulson, S. "The Effects of the Prestige of the Speaker and Acknowledgment of Opposing Arguments on Audience Retention and Shift of Opinion." *Speech Monographs* 21 (1954): 267–271.

Petrie, C. R., Jr. "Informative Speaking: A Summary and Bibliography of Related Research." *Speech Monographs* 30 (1963): 79–91.

Pettigrew, T. F. "The Measurement and Correlates of Category Width as a Cognitive Variable." *Journal of Personality* 26 (1958): 532–544.

Pines, H. A., and J. W. Julian. "Effects of Task and Social Demands on Locus of Control Differences in Information Processing." *Journal of Personality* 40 (1970): 405–415.

Redding, W. C., and G. A. Sanborn. *Business and Industrial Communication: A Source Book.* New York: Harper & Row, 1964.

Rogers, E., and F. F. Shoemaker. *Communication of Innovations.* New York: The Free Press, 1971.

Rokeach, M. *The Open and Closed Mind.* New York: Basic Books, 1960.

Rosenkrantz, P. S., and W. H. Crockett. "Some Factors Influencing the Assimilation of Desperate Information in Impression Formation." *Journal of Personality and Social Psychology* (1965): 397–402.

Scott, M. D., M. Yates, and L. R. Wheeless. "An Exploratory Investigation of Communication Apprehension in Alternative Systems of Instruction." Paper presented at the International Communication Association Convention, Chicago, April 1975.

Seiler, W. J. "The Effects of Visual Materials on Attitudes, Credibility, and Retention." *Speech Monographs* 38 (1971): 331–334.

Shamo, W. G., and J. R. Bittner. "Information Recall as a Function of Language Style." Paper presented at the International Communication Association, Phoenix, Arizona, April 1971.

Sherif, M., C. Sherif, and R. Nebergall. *Attitude and Attitude Change.* Philadelphia: Saunders, 1965.

Spielberger, C. D. *Anxiety and Behavior.* New York: Academic Press, 1966.

Thistlethwaite, D. L., and J. Kamenetsky. "The Effect of 'Directive' and 'Nondirective' Communication Procedures on Attitudes." *Journal of Abnormal and Social Psychology* 51 (1955): 3–12.

Thomas, G. L. "Effect of Oral Style on Intelligibility of Speech." *Speech Monographs* 23 (March 1956): 46–54.

Thompson, E. "An Experimental Investigation of the Relative Effectiveness of Organization Structure in Oral Communication." Ph.D. dissertation, University of Minnesota, 1960.

Thompson, E. "An Experimental Investigation of the Relative Effectiveness of Organization Structure in Oral Communication." *Southern Speech Journal* 26 (1960): 59–69.

Thompson, E. "Some Effects of Message Structure on Listener's Comprehension." *Speech Monographs* 34 (1967): 51–57.

Toch, H., and M. S. Maclean, Jr. "Perception and Communication: A Transactional View." *Audio Visual Communication Review* **10** (1967): 55–77.

Tucker, C. O., and E. L. McGlone. "Toward an Operational Definition and Measurement of Understanding." *Central States Speech Journal* **21** (1970): 41–45.

Vernon, M. D. "Perception, Attention and Consciousness." In *Foundations of Communication Theory*, K. K. Sereno and C. D. Mortensen, eds. New York: Harper & Row, 1970.

Vernon, M. D. *The Psychology of Perception*. Baltimore: Penguin Books, 1963.

Wheeless, L. R. "An Investigation of Receiver Apprehension and Social Context Dimensions of Communication Apprehension." *Speech Teacher* **24** (1975): 261–268.

Wheeless, L. R. "The Relationship of Attitude and Credibility to Comprehension and Selective Exposure." *Western Speech* **38** (1974): 88–97.

Wheeless, L. R. "The Relationship of Four Elements to Immediate Recall and Student-Instructor Interaction." *Western Speech* **39** (1975): 131–140.

Wheeless, L. R., and R. Charles. "A Review and Reconceptualization of Stereotyping Behavior." Paper presented at the Speech Communication Association Convention, New York, November 1973.

Wheeless, L. R., and J. C. McCroskey. "The Effects of Selected Syntactical Choices on Source Credibility, Attitude, Behavior, and Perception of Message." *Southern Speech Communication Journal* **38** (1973): 213–222.

Wheeless, L. R., and M. Willis. "The Relationship of Attitudes Toward Course and Instructor to Learning and Student-Instructor Interaction Assessment." Paper presented at the Speech Communication Association Convention, Chicago, December 1974.

Whorf, B. *Language, Thought, and Reality*. Cambridge, Mass.: The Technology Press, Massachusetts Institute of Technology, 1956.

Yullie, J. C., and A. Paivio. "Abstractness and Recall of Connected Discourse." Journal of Experimental Psychology **82** (1969): 467–471.

Zagona, S., and R. Harter. "Credibility of Source and Recipient Attitude: Factors for the Perception and Retention of Information on Smoking Behavior." *Perceptual Motor Skills* **23** (1966): 155–168.

Zimbardo, P. "Verbal Ambiguity and Judgmental Distortion." *Psychological Reports* **6** (1960): 57–58.

Nonverbal Communication in the Classroom

After reading this chapter, you should be able to do the following.

1. Identify the seven major nonverbal variables that impinge on communication in the classroom.

2. Distinguish between territory and personal space.

3. Identify two possible effects of violating touch norms with students.

4. Distinguish between "sparrows" and "owls" and recommend means of adapting instructional timing to both.

5. Distinguish between adults' and children's responses to conflicting verbal and vocal cues.

6. Identify five elements in a given classroom that might be made more attractive for students.

7. Distinguish between traditional, horseshoe, and modular seating patterns for classrooms in terms of their probable impact on communication in the classroom.

Up to this point, we have emphasized communication that involves the use of words—verbal communication. Another form of communication which has significant impact on the classroom is nonverbal communication. Several communication researchers have claimed that nonverbal communication constitutes over 80 percent of all our communication behaviors.

Nonverbal communication should be a significant area of concern for classroom teachers for two major reasons. The first of these relates back to the information-processing mechanisms we discussed in Chapter 5. In that chapter we pointed out the importance of obtaining communication feedback from students, so that teachers can make better judgments as to whether or not students have attained a concept. Most of that discussion centered around verbal communication feedback, as does most formal learning in the classroom. There is evidence, however, which indicates that this may not always be the best way to evaluate student learning. Research has shown, for example, that many students often attain concepts, particularly complex ones, before they can verbalize them. Thus, when a teacher demands verbal feedback, the teacher may be evaluating only whether or not a student can *verbalize* a concept, not whether or not the concept has been *attained.*

Nonverbal communication is also a critical aspect of interpersonal communication in the classroom. The most credible *messages* teachers generate as communication sources are nonverbal. Most people, including students, believe that our nonverbal communication is under less conscious control than is our verbal. Thus, our nonverbal messages are seen as more honest reflections of what we are *really* thinking or feeling at a particular time. Many of the cues students use to make judgments about a teacher's competence or character are obtained by observing the teacher's nonverbal behavior. We will discuss students' perceptions of teachers as sources in Chapter 7, but it should be stressed here that what a teacher does, the nonverbal messages that a teacher generates, have no inherent meaning, although they affect perceptions of the teacher (and teachers' perceptions of students, and students of one another). Just like verbal messages, the meanings that nonverbal messages communicate are assigned to them by receivers. We are going to look now at some nonverbal variables in the classroom and examine their impact on classroom communication.

SPACE IN THE CLASSROOM

Research in the area of *proxemics,* the study of the ways people use space while communicating, indicates that the use of space in a classroom can have a major impact on communication. To understand the impact of space on classroom communication we need to distinguish between *territoriality* and *personal space.*

The physical environment of a school can sometimes affect learning more powerfully than can the teacher.

Territory, as we are using the term here, refers to space that has a fixed or semifixed geographical location. Territorial space is, therefore, stable; for the most part, where it is today is where we would expect it to be tomorrow. Territoriality, a trait shared by human beings and lower forms of animal life, is the instinct to secure space for oneself and to defend that space against potential intruders. In the classroom, the teacher generally has a desk and chair. This desk and chair will usually be strategically located at the front or back of the room, and it is understood that this space belongs to the teacher and is to be left alone by the students. In many classrooms, the student also has a particular territory, either a desk or a particular position at a table. In some cases, particularly in the lower grades, such spaces may be assigned for a whole semester or for a year. In other instances, the student may have free choice of seating, but is very likely to choose one place at the beginning of the term and return to that space regularly throughout the term. Considerable difficulty can be forthcoming if a student has carved out a territory in the classroom and some other student seeks to take that territory over. Such invasions are likely to produce verbal aggression at the minimum and, very often, physical violence. Similarly, an invasion of the teacher's area is likely to result in a severe reprimand. Less flagrant violations of territory, such as sitting too close to another person's territory, are likely to produce tension and nervousness on the part of the person invaded, and, if the situation persists, can also lead to verbal or physical aggressive responses.

Personal space, unlike territory, has no fixed or semi-fixed geographical position. Personal space has been likened to an invisible bubble that moves with the individual and may expand in size or become smaller depending on the given situation. To exemplify its elastic nature, consider a school library that has four tables with chairs at each table. If there are three students in the library, each sitting at a different table, and a fourth student comes in, it is virtually certain that the student will go to the empty table, unless (s)he has a good friend among the three people already there. Each student will then "possess" a full table. The personal space bubble of each will be quite large. However, as more and more students enter the library, the personal space available at each table must be subdivided. Characteristically, the next few students that enter the library will sit at the end of the table opposite from the person already there. Essentially, the students will naturally divide the available personal space at the table and their personal space bubbles appropriately. If this normative behavior is not followed by someone, the result can be quite unpleasant. For example, let us presume that a student enters the library while there is a completely empty table available and chooses to sit right next to a student who is sitting alone at another table. The personal space bubble of the invaded student is unlikely to contract sufficiently to allow the intruder to sit there comfortably. The invaded student may verbally abuse the intruder or get up and move to another table.

To exemplify the kind of behavior that human beings typically engage in with reference to personal space, consider the circumstance of an elevator with one person occupying the elevator and one other person boarding the elevator. In such an instance, the two individuals will just naturally move to opposite sides of the elevator and psychologically divide it in half. The person who was on the elevator initially will contract his or her personal space bubble by half to allow room for the other person. As additional people board the elevator, each individual's personal space bubble will contract appropriately. Consider how you would feel, however, if you were the lone occupant of an elevator and an additional person got on the elevator and chose to stand on your side of an imaginary dividing line down the middle of the elevator. If you are typical, you would find this very uncomfortable. You would feel invaded and would probably generate hostile reactions toward the other individual, particularly if the other person was unfamiliar to you. Your presumed response in this instance is quite natural. As human beings grow and mature, they increasingly learn to control their responses to invasion of their personal space. However, small children have not yet learned to do so. They may respond very negatively to one another, with both verbal and physical aggression, without being aware of what exactly has produced their behavior. Teachers must be particularly conscious of this phenomenon, both in the classroom and in other school environments. While many other elements result in conflict among students, spatial invasions are some of the most frequent causes of disruptive behavior.

The classroom itself has a limited amount of space and the way that space is employed will affect the kind of communication, as well as the amount of communication, that occurs in the classroom. While there probably is an infinite number of ways of arranging a classroom, three patterns are most common. Figures 6.1 through 6.3 represent those most commonly found in American classrooms.

Figure 6.1 depicts the traditional arrangement for classrooms in most schools. We have arbitrarily included positions for twenty-five students and a teacher, but no special learning areas, such as might be found in the lower grades. This arrangement is probably most typical of upper grades, secondary-school classrooms, and college classrooms. Considerable research has been conducted regarding the nature of communication in this type of a classroom. It has been found that the people occupying the dark seats in Fig. 6.1 will account for a very large proportion of the total interaction between the teacher and the students in this type of arrangement. People sitting in the gray seats interact some, but much less frequently than those in the darkened areas. People in the white seats will participate very infrequently, if at all. Several

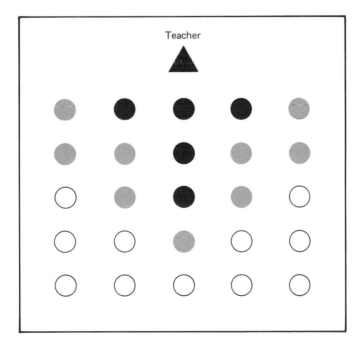

Fig. 6.1   Traditional classroom arrangement.

explanations for this variance in participation have been advanced. One of the most common is that the students sitting in the dark seats have the best visual contact with the teacher and are in comparatively closer proximity to the teacher while he or she is standing at the front of the room. As intuitively obvious as this explanation appears, there is reason to believe that it is not a satisfactory one.

Recent research has indicated that the students who choose the seats in the darkened areas differ from those who choose seats in the gray or white areas. In Chapter 9, we will consider the phenomenon of "communication apprehension" in considerable detail. At this point, we would simply note that some students are quite apprehensive about communicating with other people, particularly teachers, while other students look forward to such experiences and seek them. High communication apprehensives generally attempt to avoid interaction in the classroom and thus will gravitate to the seats depicted in Fig. 6.1 as white areas. Low communication apprehensives, on the other hand, will gravitate to the seats in the darkened areas. Students with moderate communication apprehension tend to select seats in the gray areas. Each of these different types of students, therefore, employs space in the classroom differently if they are given free choice. The question thus arises as to whether the teacher should permit the students to have free choice. Our answer is that the teacher should. If the teacher arranges the seating alphabetically or by some other arbitrary method, the interaction pattern represented in Fig. 6.1 will not usually be present. Verbal, low communication-apprehensive students will continue to participate, no matter where they are seated in such a system. Highly communication-apprehensive students will still avoid participation, even if they are put in the front row in the center. Thus, arbitrary seating arrangements will not alter the students' normal communication behavior; they will only alter where they are sitting in order to engage in it. A significant negative side effect can be produced as a result of alphabetical or other arbitrary seating arrangements. The student who wishes to participate may find it more difficult if he or she is assigned to a seat in the light area in Fig. 6.1. On the other hand, the highly apprehensive student who is assigned to the dark area may be extremely uncomfortable and develop very negative attitudes toward school and toward this particular teacher and class. If the teacher feels the need to have some kind of a seating chart, it is probably much better to allow the students to freely choose their seats for the first few days of class, and then simply assign them to the seats they have already chosen. This advice should not be taken to indicate that teachers should never move students for disciplinary reasons. However, the teacher must be very careful that he or she does not punish an innocent student by moving him or her to an inappropriate seat in order to discipline another student.

The classroom arrangement in Fig. 6.2 has been referred to as the "horseshoe" arrangement. Classes with fairly small enrollments are very often

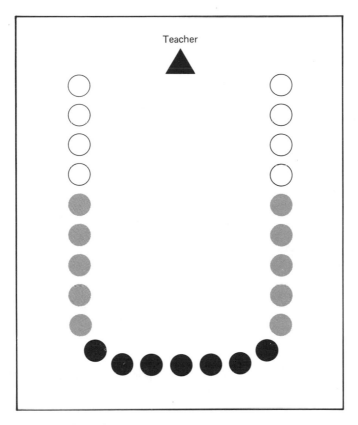

Fig. 6.2   Horseshoe arrangement.

arranged in this fashion. When students are given free choice of arranging the classroom, this is one of the most popular options. Such an arrangement provides equivalent space for each student and, at the same time, provides visual access to most other students and the teacher. Some research suggests that there is more participation in classes that are arranged in this way. Students who are at the opposite end of the horseshoe from the teacher, however, are those most likely to interact, while those at the right and left hand of the teacher are those least likely to interact. Again, students will have certain seating preferences in the horseshoe. The highly apprehensive students will tend to sit closer to the teacher on the right and left, presumably because they recognize that those seats provide less visual access to the teacher, who is trying to maintain contact with the entire group.

The classroom arrangement depicted in Fig. 6.3 has been referred to as the "modular" arrangement. This arrangement is very common in the lower elementary grades and in classes of a specialized nature in upper grades and

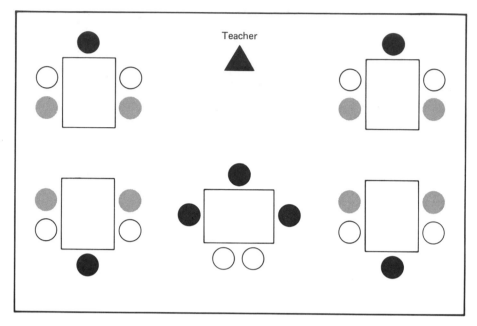

Fig. 6.3   Modular arrangement.

secondary schools. This arrangement is particularly desirable for classes requiring interaction among smaller groups of students. Modular arrangements such as the one depicted in Fig. 6.3 tend to increase the amount of student interaction, but at the same time make interaction with the teacher more difficult, unless the teacher moves from group to group. Certain seats within each of the modules will attract the more verbal students and be evaded by the apprehensive students. Again, these are indicated in the figure by the various shadings of the seats. The dark seats represent the areas where the most participation should be expected and the white seats represent the areas where the more apprehensive students will probably choose to sit.

While many other elements will determine the nature of communication in a given teacher's classroom, the arrangement of classroom space may have the largest impact. If the teacher wishes to dominate the interaction in the classroom, the traditional arrangement is probably the best. Since the students are seated side by side, the primary focal point is the teacher; thus, most interaction will go from teacher to student and from student to teacher. If the teacher desires that full-class interaction occur, the horseshoe arrangement may be the most desirable. This will encourage interaction both among the students and between student and teacher. If, however, a very important part of the learning in the class is dependent on student interaction with other students, the modular arrangement may be preferable. This arrangement permits many students to be interacting at the same time without impinging on one another. In any case, the teacher must be aware of the impact of spatial arrangement on verbal communication and on the spatial needs of the students in the classroom. Particularly in the lower grades, the teacher must be alert to the problem of spatial invasion and seek to avoid circumstances where students do invade one another's territory or personal space. If the teacher is very conscious of this problem, the interpersonal conflict that frequently occurs in any classroom can be substantially reduced.

TOUCH IN THE CLASSROOM

In North America, the use of touch to communicate feelings and emotions is a very powerful nonverbal message. Touch has differential impacts in the classroom depending on the age and sex of the students.

For younger children in the lower primary grades, touch plays an important developmental role. It can communicate a sense of belonging, security, and understanding to the child. Conversely, when a teacher withholds touch, a child may feel isolated and rejected, which can lead to the acquisition of negative attitudes toward school. Research in orphanages has revealed that in a low-touch environment, infants have a higher mortality rate and a higher level of alienation. High-touch environments produce a lower mortality rate among infants and the older children tend to be better socialized. There is also some evidence which indicates that frequent touching facilitates the development of the nervous systems of infants, making them more responsive to their environment.

Children in the lower elementary grades have a strong need to touch things around them. This is the way the child learns about her or his environment. The beginning elementary teacher may be somewhat disturbed by this behavior initially. It is not uncommon for small children to wish to touch the teacher's clothing or hair. They will also touch one another a lot. The teacher must be very careful to interpret children's touching behavior on the basis of adult touching norms. This is particularly true in the North American culture, where touching among adults is extremely limited.

As children grow older, they become more enculturated to sexual norms and touch can have a deleterious impact. In the North American culture, it is not generally considered appropriate for males to touch males, except in hand shaking, a shoulder clasp, or a pat on the back. In addition, only certain physical zones are permissible areas for males to touch females, and vice versa. Violations of these touch zones communicates sexual interest. Of course, in this culture, female-female touching is more permissible than male-male, but violations of certain zones still may communicate homosexual interest.

While certain general norms govern touching behavior in the North American culture, considerable differences exist among ethnic groups within the culture. These differences are apparent even in adults, but they are exaggerated even further among young children. While children of Northern European heritage tend to touch even less than the general North American norm, black children and children of Southern European heritage tend to touch much more. The teacher must recognize that these are set cultural variations and should be viewed in that light. The teacher of elementary-school children should keep in mind that, given a child's cultural origin, touch from the teacher can be an extremely powerful communicative message. The use of touch as a reward is very appropriate in the elementary school. A hug from the teacher can, in many cases, be much more reinforcing to the child's behavior than an A on a paper.

As children move into junior and senior high school, changes occur that require an alteration of teacher behavior. Awakening sexual interest in adolescents results in adaptation to adult touch terms. However, adolescents very often do not fully adapt to the norms of their older teachers. Hand-holding and touching in the hallways among male and female students is generally not looked on with great favor by teachers. However, such behavior merely signals an awakening sexual maturity. Children at this age have lost the freedom of touch they had learned to expect and enjoy as young children and have not yet learned to adapt fully to adult patterns. Teachers must also adapt to the particular age group. While touching is very appropriate and reinforcing for younger children, children at the junior and senior high school level will not necessarily interpret the teacher's touch in the same way. The use of touch as a reward at this stage may be greatly misinterpreted, particularly by other people who observe the touch. Most male teachers of junior- and senior-high-school students soon recognize that it is highly inappropriate to touch female students under almost any circumstance. While touch has a powerful positive impact on communication in the classroom when younger children are involved, it has too many emotional overtones to have much positive effect with other children. More than likely, the touch that was reinforcing and positive in the early years will be perceived as a sexual advance during the junior and senior high period.

BODY MOVEMENT AND GESTURE IN THE CLASSROOM

Movement and gestures by the hands, arms, legs, and other parts of the body and face are the most pervasive types of nonverbal messages and the most difficult to control. One social scientist has estimated that there are over 700,000 physical signs capable of stimulating meaning in another person. For example, there are twenty-three distinct eyebrow movements, each capable of stimulating a different meaning.

The variety of ways in which teachers and students walk, stand, or sit can all affect interpersonal perception. The teacher who slouches or twitches when talking to students is not likely to be perceived as a composed person.

Conversely, the teacher who always appears unruffled regardless of the circumstances is likely to be perceived as cold and withdrawn.

Facial expression involves some of the smallest bodily movements, but its impact in the classroom may be greater than any other body language the teacher exhibits. The teacher probably communicates more accidentally by his or her facial expression than by any other means. Scientists who study facial expression refer to "micro-momentary movements," changes in expression that constantly occur in all human communicators and are usually so fleeting that it requires highly technical photography to be able to isolate them for study. However, as quickly as they pass across a person's face, they are picked up by other people and produce responses.

When teachers are responding to students, these changes in facial expression can serve as reinforcers to the student or as nonreinforcers. Unfortunately, the teacher normally has very little control over such micro-momentary movements, but should be able to control more long-lasting expressions, such as smiles or frowns. Although it may seem surprising, it has been our experience that few teachers really do control their use of smiles and frowns in the classroom in order to reinforce students. More commonly, teachers simply respond to the student without thinking about what their nonverbal physical response may be communicating. Often a teacher does not want to communicate what he or she is thinking to the student. A student who gives a response that is not correct, but is in the right direction, probably should be rewarded, but the teacher's initial response is likely to register that the student's answer was not fully correct. While the teacher may not say that, his or her facial expression may communicate it very clearly. We cannot suggest here a bag of tricks for the teacher to employ in controlling his or her facial expression. Rather, we can only suggest that the teacher strive to be as aware as possible of the expressions he or she has in the classroom. Increased sensitivity to one's nonverbal bodily and facial movements can lead to more desirable classroom communication. But no one ever has, and probably no one ever will, be able to control completely all of the bodily and facial movements in which they engage.

Body type also communicates a variety of meanings, particularly as it relates to physical attractiveness. Three general body types, each capable of arousing several stereotypes about personality, can be identified. The first of these is the *ectomorph*. Ectomorphs are tall, thin, and fragile looking and are thought of as being tense, anxious, reticent, and self-conscious. *Mesomorphs* are bony, muscular, and athletic and are thought of as being dominant, energetic, and talkative. *Endomorphs* are described as soft, round, and fat and are thought of as complacent, warm, and sociable. Whether these adjectives are accurate is irrelevant; they represent the real stereotypes these body types arouse.

The reason we stress these various body types is because teachers, like other people, tend to stereotype students on the basis of their physical characteristics. The body type considered most physically attractive to most people in this culture is the mesomorph. Mesomorphs tend to get higher grades, not because they are more intelligent, but because they are more attractive and are likely to be targets of interaction. They are more popular with other students and teachers and often are the opinion leaders among their peers. Teachers must be very careful about the stereotypes. Intelligent students don't all look alike, they don't all wear glasses, and they are not all thin. Plump children are not all happy and contented and easy-going. Athletically built young people are not all "jocks." While few teachers would argue the validity of any of these body-type stereotypes, many *behave* as if they were valid. Thus, we should be aware of the impact of these variables on interpersonal communication in the classroom, particularly as they affect teachers' responses to students.

USE OF TIME IN THE CLASSROOM

In the North American culture, time is viewed as a commodity, as is reflected in such statements as, "Time is money" or "We've run out of time." Teachers tell students not to waste time, or to use their time more efficiently. Classes are scheduled to meet at certain times during the day. Tardiness is a punishable offense and students are required to have tardy slips. Colleges and universities have carried time considerations to their absurd extreme; undergraduate degrees are awarded partially on the basis of a minimum number of credits which are computed in terms of the number of contact hours a week students spend in classes. In many states, pay increases for public school teachers are based on a "thirty hours, plus," model.

While some people argue that formal time is really a type of verbal communication (we "read" clocks, "tell" time, etc.), the expectancies we have about "waiting" for people may be more clearly nonverbal. We have encountered a waiting norm at nearly all of the universities with which we have been associated (among the three of us, that comes to sixteen). It is a norm relating to how long students are expected to wait for "tardy" instructors, and it varies according to rank. For full professors, the maximum time is twenty minutes; for associate professors, the maximum time is fifteen minutes; for assistant professors, ten minutes; and for graduate teaching assistants, five minutes. We have no idea where these norms originated, but they seem well known, with minor variations, to all students. Nowhere do we know of an official policy that specifies such waiting time.

Since students are accustomed to classes running for a certain amount of time, they tend to be less than enthralled when their expectancies are violated. If reading is scheduled to end at 9:50 A.M. and arithmetic to begin at 10:00 A.M., students will start to engage in some nonverbal "leave-taking" behaviors around 9:45, such as putting away pens and pencils, closing notebooks, shuffling feet, and looking at the clock. It is probably not good to introduce new material near the end of a class period, since the time for attentiveness has in all likelihood passed its peak.

In such a time-conscious society, it should be no surprise that time impinges strongly on communication in the classroom. One of the more important uses of time on the part of the teacher is the use of the pause. Pausing while presenting information usually emphasizes the content that has just preceded or will immediately follow. Similarly, the amount of time a teacher spends on a certain topic will communicate to the students the relative importance of that topic. If in the elementary school only fifteen minutes during the entire day is spent on reading, the young person will quickly conclude that reading is not a very important part of the whole school program. In a very real sense, then, the use of time itself communicates in the classroom.

Most classrooms involve interaction between teachers and students, with the teacher asking questions to which the student is expected to respond. One of the hardest things for teachers to learn is to take sufficient time between asking the question and expecting an answer. All too often, the teacher expects an instant response. Frequently, no such response is forthcoming. The teacher may then give the answer, or may call on some poor student who is not ready to answer. Voluntary responses to questions in the classroom almost always occur if the teacher is willing to wait long enough. We are not suggesting, of course, a ten-minute waiting period, but the time may seem almost that long to the teacher at first. Few teachers would think that fifteen seconds is a long time to wait. Yet if we examine teacher behavior, we find that teachers seldom wait as long as five seconds! In addition, children have different response rates. Some children can process a question and determine what their answer will be quickly, while other children take two or three times as long to determine their response. This does not indicate a difference in intelligence or preparation on the part of the children, only a difference in response pattern. Children who respond quickly, of course, tend to become favorites of the teacher. Those who wait a long time probably participate much below average in most teachers' classrooms. Our advice to the teacher is to learn how to wait for a response and not to always call on the first student who is ready to respond.

In addition to response-time differences, children vary even more markedly in their basic time orientation. Such differences are almost universally ignored in elementary and secondary education in the United States. These differences relate to the bodily time of the individual. Most children, as well as most adults, can be placed into one of two categories relating to their bodily time: "sparrows" and "owls." Like their namesakes, sparrows are early risers and are at their best in the morning. Conversely, owls, like their namesakes, do not function well in the morning, but begin functioning better as the day proceeds and are at their best in the evening. While the largest percentage of both children and adults fall into the owl category, our elementary and secondary schools in the United States almost exclusively follow a sparrow pattern. Children are asked to be up and ready for the bus early in the morning, sometimes as early as 6:30 or before. Classes typically start between 7:30 and 8:30 in the morning. This is fine for little sparrow children, but it is dreadful torture for little owl children. It should come as no surprise, therefore, that sparrow children do much better in classes in the early morning than do owl children. Nor should it be surprising that owl children, for the most part, have lower overall academic averages than sparrow children, since they are seldom allowed to have important classes at the time when they are at their peak. As if this were not bad enough, teachers, as representatives of our society's culture, tend to preach the virtues of the sparrow existence. Expressions such as, "The early bird catches the worm," and "Early to bed, early to rise, makes a person healthy, wealthy and wise," are rigorous sparrow orientations that owls find to be of little value.

An interesting phenomenon occured in California during the early 1960s. Many schools were overcrowded as a result of the postwar baby boom. Some were placed on split shifts, with half the students coming in the morning and half coming in the afternoon. In one school district where this occurred, achievement data were examined to see what impact the split-shift system had on children's learning. The results of that examination should disturb us all. Children in this district were given their choice as to whether they would come in the morning or in the afternoon. What was found was that achievement of students overall increased dramatically after the school had gone on split shifts. Of course, when funds became available, an additional school was built and everything reverted back to the traditional norm, with everybody starting school at 8:00 A.M. and getting out at 2:30 P.M. An examination of the achievement levels of students after the reversion of the traditional norm indicated that achievement had also reverted to its pre–split-shift levels.

What we should have learned from that experience is that children will learn more if they are allowed to learn during the time of day when they are at their peak, rather than at some arbitrary time set by the school district. Sparrow children learn more in the morning, owl children learn more in the afternoon. But our society has for some reason determined that we should all act like sparrows, even when we are little children. Unfortunately, this is a cultural norm we are probably not going to be able to overcome at any foreseeable point in the future, and we will continue to retard the educational development of our children because of this norm. However, individual teachers, particularly in the elementary schools, can make a major step toward improving this situation by careful scheduling of the school day. Either of two policies can be implemented to advantage. The first would be to change the schedule periodically, even daily, as to when a certain subject will be taught. Thus, reading may be at 9:00 A.M. one day, 11:00 A.M. another day, and 2:00 P.M. a third day. This will provide a more equal opportunity for sparrow and owl children to make strides in each subject. Another option available to the teacher is to place the classes that are considered most important (perhaps the traditional reading, writing, and arithmetic) in the late morning and early afternoon, while scheduling the subject of somewhat less importance during the early and late hours. This will be a major step toward making it possible for both owl and sparrow children to have maximum learning of the important subjects. At the least, the teacher should be aware that the amount he or she will communicate in a certain subject will depend on the interaction between the time of day at which that subject is taught and the particular bodily time of the student who is to learn.

VOCAL BEHAVIOR IN THE CLASSROOM

The use and quality of the voice in human communication has considerable potential for influencing the meanings receivers assign to verbal messages. The voice communicates our attitudes about the content of our verbal messages. In that regard, it may be called *meta-communication:* communication about communication. If a teacher examines a student's work and says, "*That* is good?", the emphasis on "that" and the rising inflection of the voice at the end of the sentence communicates a completely different meaning than "That *is* good." Although the words are the same, the former instance is usually taken to mean, "That is bad," while the latter is interpreted literally. We have already discussed the importance of vocal behavior in information processing. Teachers should strive to avoid contradictory vocal and verbal messages. The student, particularly the older student, is more likely to believe the former than the latter.

There is a major distinction between a child's response to nonverbal behavior and that of an adult, particularly in terms of nonverbal vocal behavior. While the adult will almost universally accept the nonverbal vocal behavior as the correct cue when vocal behavior and verbal behavior are in conflict, young children often operate in the reverse manner. The young child has not yet learned that we use vocal behavior to change the meaning of our words. This learning process occurs somewhere between the ages of six and twelve, so the typical twelve-year-old will be operating at adult norms. But for the small child, conflicting verbal and nonverbal messages will cause considerable trouble. One of the best examples of this is the use of satire, where we intentionally suggest a meaning opposite from the literal meaning of our words through our vocal behavior. The child in the early elementary grades may miss this completely and accept our words in terms of their literal rather than satiric meaning. Satire and sarcasm, since both depend on vocal behavior, are generally inappropriate means of communicating with small children.

Vocal behavior is also capable of arousing stereotypes about either a teacher or a student. For example, a teacher who has a very nasal speaking voice is often perceived as having a variety of undesirable personal and physical characteristics. Female teachers with very tense voices are often perceived as being younger, feminine, more emotional, high strung, and less intelligent. Male teachers with the same vocal characteristics are often perceived as being older, more unyielding, and cantankerous.

Of course, vocal characteristics affect teachers' perceptions of students as well, and the stereotypes noted above can also be applied to students. Fortunately, as students and teachers get to know one another better, they are able to overcome some of these stereotypes. However, in the upper grades and secondary schools, students and teachers may never interact frequently enough to overcome the stereotypic responses based on vocal behavior. Many teachers would be shocked at students' imitations of them, often imitations mimicking the teacher's vocal pattern. While teachers may be somewhat less exhibitionistic about their impressions of students, the attitudes are not always that different.

Ethnic or regional accents and dialects in the classroom can often cause problems of perception. A child with a Puerto Rican or Appalachian dialect may be perceived as less intelligent and more backward by many teachers. Teachers naturally assume that the accent with which they speak is the best one, and it is often very difficult for them to realize that there is no one best accent or dialect in the English language—there are only some that are more common than others. When the teacher does not speak the same accent or dialect as the children in his or her classroom, a conscious or unconscious bias may develop. In some instances, this bias is carried so far as to permeate the whole school system. When this occurs, there are frequently attempts to "improve" the accent or dialect of the students. Often this is considered to be very offensive to the children and their parents, with good reason. The underlying assumption is that there is an "ideal" dialect and accent; thus, those who do not speak that way are perceived as being deficient. While it is certainly true that children who leave their ethnic or regional background in order to gain employment and acceptance in other areas of the community will have difficulty because of their accent or dialect, it is also true that most young people do not leave their home environment. But even more importantly, a child's speech pattern is an intrinsic part of the child's personality and self-image. Children learn their speech from their parents and the other people in their environment. Their assumption is that the accent or dialect they have learned is the "correct" one. To find that accent or dialect rejected by the teacher and/or the school is usually interpreted by the child as a personal rejection. Frequently this leads to a rejection of self and a lowered self-image and/or a rejection to teacher and school.

A child's speech pattern should not be tampered with. If the child has a speech correction problem, of course, then the child should be referred to the appropriate specialist in the school district. Similarly, if it is deemed desirable that the child learn to speak with more than one dialect, the child should be referred to the appropriate specialist in speech improvement. Classroom teachers typically are not trained to handle either of these problems, and their attempts to modify children's accents and dialects will normally lead only to negative results for both the child and the school.

EYE BEHAVIOR IN THE CLASSROOM

The use of eye movement is perceived as being one of the most meaningful cues in nonverbal communication, for it signals a willingness to interact and communicate. Direct eye contact with another in our culture normally communicates interest and attention. Conversely, lack of eye contact communicates lack of interest and attention.

Eye contact is often used to control an interpersonal interaction. When people do not wish to be interrupted, they will often glance away and continue talking. When they wish the other person to speak, they will pause, making direct eye contact. Teachers often use eye contact in the classroom to decide who is prepared to answer a question, or who has completed a homework assignment. We know of teachers who, from time to time, deliberately call on students who will not look them in the eye when they ask for volunteers, or for the answer to a question. In straight-row classes, as we discussed previously, one of the reasons certain students have less interaction with teachers is because their physical location in the class makes eye contact difficult. In fact, the "interaction wedge" in Fig. 6.1 demonstrates this effect clearly.

In addition, eye contact is often used as an indicant of whether or not a person is lying. The stereotype has it that a person who is dishonest will not look you in the eye. Many teachers who suspect a student is cheating on a test may, in the absence of other evidence, decide a student is lying because the student fails to look them in the eye when answering a direct question about the test. Unfortunately, there seems to be little validity to this theory. Research has actually found the reverse to be true—people who are lying are *more* likely to look the other person directly in the eye, probably as a conscious response to the stereotype.

Better nonverbal cues for determining lying are the kinesic variables relating to hand, foot, and leg movements. Rapid, jerky movements of these limbs may be a sign of lying. But no single nonverbal cue will always predict the honesty of a student. In the absence of other evidence, it is best to give the student the benefit of the doubt.

OBJECTS IN THE CLASSROOM

In the classroom, many objects impact on communication. Some of these are intrinsic to the classroom itself, while others are objects that the inhabitants bring with them. Such objects may have either a very negative or a very positive effect on what occurs in the communication between teacher and student.

The physical environment of the classroom is determined in large measure by the objects in that classroom. We can walk through almost any school at random and find some classrooms that appear much more conducive to learning and positive communication between teachers and students than do other classrooms. Environmental research has clearly indicated that communication differs greatly from one physical environment to another.

In an interesting study of the impact of environment on communication, students were randomly assigned to one of two different rooms. One room, known as the "beautiful room," was well decorated, carpeted, and had sufficient but subdued lighting. The room was clean and attractive. The other room, known as the "ugly room," was devoid of carpeting, was painted in a drab color, and had brilliant lighting. The room was dirty and cobwebs were noticeable in the corners. The students were engaged in an interaction task for about a half hour. Subsequently, they were removed to a third room that was moderately attractive. They then completed questionnaires indicating how pleasant they found their interaction to have been, whether they would like to continue interacting with the same people with whom they had been interacting, and whether they would like to return to the same room for future discussions. The differences between the two groups were dramatic. The people in the "beautiful room" enjoyed their experience, liked the people they interacted with, and looked forward to interacting in that environment further. The students who had been in the "ugly room," however, did not like the people with whom they interacted, did not enjoy the task, and did not want to return to that place for future discussions.

Unfortunately, many of the classrooms with which teachers must cope more closely fit the description of the "ugly room." And, citing the study that we noted above will not persuade voters to pass a bond issue to build a new school! The teacher can, however, do a great deal to overcome the negative elements of the environment which can adversely affect communication. Unfortunately, though, many teachers seem to be totally unaware of the problem, or have simply given up on it. If the room has movable chairs, it is easy to arrange them so that the students do not have to cope with excessive glare from outside windows. It is also often possible to adjust the lighting in the room. Brilliant lighting may make it easier for the children to see the paper on their desks, but over a period of time it tends to increase the irritability of both the teacher and the student. Even in the most dismal classroom, it is usually possible for the teacher to add decorations to make the room a more pleasant environment. Many teachers employ bulletin boards for this purpose and also display students' work around the room. The addition of inexpensive photographs and paintings can also greatly alter the appearance of the room. While the ideal classroom may be carpeted, soundproofed, have excellent control of heating and air-conditioning, and have adequate but subdued lighting, it is usually possible for the creative teacher to produce a reasonably attractive environment, even in the oldest of buildings.

In addition to the objects characteristic of the classroom environment it-self, both students and teacher may wish to bring in more personal objects to enhance their classroom. All too often, teachers discourage such contribu-tions. In doing so, they limit the students' attempts to express their individual-ity. When possible, the teacher should allow students to alter and decorate the small part of the room which is theirs, whether that be their desks or whatever. This may need to be restricted because of potential damage to school property, but usually this is not a problem. We have observed teachers who even allowed students to alter areas outside of their own small desk area. In one classroom we visited, the teacher encouraged the children to bring their favorite poster, photograph, or painting to be displayed in the room. This created a more intimate atmosphere for the young people and made school seem more a part of them rather then something imposed on them.

Finally, we should consider the objects that are clearly intrinsic to the individual student—that is, the students' wearing apparel and adornment. The teacher should allow as much individuality in this area as the school permits, within limits. Given free rein, junior- and senior-high-school students may choose to outfit themselves in outlandish wearing apparel, but, if sufficient tolerance for this deviation is permitted, there is usually movement toward more restraint fairly soon. The best policy for the individual teacher is to not interfere with the individuality of the student in this area unless forced to by the administration or because an individual's extreme behavior is proving to be a disturbance to the other students. Limiting a young person's freedom of expression almost ensures rebelliousness on his or her part, and consequently interferes in the communication between teacher and student.

In this short space, we have only been able to highlight certain aspects of nonverbal classroom communication. There is certainly much more to explore in this area, and we hope this brief discussion has encouraged you to pursue the topic further on your own. The several references that follow should provide an excellent starting point for your further reading.

SELECTED REFERENCES

Addington, D. W. "The Effect of Vocal Variations on Ratings of Source Credibility." *Speech Monographs* **28** (1971): 242–247.

Allport, G., and H. Cantril. Judging Personality from Voice." *Journal of Social Psy-chology* **5** (1934): 37–54.

Ball, J., and F. C. Byrnes. *Principles and Practices in Visual Communication*. Wash-ington, D.C.: Department of Audiovisual Instruction, National Education Associa-tion, 1964.

Birdwhistell, R. L. *Kinesics and Context*. Philadelphia: University of Pennsylvania Press, 1970.

Bosmajian, H. A., ed. *The Rhetoric of Nonverbal Communication*. Glenview, Ill.: Scott Foresman, 1971.

Darwin, C.   *The Expression of Emotions in Man and Animals.* London: John Murray, 1872.

Davitz, J. R.   *The Communication of Emotional Meaning.* New York: McGraw-Hill, 1964.

Dittmann, A. T., and L. G. Llewellyn.   "Body Movement and Speech Rhythm in Social Conversation." *Journal of Personality and Social Psychology* **11** (1969): 98–106.

Duncan, S., Jr.   "Nonverbal Communication." *Psychological Bulletin* **72** (1969): 118–137.

Efron, D.   *Gesture and Environment.* New York: King's Crown, 1941.

Eisenberg, A. M., and R. R. Smith.   *Nonverbal Communication.* Indianapolis: Bobbs-Merrill, 1971.

Ekman, P.   "Universals and Cultural Differences in Facial Expressions of Emotions." In *Nebraska Symposium on Motivation,* J. Cole, ed. Lincoln: Universities of Nebraska Press, 1972.

Ekman, P., and W. V. Friesen.   "The Repertoire of Nonverbal Behavior: Categories, Origins, Usage, and Coding." *Semiotica* **1** (1969): 48–49.

Exline, R.   "Explorations in the Process of Person Perception: Visual Interaction in Relation to Competition, Sex and Need for Affiliation." *Journal of Personality* **31** (1963): 1–20.

Frank, L. K.   "Tactile Communication." *Genetic Psychology Monographs* **56** (1957): 209–255.

Goffman, E.   *Behavior in Public Places.* New York: The Free Press, 1963.

Hall, E. T.   *The Silent Language.* New York: Doubleday, 1959.

Hall, E. T.   *The Hidden Dimension.* Garden City: Doubleday, 1966.

Harms, L. S.   "Listener Judgments of Status Cues in Speech." *Quarterly Journal of Speech* **47** (1961): 164–168.

Harrison, R. P.   *Beyond Words.* Englewood Cliffs, N.J.: Prentice-Hall, 1974.

Harrison, R.   "Nonverbal Communication." In *Handbook of Communication,* I. DeSola Pool, W. Schramm, N. Maccoby, F. Fry, E. B. Parker, and L. Fein, eds. Chicago: Rand-McNally, 1973.

Hinde, R. A.   *Non-Verbal Communication.* Cambridge: Cambridge University Press, 1972.

Izard, C. E.   *Face of Emotion.* New York: Appleton-Century-Crofts, 1971.

Journal of Communication, December 1972.

Knapp, M. L.   *Nonverbal Communication in Human Interaction.* New York: Holt, Rinehart and Winston, 1972.

Mehrabian, A.   *Silent Messages.* Belmont, Cal.: Wadsworth, 1971.

Mehrabian, A.   *Nonverbal Communication.* Aldine-Atherton, 1972.

Meyer, L. B.   *Emotion and Meaning in Music.* Chicago: University of Chicago Press, 1956.

Montagu, A.   *Touching: The Human Significance of Skin.* New York: Columbia University Press, 1971.

Pearce, W. B., and F. Conklin. "Nonverbal Vocalic Communication and Perceptions of a Speaker." *Speech Monographs* 38 (1971): 235–241.

Ruesch, J., and W. Kees. *Nonverbal Communication: Notes on the Visual Perception of Human Relations.* Berkeley: University of California Press, 1956.

Ryan, M. S. *Clothing: A Study in Human Behavior.* New York: Holt, Rinehart and Winston, 1966.

Scheflen, A. E. *Body Language and the Social Order.* Englewood Cliffs, N.J.: Prentice-Hall, 1972.

Schutz, W. *Joy.* New York: Grove Press, 1967.

Sommer, R. *Personal Space.* Englewood Cliffs, N.J. Prentice-Hall, 1969.

Sommer, R. *Design Awareness.* San Francisco: Holt, Rinehart and Winston, 1972.

Starkweather, J. "Content-Free Speech as a Source of Information About the Speaker." *Journal of Abnormal and Social Psychology* 52 (1956): 394–402.

Watson, O. M. *Proxemic Behavior: A Cross-Cultural Study.* The Hague: Mouton, 1970.

Weiner, M., S. Devoe, S. Rubinow, and J. Geller. "Nonverbal Behavior and Nonverbal Communication." *Psychological Review* 79 (1972): 185–214.

7

Perception of Teachers as Communication Sources in the Classroom

After reading this chapter, you should be able to do the following.

1. Explain the impact of the ways students perceive teachers on:
   a. exposure to communication with the teacher
   b. perception of the teacher's messages
   c. cognitive learning
   d. the teacher's influence over the student
2. Identify the dimensions of credibility.
3. Identify the dimensions of attraction.
4. Identify the dimensions of homophily.
5. Distinguish between ''legitimate'' and ''illegitimate'' power.
6. Distinguish between effective and ineffective methods a teacher may employ to build a positive image.
7. Indentify four significant sources that impact on communication in the classroom (beyond the teacher).

Possibly the single best predictor of how well students will do in a teacher's class is the way the teacher is perceived by those students. Yet most teachers seldom think about how they are perceived by the individual students in their classroom, and those who do think about this problem seldom do much to alter their image. One of the most common misconceptions about teaching is the assumption that a person who is well qualified in subject matter and sincerely wishes to be an effective teacher will be perceived positively by his or her students. Unfortunately, the way the person really is and the way that person is perceived to be by others have no necessary correlation at all. Frequently, when beginning teachers or practice teachers first discover how their students perceive them, they are somewhat shocked and are likely to exclaim, "But I'm not like that at all." That teacher might be correct, but the issue is moot. Communication in the classroom depends not on how the teacher really is, but on how the students perceive the teacher to be. The perceptions *are* the reality.

THE IMPACT OF STUDENTS' PERCEPTIONS OF TEACHERS

Students' perceptions of their teacher have a major impact on four aspects of communication in the classroom: exposure to communication, perception of messages, cognitive learning, and influence. We will consider each of these in turn.

Exposure to Communication

One of the most important effects students' perceptions of their teacher has on communication in the classroom is the degree to which the student is willing to expose herself or himself to communication with the teacher. As we pointed out in Chapter 4, if the student views the teacher positively, there is a much greater probability that the student will seek to communicate with the teacher. This is a common phenomenon in all communication, so it should not be surprising to find it operating in the classroom as well.

This impact is felt in two ways. The first relates to the students' choice of whether or not to take a class with the teacher. In the lower grades, students generally have less freedom of choice as to what classes to take and what not to take. Often the student will have the same teacher for all classes for the whole year. But as the student progresses into the middle and upper grades, more choice is available. He or she may elect some courses and avoid others. Similarly, student activities are generally voluntary, so the student can choose to participate in them or choose not to participate. Such student decisions are heavily affected by the students' perception of or attitude toward the teacher, or prospective teacher.

It is not uncommon to find one school having a large enrollment in course A, while another comparable school has a low enrollment in course A. While other elements in the educational atmosphere may have an impact on such a comparison, the best predictor of such a difference will normally be the students' attitudes toward the two different teachers. Since exposure to the teacher is obviously necessary for any communication in the classroom to occur, this impact is of particular importance. Once a student has chosen to expose herself or himself to a teacher in a voluntary course or activity, or has been informed that he or she will be taking a certain required course, the student still has a lot of freedom in determining how many communication attempts will be permitted. Will the student ask a question in class? Will the student respond to a question in class? Will the student come to see the teacher outside of class? All of these questions depend heavily on the way the teacher is perceived by the student. Such perceptions will even have an impact on how regularly the student chooses to attend school, rather than coming up with a variety of "illnesses" to stay at home.

Perception of Messages

One of the cardinal principles of human communication is that messages do not exist in and of themselves. Rather, the way students choose to interpret teacher messages is heavily influenced by the students' perception of the teacher. Would the same material being taught in a sex-education class be interpreted the same way if the teacher was perceived as "young, single, and the swinger of the school" as it would be if the teacher was perceived as the "old-maid"? The answer seems obvious, but our observation of teacher behavior and interaction with teachers suggests that very seldom does the teacher take this into account.

Cognitive Learning

Students' perceptions and attitudes toward their teacher have a major impact on how much cognitive learning occurs in the classroom. This effect appears to be related to attention. Students pay more attention to teachers they regard positively, and, as a result, receive more messages from such teachers. We all have observed classrooms in which the students do not have a positive attitude toward the teacher and have noted the general lack of attention—students spend time looking out the window, talking to neighbors, writing letters, and so on. But when students have a positive attitude toward their teacher, they tend to be more interested in what the teacher is saying than in other elements of their environment. Consequently, they will acquire more information under such circumstances.

Influence

Few teachers have as their ultimate goal simple cognitive learning. Rather, teachers normally seek to influence their students. Such influence may be directed toward either affective learning or actual behavioral change, or both. One of the clearest results from research in communication is that people are influenced primarily by those toward whom they have a positive attitude; we do not adopt the attitudes or behavioral recommendations of people whom we do not like or respect. While we may learn to verbalize or even be able to exhibit the behaviors they insist we exhibit, neither the attitudes nor the behaviors become a part of us.

Similarly, in the classroom, the student may be able to give evidence of cognitive learning on an examination or project, but once a student leaves the classroom, he or she may no longer exhibit the attitudes or the behaviors for which the course was designed. Thus, for a teacher to accomplish "real learning," positive student regard is essential.

THE WAYS TEACHERS ARE PERCEIVED BY STUDENTS

The ways students perceive their teachers can be divided into four major categories: credibility, attraction, homophily, and power. We will look at the perceptions that are included in each of these categories individually.

Credibility

"Credibility" is a general term used to encompass five different perceptions students may have of their teachers. Three of these perceptions (competence, character, and sociability) are highly evaluative in nature. The other two (composure and extroversion) are somewhat evaluative, but apply primarily to the ways the student perceives the teacher to communicate.

Competence refers to the degree to which a student perceives the teacher to be knowledgeable or expert in a given subject matter. If the student perceives the teacher to have little knowledge about the subject, the teacher will probably have little impact on the student's thinking as a result of their communication in the classroom. Perceptions of competence can range across a continuum from completely incompetent to extremely competent. But these perceptions are mediated by the student's perceptions of his or her own competence. If, on a scale from 0 to 10, the student visualizes his or her own competence as a 7, and if the teacher is perceived to be an 8, then the teacher is probably perceived to be reasonably competent. However, if the student perceives her or his own competence to be a 5 and the teacher's competence to be a 4, the teacher's competence is probably judged to be insufficient. Perceptions of competence significantly affect communication in the classroom. Students tend to accept opinions of teachers they judge to be more competent than themselves and to reject the ideas of those perceived as not sufficiently competent.

The role of perceived competence cannot be underestimated. Very often teachers perceive themselves as presenting information to the students that the students should learn. However, the student may perceive these messages as being opinions rather than information. To a major extent, this difference in perception can be a function of the student's perception of the teacher's competence. When we perceive a person to be highly competent, we tend to view their opinions as information. On the other side of the coin, people whose competence we question tend to be treated in the opposite manner. When they present what they perceive to be information, we may perceive that to be simply their opinion. A crude but fairly accurate way of determining how competent students perceive their teachers to be, at least at upper grade levels, is to obtain an answer to the following question: If the teacher and the textbook are in disagreement, which will the student believe?

The importance of perceived competence grows as the student progresses from the lower grades to the upper grades. At the very low level of the educational continuum, teachers are granted competence by almost all students—most kindergarteners don't stop to question whether the teacher knows what he or she is talking about. But as children obtain more information and become more confident in their own abilities, the question of teacher competence arises more frequently. In the upper grades, and even more often at the college level, teacher competence is questioned by students. Quite simply, if the student does not perceive the teacher to be competent enough, the student will learn little from that teacher.

Although the first judgment a student may make about a teacher's credibility is in terms of competence, the second dimension of judgment, *character,* is frequently as important or more important to successful communication in the classroom. Judgments of character are concerned with the perception of a person's essential goodness, trustworthiness, and decency. Even though a student may recognize that a teacher is highly competent in the subject matter, if the student does not trust the teacher to tell the truth, the student will have a low opinion of the teacher's credibility. While competence is usually judged on a comparative basis, as we noted above, character is more likely to be judged on an absolute basis. In other words, the student is probably not taking into consideration how trustworthy he or she is when judging the trustworthiness of the teacher. Even a totally dishonest student will tend to discount communication from a teacher perceived as being dishonest. In short, students tend to discount messages from teachers who they feel lack integrity.

The importance of perceived character is most apparent when the teacher is attempting to modify student behavior outside the classroom. While students may conform to the teacher's requests within the classroom, they are very unlikely to engage in teacher-recommended decisions and behaviors outside the classroom unless they believe the character of the teacher to be high. Thus, for meaningful learning to generalize beyond the classroom setting, the student must perceive the teacher to be of high character.

A very important dimension of credibility in elementary and secondary school classrooms is *sociability.* Class enrollments at these levels are generally lower than in many college classrooms, usually between twenty and thirty-five students per class. In classroom environments with this comparatively low number of students, it is not only expected, but also very probable, that the teacher and the students will get to know one another quite well. Sociability refers to the degree that the student perceives the teacher as being friendly, pleasant, and likable. In general, students will seek contact with teachers whom they rate high on sociability. This dimension has a major impact on communication that takes place outside the formal classroom environment. The teacher that is perceived as sociable is very likely to be sought outside of regular class hours for extra help or for further clarification of information communicated during class. However, the teacher who is not perceived as sociable will generally be avoided outside of the classroom. Since some of the most meaningful teaching that can occur in school occurs outside of the formal teaching environment, a teacher's perceived sociability can significantly affect student learning.

The three dimensions of credibility discussed so far are highly evaluative in nature—i.e., there is a "good" perception and a "bad" perception. Teachers who are perceived to be highly competent, of high character, and sociable are much more likely to be effective in their classroom communication and in their outside-of-class communication than are teachers who are perceived as being less competent, of lower character, and nonsociable. The next dimension of teacher credibility is less clearly evaluative. *Composure* refers to the student's perception of a teacher's emotional control—that is, whether the teacher is perceived as being poised, relaxed, and in control or nervous, tense, and uptight. In general, students perceive teachers who are more composed as being more credible as a whole, but there is such a thing as being *too* composed. A teacher who is so completely in control of his or her emotions as to be at the extreme end of the composure scale is likely to be perceived as cold and unfriendly. Teachers who are highly communication apprehensive (a problem we will talk about in Chapter 9) are very likely to exhibit considerable tension and lack of confidence in their classroom communication. Students are likely to interpret such obvious tension as a lack of composure, and this can negatively influence the teacher's credibility. Thus, either too much composure or too little composure will tend to negatively affect teacher-student communication. Too little composure will tend to lead to negative perceptions of competence, while too much composure will tend to lead to negative perceptions of sociability.

Extroversion is the final dimension of credibility we will consider. Extroversion concerns the degree to which the student perceives the teacher to be talkative, bold, and outgoing. The very introverted or shy teacher is generally perceived by students as being less credible. On the other hand, the person who is extremely extroverted may also be judged low in credibility (as the stereotypical used-car salesman). The teacher may be just too outgoing, to the point of being overbearing. The most credible teacher probably falls somewhere near the middle of the extroversion continuum, perhaps a little more extroverted than introverted, but not too much so.

Extroversion is a perception that is closely associated with the perceived self-esteem of the teacher; it is a signal students pick up on to judge whether the teacher has confidence in her or his own ability. The image we project to others is very often accepted by others. Thus, the very introverted and shy teacher tends to project an image of lack of confidence and ability and this is often accepted by that teacher's students. On the other hand, the extremely extroverted teacher may come on so strong as to frighten away many students, particularly students who are normally apprehensive about communicating with teachers. Therefore, a moderate degree of extroversion will probably generate the most positive relationship between teacher and student.

Teacher credibility is a *perception* on the part of the student, and does not necessarily correspond to reality. A teacher can be extremely competent, but if the teacher is not perceived to be competent by the student, the teacher is not credible. Since credibility is a multidimensional set of perceptions, the teacher can be perceived positively on some of the dimensions and not on others, and thus not be perceived as credible. For example, the student may perceive a teacher as being very friendly, composed, and moderately extroverted, but also as being a compulsive liar, and thus will tend to reject the opinions or information provided by that teacher. Or, the student may perceive a person to be highly competent and trustworthy, as well as composed and moderately extroverted, but to be unfriendly. Thus, the student is not likely to seek communication with that teacher or establish any kind of communication relationship outside the formal demands of the classroom. To be completely credible, therefore, a teacher needs to be perceived as competent, of high character, sociable, moderately composed, and moderately extroverted. If any of these dimensions are lacking, teacher credibility suffers and he or she will be much less effective in classroom communication with students.

Interpersonal Attraction

Interpersonal attraction, like credibility, is composed of several perceptions. At least three dimensions are involved for teachers: physical, task, and social. Let us consider each of these in turn.

Physical attraction relates specifically to students' perceptions of a teacher's physical appearance. During initial contacts between teacher and students, students tend to view the teacher more as an object than as a human being. Research has clearly indicated that physical attractiveness is the single most important perception in initial communication encounters. This dimension of attraction, however, becomes less important as the teacher and student become more familiar with one another. Over time, the other dimensions of attraction increase in importance; however, initially the physical dimension is vital.

Although it is popular within the American culture to discount the importance of physical appearance by saying things like "Beauty is only skin deep," our behavior belies this maxim. As one writer put it, "Beauty is only skin deep, but people are only interested in skin!" Physical attractiveness is affected not only by the physical makeup of a person's body, but also by the clothing and accessories the person wears. It is difficult to say what a teacher should look like, because any generalization would not apply to all grade levels. Kindergarten children and high-school seniors do not judge physical attractiveness in exactly the same way. About the only principle that is generalizable across all grade levels is that if the teacher is perceived as "old" the importance of physical appearance is probably greatly reduced. But what do we mean by "old"? To a kindergartener, a thirty-year-old is ancient, but to a high-school senior boy a twenty-two-year-old female English teacher is definitely not old. Prepuberty students are probably much less aware of the actual physical properties of the teacher than they are of the teacher's demeanor and bearing—they expect a teacher to fit the "role" of teacher. Older students, however, may react to quite different aspects of the physical characteristics of the teacher. High-school students are very sexually conscious; possibly more so than they ever again will be in their lives. A teacher of the opposite sex whom they perceive to be very sexually attractive may be both helped and hindered by this perception. Although the student will be more likely to seek interaction with that teacher, the teacher's perceived attractiveness will very likely distract the student from that which the teacher wishes to communicate.

An important point to remember about physical attraction is that at the beginning of the classroom relationship, the teacher is simply an object to the student. The student will generate many other perceptions of the teacher based on this initial physical judgment. As time wears on, many of these perceptions can be altered, but they may set a tone for later interaction which is irreversible.

Task attraction refers to the degree to which the student perceives it to be desirable to establish a work relationship with the teacher. If the student perceives the teacher as a person with whom it would be easy to work, who would probably be productive at work, and who is motivated to help the student achieve, the student is likely to perceive that teacher to be task attractive. When there is strong task attraction, classroom communication between the two will be goal directed and quite effective. When students perceive a teacher as task attractive, they believe that working with that teacher will result in a desirable outcome. This perception is likely to be a self-fulfilling prophecy. Since students expect to communicate effectively with the teacher, it is much more likely that their communication will actually be effective.

The final dimension of interpersonal attraction is *social attraction*, or the degree to which a student perceives a teacher to be someone with whom he or she would like to spend time at a social level. As with perceived task attraction, perceived social attraction is very likely to be a self-fulfilling prophecy. If the student expects to have a pleasant relationship with the teacher, such a relationship is likely. While teachers very often do not seek or desire social contact with their students, such contact can have a very positive impact on subsequent communication within the classroom. If a good interpersonal relationship has been established outside the classroom, it is generally quite easy to maintain that relationship within the classroom. However, it is often difficult for the teacher to initiate such a social relationship. Usually the initiation must come from the student. If the teacher is not perceived to be socially attractive, it is very unlikely that the student will initiate such a contact.

While it is possible for a student to perceive a teacher as highly attractive on all three dimensions, it is not necessary that a teacher be perceived as attractive on one dimension in order to be perceived as attractive on another. Students may perceive a teacher to be quite low on physical attraction and social attraction, and yet be highly task attracted to that teacher. In this case, communication in the classroom will probably be quite effective. On the other hand, a student may find a teacher very physically attractive and may wish to establish a social relationship outside of the classroom, but may not be task attracted to the teacher. Given these perceptions, communication in the classroom might be very ineffective. Again, we are dealing here with student perceptions, not reality. The teacher is attractive if *perceived* as attractive by the student. The "attractive" teacher is much more likely to be sought for communication than is the teacher considered less attractive.

HOMOPHILY

Homophily refers to the degree of similarity between teacher and student on any given attribute or group of attributes. The term "homophily" may be roughly translated as "similarity." A very important principle of human communication, often referred to as the "principle of homophily," states that the more similar two people are the more likely they are to attempt to communicate with one another, and the more likely their communication attempts will be successful. Homophily has a major impact on communication in the classroom. Specifically, students are more attracted to teachers they perceive as being similar to themselves, they tend to learn more from such people, and such teachers are very influential with those students.

Homophily may be considered from two vantage points. We may consider homophily on the basis of what an external observer can perceive, what we might call "real homophily," or we may examine homophily on the basis of what students perceive about their teachers, or "perceived homophily."

Many of the similarities and dissimilarities between teachers and students can be observed by people outside the classroom. The degree to which the teacher and student share the same sex, age, culture, religion, race, and the like is an indication of the degree to which they have homophily. We can make many predictions about the probable success of classroom communication on the basis of such observable characteristics. And many of these predictions will be found to be accurate. For example, we can predict that a black teacher raised in a black ghetto would be a more effective classroom communicator in a ghetto school that is predominately black than would be a white teacher born and raised in suburbia. Although such a prediction is obvious, given knowledge of the principle of homophily in human communication, this prediction is often ignored in attempts to establish racial balance in schools. It is not uncommon to find a classroom in which the overwhelming majority of students are black but the teacher is white. Or the reverse. We do not wish to comment on the advisability of integrating schools, for the issues are complex and are far beyond our scope of competence. However, it is clear that effective classroom communication is certainly not facilitated by having students taught by teachers from a drastically different culture than their own. As was pointed out in Chapter 2, research on human communication clearly indicates that the probable success of a teacher in this environment is extremely low.

Most of the early research on the effects of homophily and human communication examined homophily as determined by observers outside the communication system. More recently, attention has been focused more on perceived homophily. As with credibility and attraction, perceived homophily has been found to be multidimensional. At least three dimensions of perceived homophily can be identified: attitude, background, and value.

Attitude homophily refers to the degree to which the student perceives the teacher's attitudes and beliefs about reality to be similar to her or his own. Since it is generally impossible for a student to completely know a teacher, no matter how much communication occurs between the two, attitude homophily perceptions tend to fluctuate somewhat over time. During the opening days of class, for example, a student may discover that the teacher belongs to the same political party as the student's parents, adheres to the same religion as the student, and has some of the same opinions about life. The student, therefore, mày perceive a considerable degree of attitude homophily with the teacher. Later the student may discover that the teacher has a very different attitude about homework than the student has and thus have a reduced perception of attitude similarity. Or, the student may find that the teacher's attitude about the value of an athletic program differs sharply from the student's, and, again, a reduction in attitude similarity may occur. Thus attitude homophily is somewhat more variable than the other perceptions we have discussed.

The importance of perceived attitude homophily cannot be overstated. Whenever students hear a message from a teacher, students must interpret that message in light of what *they* think and in light of the way they think the *teacher* thinks. If there is high perceived attitude homophily, this will not be a severe problem. But if the perception of attitude homophily is not present, distortion of the teacher's message is probable. Even beyond this, students seek communication and information from teachers who they believe share their attitudes, but will not seek information from teachers whom they perceive as being attitudinally very different from them.

One of the authors recalls his first teaching experience in high school, teaching English grammar at the sophmore level. There was a student in his class who could have been described as a "leather-jacketed hood." The author was having little or no success teaching grammar to this boy, and the boy wanted no part of the class or the instructor. Several weeks after the term began, the author was sitting in a restaurant and talking with some friends, including one student from the class. The problem student joined the group. The conversation eventually included a discussion of what people had done when they were in high school. When this student found that the author had worn a black leather jacket and driven a hot rod as a teenager, there was a dramatic shift in the relationship between the two. From that time on, the problem student was no longer a problem student. His grades moved from the D-F level to the A-B level, and eventually that student went on to complete college and become an English teacher! The key to this changed relationship was the discovery by both people of a considerable degree of attitude homophily. The student's thinking, relayed to the author several years later, went something like this: "If McCroskey likes hot rods and hell-raising like I do, then maybe there is something to this English stuff after all." While this example may be an unusual case, it does not represent an unusual relationship between student and teacher. If students perceive strong attitudinal similarity with the teacher, they will tend to generalize that perception to that which the teacher is attempting to communicate. But if the student sees the teacher as being worlds apart, the student will also see the subject matter the teacher is attempting to communicate as being irrelevant.

Another important homophily perception is the dimension of *background*. We perceive those people who have backgrounds similar to our own as more homophilous with us than people with different backgrounds. Students in New York City perceive other New Yorkers to be more homophilous than people from the West. People born and raised in a ghetto tend to perceive other ghetto dwellers as more homophilous than suburbanites. A student with a southern accent perceives another person with a southern accent as being more homophilous than a person with a midwestern accent. All of these perceptions lead to an increase in perceived homophily with the teacher, more communication with the teacher, and a greater likelihood that the communication between student and teacher will be effective. Obviously, of course, certain background differences are inherent in teacher-student communication relationships. At a minimum, there is an age difference and an educational difference. Thus, to establish a strong degree of perceived background homophily, it is important that the student be aware of what shared experiences the teacher and student do have. Usually, since the teacher has also passed through the educational system, they will have a number of experiences in common.

The third dimension of perceived homophily, *value* homophily, refers to the degree to which the student perceives the teacher to share the student's basic orientation on such things as moral questions. Behavioral decisions are heavily influenced by an individual's values. And, since teachers are frequently asking students to alter their behaviors, it is very important that the student perceive a sharing of values between teacher and student. Otherwise, the student may perceive the recommended behavior as being in keeping with the teacher's values, but not in keeping with his or her own values. Ironically, teachers who come off as too moralistic may defeat their own purposes. Students may judge teacher-recommended behaviors in light of that extremely moralistic view and decide that the behaviors do not fit within their own system.

To summarize: to the extent that students perceive their teachers to be similar to them, they are increasingly likely to attempt to communicate with their teachers. To the extent that their perceptions of homophily are accurate, there will be a much greater likelihood of having effective communication, primarily because the more similar teacher and student are, the more likely they are to perceive verbal and nonverbal messages in a similar manner. Simply put, students prefer to communicate with teachers perceived to be similar to themselves, and to avoid communication with teachers they perceive to be dissimilar. A word of caution, however, is in order here. There is such a thing as *too much* perceived homophily. The teacher must always remember that there are *real* differences between teachers and students. To attempt to break down those differences completely may destroy the teacher's real potential to be a senior guide and counselor. The teacher cannot be the student's best friend and still be the student's teacher, at least in most circumstances. The desired perception is considerable similarity, not a perception of being "the same."

POWER

Power refers to a teacher's ability to affect in some way the students' well-being, beyond the students' own control. As with homophily, power can be examined either on a basis of "reality" or on the basis of perception. We will consider both.

Real power has an impact on classroom communication whenever the power is used in a coercive manner or whenever the threat of coercion is present. The presence of power tends to inhibit communication. When one person has power over another, it is common for that person to perceive less need to communicate with the other person. What communication exists frequently takes the form of simple instructions, which the power source assumes will result in receiver compliance. In the classroom communication environment, a certain degree of teacher power is always present. The teacher does have, within limits, the ability to threaten and coerce students into conforming to the behaviors that the teacher requests. It is a rare classroom, indeed, in which the teacher never exerts power over the students. However, the extent to which power is used by the teacher is highly predictive of how the students perceive the teacher on other dimensions, such as sociability and task attraction. Simply put, the use of power in the classroom tends to increase the likelihood that power will be needed later to insure conformity. The more it is used, the more it will need to be used.

Perceived power is likely to have an even greater impact within the classroom communication atmosphere than real power. Perceived power refers to the degree to which the student perceives the teacher as having the ability to influence the student's existence. The crucial aspect of this perception is whether or not the student perceives the teacher's power to be *legitimate* or *illegitimate*. In a democratic society, the perceived legitimacy of one's power is crucial to maintaining that power. We believe in democratic elections, for example. Even though our candidate does not win, we still normally perceive the person who is elected to have assumed power legitimately, and we will follow the requests or demands of that individual. Similarly, if we choose to accept a particular job, we generally perceive our supervisor as having legitimate power over us. We have the choice, if we don't like the way our supervisor exerts his or her power, to resign and take a position elsewhere. Small children generally perceive their parents as having legitimate power over them and follow their requests without much question. This perception is often transferred to the elementary teacher when the child begins school. However, as the child moves into the teenage years, this perception of legitimacy tends to diminish to the point where, in some cases, the teenager does not perceive the parent or teacher as having any legitimate power whatsoever.

The impact of legitimate power and the impact of illegitimate power differ markedly. To the extent that students perceive the teacher to have legitimate power, they will follow the instructions and requests of that teacher without giving the request too much consideration. In fact, students will often turn to the teacher to ask for directives, particularly if they are uncertain about what should be done. Perceived legitimate power, therefore, can be very helpful to the teacher in improving communication in the classroom. Perceived illegitimate power, however, produces a very different result. Students will attempt to avoid influence from the teacher holding such power, and will make an effort to circumvent the regulations and instructions that teacher gives. This is highly disruptive, of course, to communication within the classroom. In such circumstances, useful student-teacher communication is effectively ruled out.

The type of course being taught can also have a considerable impact on the degree of legitimacy a teacher is perceived as having. At grade levels where students have no real choice in what subjects to take, the student has little opportunity to grant the teacher power. Under these circumstances, the likelihood that the perception of power will be legitimate is greatly reduced. At upper grade levels, however, where students have an option of what courses to elect, their choice of an elective course will tend to grant more legitimate power to the teacher of that course. Teachers often indicate their preference for teaching elective courses over required courses, and with good reason. Instructions and requests by teachers of elective courses are much more likely to be received by the students than are similar instructions or requests communicated in a required course.

Whether the teacher's power is perceived to be legitimate or illegitimate, the teacher must be careful to avoid abusing the power that he or she has. The abuse of power by teachers is probably more resented by students than any other single thing a teacher can do. There is little question that the teacher has the power to make a major assignment that must be completed by the morning after an important ball game. But the important question is: Should the teacher exert her or his power in this way? Such a use of power would almost certainly be perceived as an abuse of power by the students involved. By the same token, the teacher certainly has the power to require a student to stay after school for misbehavior. But should the teacher do so? There is certainly no one answer to this question, because it will depend on the circumstances involved. The point is simple: the legitimate use of power may still be perceived as an abuse of power by the students. Whenever the teacher must resort to power in order to influence students' behavior, the teacher sacrifices much more than he or she gains in most circumstances. Teachers who rely heavily on their power are seldom perceived to be credible, attractive, or homophilous. Rather, they are perceived as people to steer clear of and avoid communicating with as much as possible.

BUILDING THE TEACHER'S IMAGE

Considering the many ways in which students perceive their teachers, it is reasonable to ask what kind of image a teacher ought to try to project to students. Today, most teachers' images are built almost at random; few systematically work to create a certain image. In years gone by, of course, the educational system more or less defined the teacher's image and forced the teacher to conform to behaviors that would enhance and protect that image. There were dress rules and hours after which teachers should not be seen on the streets. Teachers were told never to be seen smoking or drinking, and were expected to adhere to all manner of specific regulations designed to create the "teacher image" in students' minds, as well as in the community at large. In most areas these days are gone. Teachers will no longer tolerate such regulations. But what has taken the place of these formalized images? Let's look at some of the images teachers try to project, or images that students pick up even if teachers have not consciously tried to project them.

The "Tough Guy" Image

The tough-guy image is often projected by the beginning teacher, particularly the beginning male teacher. Underneath such an image is usually an insecure person who is not sure that he is able to cope with the teaching situation. In order to compensate for their own basic insecurity, teachers who try to project the tough-guy image make a big thing out of how thoroughly they can control and discipline the class. Students are made to feel that if they get out line, punishment will be swift and severe. Communication in the tough-guy teacher's classroom is normally very strained and primarily one-way—teacher to student. Student-initiated communication is minimal. The student may answer questions the teacher asks, but that's about all. Even the word "communication" is a misnomer; the tough guy doesn't want any communication and will have very little. There may be considerable cognitive learning in this teacher's classroom, but its carry-over outside the classroom will be approximately zero.

The "Everybody's Buddy" Image

This type of teacher is the opposite of the tough guy. More than anything else, he or she wants to be liked. Such individuals operate on the assumption that if a teacher is socially attractive and homophilous, everything else will work itself out. That, of course, is just not true. This teacher may have a great deal of talking going on in the classroom, but possibly very little instructional communication occurring. Often, the "everybody's buddy" teacher is taken advantage of by the students—to the detriment of their intellectual development. It is perfectly acceptable for a teacher to be friendly with students, in fact it is highly desirable, but a teacher is not a buddy, and a buddy is not a teacher.

The "Sensitive Human Being" Image

In these days of encounter groups and sensitivity training, some teachers try to project a "sensitive human being" image by conveying the idea that they can feel what the student feels and by pretending great empathy for the student. While the teacher may actually feel that he or she is a sensitive human being, the student is likely to see this teacher as a shallow fraud, particularly students in the upper grades. Being sensitive to students' needs and feelings is, of course, very important to successful communication in the classroom, but it can never be a substitute for the learning that must go on in the classroom. When it becomes a substitute, the classroom is no longer functional.

This teacher projects an "everybody's buddy" image. Can you think of any learning problems this image might cause?

The "Reluctant Dragon" Image

The "reluctant dragon" teacher makes it very clear to students that he or she does not want to be teaching in this classroom, but since he or she is forced to do so, "By golly, you're going to learn." With the increasing surplus of teachers at the elementary and secondary level, as well as the college level, there are more and more reluctant dragons in the classroom. The people that have jobs that they really don't want, because they couldn't get the jobs that they wanted, are prime candidates for the reluctant-dragon image. Such teachers are very likely to be perceived as less competent and task attractive than are other teachers, and are prime candidates for perceptions of abuse of power. Better for our school systems that such teachers be unemployed rather than be in our classrooms.

The "Genius" Image

This type of teacher has long populated the classrooms of secondary and elementary schools. It is the teacher who tries to impress students with his or her vast knowledge, the teacher who is overly concerned with perceived competence to the exclusion of all other important perceptual dimensions. Communication is likely to suffer if a teacher is perceived as being "too competent." People do not normally turn to the most competent person around for their information, and students are no different. So the "genius," even if successful in projecting the image, is working against effective communication in the classroom. People who try to project the genius image generally are not all that bright, and students are quick to see through the facade. At this point, perceived competence will hit an all-time low.

The "Grandmother" Image
Although children in the lower elementary grades generally appreciate teachers who project a grandmotherly image, older students do not share their enthusiasm. The grandmother teacher is truly very sensitive to the students' needs and tries to adapt everything to the individual student. It is a basically good image, but very hard for a twenty-four-year-old teacher to make work. And to try this approach with teenagers is to guarantee failure. Grandmothers are grand for kindergarten and the lower grades. But they are generally not perceived as competent or task attractive by older children.

The "Liberated Person" Image
This is a new teacher image that is becoming increasingly popular in our classrooms, primarily as an offshoot of the women's liberation movement. While we view the women's movement as a very positive thing, the liberated-person image in the teacher is not. The liberated-person teacher is the one who makes too big an issue of the fact that he or she is a unique human being and "not just another teacher." While this may be an appropriate role in the teacher's lounge, the classroom should not be used as a personal soapbox or a testing ground for one's new-found self. The individual teacher who presumes to do this will succeed only in conveying a negative impression to his or her students. That impression frequently will be a negative perception of sociability and social attraction, as well as of homophily.

The "Cool Dude" Image
The "cool-dude" teacher is usually male, but some females also attempt to project this image. This kind of teacher wants the students to perceive the teacher as "relevant" and will make every effort to indicate that he or she is "with it," often by using the current slang, identifying with the students' music, dressing in a "hip" fashion, and so forth. This teacher just can't face the fact that there are differences in generations and that the gaps cannot be completely bridged. Such a teacher is almost certain to be perceived as phony and dishonest. A fifty-year-old man with gray hair falling below his shoulders talking jive talk is an object of student scorn, not an object of admiration.

The "Sex-Symbol" Image
For obvious reasons, this is an image attempted only by comparatively young teachers, in most circumstances. This teacher perceives physical attractiveness to be the key to success in teaching, and dresses and acts accordingly.

Unfortunately, physical attractiveness, while important, cannot guarantee efficacy in the classroom. In fact, as we noted previously, a sexy image may even get in the way of student-teacher communication, especially in the upper grades.

The "Teacher" Image

Anyone who has taught for a while has probably encountered several of the images described above in people with whom they have worked. Students can certainly identify former teachers that fit in several of these categories. All of these images have one thing in common: they are the result of being overly concerned with one aspect of student perception to the exclusion of other important perceptions.

What, then, is a good image to project? There is no simple answer to that question, but we can suggest general guidelines. The teacher should attempt to be perceived as reasonably competent, honest, friendly, composed, moderately extroverted, and moderately physically attractive. He or she should be viewed as a person with whom it would be pleasant to work; a person with whom it would be pleasant to talk in a nonclassroom environment; a person with similar attitudes, background, and values; and a person who uses power sparingly, but is able to use it to some extent. All that is very easily said, but for most teachers, it is somewhat more difficult to accomplish. The best advice we can give to teachers who wish to improve their image is to determine systematically how the students perceive them initially. The questionnaire in Fig. 7.1, the "Teacher Evaluation Questionnaire," is designed for this purpose. Once the teacher has determined how the students do perceive her or him, problem areas can be identified and worked on specifically. A note of caution: formal information of the type collected in Fig. 7.1 is essential in determining how one is actually perceived. Students are able to project false perceptions to their teachers in order to guard against possible retaliation, should their true feelings be known. Thus, the teacher may perceive that the students' perceptions are very positive while, in fact, they are quite the opposite. There is no substitute for formal measurement of student perceptions.

ALTERNATE SOURCES OF COMMUNICATION IN THE CLASSROOM

Up to this point, we may have given the impression that the teacher is the only source of communication in the classroom. This is obviously not a true picture, but we have chosen to emphasize the teacher for purposes of this discussion. However, we would be derelict if we did not point to other sources of communication that exist in the classroom and talk about their impact on communication.

Circle the number that represents how you perceive your teacher. Mark in the direction, toward either end of the scale, that is most compatible with your perceptions. Circle only one number per scale and complete all scales. Please give an honest, frank response. There are no right or wrong answers.

																		For teacher use
Expert	:	7	:	6	:	5	:	4	:	3	:	2	:	1	:	Inexpert		
Unintelligent	:	1	:	2	:	3	:	4	:	5	:	6	:	7	:	Intelligent		
Narrow	:	1	:	2	:	3	:	4	:	5	:	6	:	7	:	Intellectual		
Qualified	:	7	:	6	:	5	:	4	:	3	:	2	:	1	:	Unqualified	Competence
																	Total _____

Nervous	:	1	:	2	:	3	:	4	:	5	:	6	:	7	:	Poised	
Tense	:	1	:	2	:	3	:	4	:	5	:	6	:	7	:	Relaxed	
Calm	:	7	:	6	:	5	:	4	:	3	:	2	:	1	:	Anxious	
Excitable	:	1	:	2	:	3	:	4	:	5	:	6	:	7	:	Composed	Composure
																	Total _____

Honest	:	7	:	6	:	5	:	4	:	3	:	2	:	1	:	Dishonest	
Bad	:	1	:	2	:	3	:	4	:	5	:	6	:	7	:	Good	
Kind	:	7	:	6	:	5	:	4	:	3	:	2	:	1	:	Cruel	
Undependable	:	1	:	2	:	3	:	4	:	5	:	6	:	7	:	Responsible	Character
																	Total _____

Bold	:	7	:	6	:	5	:	4	:	3	:	2	:	1	:	Timid	
Quiet	:	1	:	2	:	3	:	4	:	5	:	6	:	7	:	Verbal	
Silent	:	1	:	2	:	3	:	4	:	5	:	6	:	7	:	Talkative	
Aggressive	:	7	:	6	:	5	:	4	:	3	:	2	:	1	:	Meek	Extroversion
																	Total _____

Awful	:	1	:	2	:	3	:	4	:	5	:	6	:	7	:	Nice	
Unpleasant	:	1	:	2	:	3	:	4	:	5	:	6	:	7	:	Pleasant	
Irritable	:	1	:	2	:	3	:	4	:	5	:	6	:	7	:	Good Natured	
Cheerful	:	7	:	6	:	5	:	4	:	3	:	2	:	1	:	Gloomy	Sociability
																	Total _____

Fig. 7.1   Teacher evaluation questionnaire.

The Peer Source

Most classroom communication is not between student and teacher; rather, it is between student and student. There is more homophily among students than there can ever be between teacher and student and, consequently, the principle of homophily dictates this preponderance of student-student communication. In the middle and upper grades, peers are by far the most influential sources of student behavior, both inside the classroom and outside. The sensitive teacher will make use of this fact rather than trying to overcome it. One of the things we learned many years ago when there were lots of one-room schools in the nation (something that seems to have been forgotten since then) is that peers can teach one another very well. The effective teacher in the classroom will use peer teaching whenever possible, because students enjoy it and learn from it.

The Parent Source

We often don't think of the parent as having a role in classroom communication. But when we stop to think about it, we recognize that the influence of the parent is extremely strong, particularly in the early grades. If the parent and the teacher disagree, the lower-elementary-school student will generally go along with the parent and reject the teacher. The impact of the parent as a source declines through the middle and into the upper grade levels, but never is completely absent. Remember: the student generally develops her or his values and basic beliefs and attitudes from the parent, not from the school. A challenge to these values, beliefs, and attitudes is likely to be rebuffed by the student and taken to the parent for disconfirmation. A skilled teacher will establish a good relationship with the parents of the student, so that a coordinated effort can be made to enhance this student's learning.

The Book Source

The textbook is omnipresent in the classroom, and is often regarded by students as a virtual fountain of all wisdom. After a student has absorbed this orientation for several years, the book becomes paramount to the teacher, and, if there is disagreement, the student tends to believe the book, no matter what the teacher says. This is both understandable and unfortunate. In the lower grades, textbook writers and teachers rarely disagree. Thus, the book is "always right." The student very quickly learns this principle. Then, in the upper grades, where there are legitimate grounds for disagreement between textbook writers and teachers, this principle is still adhered to by the student.

If the textbook is not to become a barrier to communication in the classroom, particularly in subjects dealing with the social sciences, the teacher must confront this problem directly. In many instances, the goal of the class is for students to think through an idea and come to their own conclusion rather than to accept somebody else's conclusion. This is difficult with the ever-present book source saying, "Here's the answer." The teacher who tries to communicate in such a classroom and is not aware of the impact of the textbook is likely to be very ineffective.

The Student Source

The most important sources of communication in the classroom are the students themselves. And they are perceived by teachers and other students on the same dimensions that we have discussed above in regard to students' perceptions of teachers. Both teachers and students respond to other students on the basis of those perceptions. If we perceive a student to lack competence, how do we as teachers respond to ideas that the student suggests? If we perceive a student to be of low character or dishonest, how do we respond when the student gives an explanation for his or her absence or for not having an assignment completed on schedule? If we perceive a student to be unfriendly and hostile, how likely are we to seek communication with that student inside or outside the classroom? What we are driving at here is the same point we made in the first chapter: communication is a two-way street. Teachers and students perceive one another and, to the extent that they perceive one another positively, they will communicate with one another and communicate effectively. But, if *either* the student or the teacher has a negative perception of the other individual, communication in the classroom is severely disturbed. As teachers we can work on our own images with our students. But we cannot expect the student to be as sensitive to communication problems as we must be. Consequently, we must do some of their work for them by recognizing our own perceptions about students and attempting to remove the negative impact of these perceptions on the way we communicate with them. It will be a difficult task. But while students have the option of turning teachers off, teachers do not have that alternative. Teachers are paid to teach all students, whether they like them or not, whether they believe that they are competent or not. We will consider this problem in more depth in Chapter 10.

SELECTED REFERENCES

Abrahamson, M.   *Interpersonal Accommodation*. Princeton, N.J.: D. Van Nostrand, 1966.

Alpert, M. I., and W. T. Andersen, Jr.   "Optimal Heterophily and Communication Effectiveness: Some Empirical Findings." *Journal of Communication* **23** (1973): 328–343.

Andersen, K., and T. Clevenger, Jr.   "A Summary of Experimental Research in Ethos." *Speech Monographs* **30** (1963): 59–78.

Aronson, E., and F. Cope.   "My Enemy's Enemy Is My Friend." *Journal of Personality and Social Psychology* **8** (1968): 8–12.

Aronson, E., and B. W. Golden. "The Effect of Relevant and Irrelevant Aspects of Communicator Credibility on Opinion Change." *Journal of Personality* **30** (1962): 135–146.

Burger, C. H., and R. J. Colobrese. "Some Explorations in Initial Interaction and Beyond Toward a Developmental Theory of Interpersonal Communication." *Human Communication Research* **1** (1975): 99–112.

Berger, E. M. "The Relation Between Expressed Acceptance of Self and Expressed Acceptance of Others." *Journal of Abnormal and Social Psychology* **47** (1952): 778–782.

Berlo, D. K., J. B. Lemert, and R. Mertz. "Dimensions for Evaluating the Acceptability of Message Sources." *Public Opinion Quarterly* **33** (1969): 563–576.

Berscheid, E., D. Boye, and J. Darley. "Effect of Forced Association Upon Voluntary Choice to Associate." *Journal of Personality and Social Psychology* **8** (1968): 13–19.

Berscheid, E., and E. Walster. *Interpersonal Attraction.* Reading, Mass.: Addison-Wesley, 1969.

Brewer, R. E. "Attitude Change, Interpersonal Attraction, and Communication in a Dyadic Situation." *Journal of Social Psychology* **75** (1968): 127–134.

Brewer, R. E., and M. B. Brewer. "Attention and Accuracy of Perception in Dyads," *Journal of Personality and Social Psychology* **8** (1968): 188–193.

Brislin, R. W., and S. A. Lewis. "Dating and Physical Attractiveness." *Psychological Reports* **22** (1968): 976.

Byrne, D., and W. Griffitt. "A Developmental Investigation of the Law of Attraction." *Journal of Personality and Social Psychology* **4** (1966): 699–703.

Byrne, D., and W. Griffitt. "Similarity Versus Liking: A Clarification." *Psychonomic Science* **6** (1966): 295–296.

Byrne, D., O. London, and K. Reeves. "The Effects of Physical Attractiveness, Sex, and Attitude Similarity on Interpersonal Attraction." *Journal of Personality* **36** (1968): 259–271.

Clore, G. L., and B. Baldridge. "Interpersonal Attraction: The Role of Agreement and Topic Interest." *Journal of Personality and Social Psychology* **9** (1968): 340–346.

Daly, J. A., J. C. McCroskey, and V. P. Richmond. "The Relationship Between Vocal Activity and Perception of Communicators in Small Group Interaction." Paper presented to the convention of the Speech Communication Association, Chicago, 1974.

Festinger, L., S. Schachter, and K. Back. *Social Pressures in Informal Groups.* New York: Harper and Brothers, 1950.

Haimen, F. "An Experimental Study of the Effects of Extos in Public Speaking." *Speech Monographs* **11** (1949): 190–202.

Heider, F. *The Psychology of Interpersonal Relations.* New York: Wiley, 1958.

Horowitz, H. "Interpersonal Choice in American Adolescents." *Psychological Reports* **19** (1966): 371–374.

Hovland, C. I., I. L. Janis, and H. H. Kelley. *Communication and Persuasion.* New Haven, Conn.: Yale University Press, 1953.

Hovland, C. I., and W. Weiss. "The Influence of Source Credibility on Communication Effectiveness." *Public Opinion Quarterly* **15** (1951): 635–650.

Iliffe, A. H. "A Study of Preferences in Feminine Beauty." *British Journal of Psychology* **51** (1960): 267–273.

Inglis, R. "The Effects of Personality Similarity on Empathy and Interpersonal Attraction." Ph.D. dissertation, Duke University, 1965.

Iverson, M. A. "Attraction toward Flatterers of Different Statuses," *Journal of Social Psychology* **74** (1968): 181–187.

Katz, A. M., and R. Hill. "Residential Propinquity and Marital Selection: A Review of Theory, Method, and Fact." *Marriage and Family Living* **20** (1958): 27–35.

Katz, E., and P. F. Lazarsfeld. *Personal Influence.* New York: The Free Press, 1955.

Landy, D., and E. Aronson. "Liking for an Evaluator as a Function of His Discernment." *Journal of Personality and Social Psychology* **9** (1968): 133–141.

McCroskey, J. C. "Scales for the Measurement of Ethos." *Speech Monographs* **33** (1966): 65–72.

McCroskey, J. C., P. R. Hamilton, and A. N. Weiner. "The Effect of Interaction Behavior on Source Credibility, Homophily, and Interpersonal Attraction." *Human Communication Research* **1** (1974): 42–52.

McCroskey, J. C., W. E. Holdridge, and J. K. Toomb. "An Instrument for Measuring the Source Credibility of Basic Speech Communication Instructors." *Speech Teacher* **23** (1974): 26–33.

McCroskey, J. C., T. Jensen, and C. Todd. "The Generalizability of Source Credibility Scales for Public Figures." Paper presented at the Speech Communication Association Convention, Chicago, December 1972.

McCroskey, J. C., T. Jensen, C. Todd, and J. K. Toomb. "Measurement of the Credibility of Organization Sources." Paper presented at the Western Speech Communication Association Convention, Honolulu, November 1972.

McCroskey, J. C., and T. Jensen. "Measurement of the Credibility of Mass Media Sources." *Journal of Broadcasting* **19** (1975): 169–180.

McCroskey, J. C., and T. Jensen. "Measurement of the Credibility of Peers and Spouses." Paper presented at the International Communication Association, Montreal, April 1973(b).

McCroskey, J. C., and T. A. McCain. "The Measurement of Interpersonal Attraction." *Speech Monographs* **41** (1974): 261–266.

McCroskey, J. C., V. P. Richmond, and J. A. Daly. "The Measurement of Perceived Homophily in Interpersonal Communication." *Human Communication Research* **1** (1975).

McCroskey, J. C., M. D. Scott, and T. J. Young. "The Dimensions of Source Credibility for Spouses and Peers." Paper presented at the Western Speech Communication Association convention, Fresno, California, November 1971.

Meyer, W. J., and M. A. Barbour. "Generality of Individual and Group Social Attractiveness Over Several Rating Situations." *Journal of Genetic Psychology* **113** (1968): 101–108.

Mills, J., and E. Aronson. "Opinion Change as a Function of the Communicator's Attractiveness and Desire to Influence." *Journal of Personality and Social Psychology* **1** (1965): 173–177.

Newcomb, T. M. *The Acquaintance Process.* New York: Holt, Rinehart and Winston, 1961.

Priest, R. F., and J. Sawyer. "Proximity and Peership: Bases of Balance in Interpersonal Attraction." *The American Journal of Sociology* **72** (1967): 633–649.

Rogers, E. M., and F. F. Shoemaker. *Communication of Innovations.* New York: The Free Press, 1971.

Shrauger, J. S., and S. C. Jones. "Social Validation and Interpersonal Evaluations." *Journal of Experimental Social Psychology* **4** (1968): 315–323.

Walster, E., V. Aronson, D. Abrahams, and L. Rottmann. "Importance of Physical Attractiveness in Dating Behavior." *Journal of Personality and Social Psychology* **4** (1966): 508–516.

Warr, P. B., and C. Knapper. *The Perception of People and Events.* New York: Wiley, 1968.

Widgery, R. N., and B. Webster. "The Effects of Physical Attractiveness upon Perceived Initial Credibility." *Michigan Speech Association Journal* **4** (1969).

Motivations to Communicate in the Classroom

After reading this chapter, you should be able to do the following.

1. Identify five major reasons why students and teachers attempt to communicate.

2. Identify five major reasons why some students avoid communication in the school.

A teacher must communicate in the classroom in order for a maximal amount of learning to occur. However, a sizeable portion of the communication that occurs in a classroom in a given day is initiated by students rather than by the teacher. Frequently, the teacher will have little choice as to whether or not to communicate. A student walks into a room or raises a hand and asks a question. The teacher must communicate in return, even if all he or she does is ignore the student. Of course, that behavior in itself will certainly communicate something very strongly to the student. Nevertheless, both students and teachers exert considerable control over the extent to which they communicate with each other. Why, in some instances, do students choose to communicate, and, in other instances, choose not to?

A student's decision to communicate is normally based on a projection of the outcome of communicating in the given instance. Generally, if the student predicts that the outcome will be to her or his advantage, the student will choose to communicate. If the projection is negative, however, the student will be more likely to avoid communication. The outcomes with which students are concerned are affinity, information and understanding, influence, decision making, and confirmation. We will examine each of these outcomes as they apply to the motivations of students as communication sources in a classroom.

WHY STUDENTS COMMUNICATE IN THE CLASSROOM

Affinity

Affinity between two people is often a desired outcome of communication. Most students have an inner need for warm relationships with other people, including teachers. Almost no one wants to be isolated from fellow human beings. Consequently, students often seek to communicate with others in order to establish close affinity relationships with people. Some students have a lower need for affinity than others, and they will probably initiate less communication on a social level than will students with higher affinity needs.

Most students do desire to establish an affinity relationship with their teacher. This is a particularly strong motivation for communication at the lower levels and only declines slightly as the student moves through the educational system. Thus, the student will often initiate communication with the teacher that has little to do with the subject matter at hand. The student will also initiate communication with other students in the classroom in order to establish affinity relationships with them. These are normal outcomes of normal communication motivations. However, problems can occur as a result of this affinity need.

One problem that may occur when students seek communication with their teacher in order to establish an affinity relationship is that such an attempt may be misperceived by either the teacher or other students. We are all familiar with the label "apple polisher." Whether it be true or not, most students believe that if a student has a friendly relationship with a teacher, the student will get more rewards from the teacher. If the teacher perceives the student initiating an unusually large number of social interactions, the teacher may be turned off. He or she may perceive the student as being a "phony," interested only in garnering the benefits that come from being pals with the teacher. Similarly, other students who observe these interactions may develop a negative attitude toward the student involved. Since most students are somewhat lacking in maturity, it is very difficult for them to know when they are approaching the line of normal affinity interaction and when they pass the point at which they would be perceived as apple polishing.

Another problem arising from the need for affinity is that the student may become a "social butterfly" in the classroom—that is, a person who seeks to communicate a great deal with other students in order to satisfy a high affinity need. Again, there is nothing abnormal about this motivation or behavior, but it can get in the way of effective learning. Such communication attempts are often reprimanded by the teacher, particularly in the self-contained classrooms in the lower grades. While there is a definite need to keep such interactions under control, regulating them may cause problems in communication between the teacher and the student. The student sees nothing wrong in her or his behavior (and indeed there is nothing intrinsically wrong with it) and is likely to interpret the teacher's attempts to regulate the extent of affinity-seeking communication behavior as an abuse of power. Probably the biggest problem that arises from communication motivated by the need for affinity is poor timing on the part of the student. Few teachers would object if Billy wants to talk to Mary in order to establish a better affinity relationship. But most teachers do object if Billy tries to do this while the teacher is explaining the next arithmetic assignment. While Billy's motivations are normal, his behavior is potentially disruptive, and interferes with teacher-student communication.

While several other factors also motivate students to communicate, the desire to establish affinity relationships with others may well be the strongest force. A positive classroom atmosphere will permit the student to engage in the satisfaction of this motivation, at least to some extent. The problem for the teacher is to regulate that extent without generating negative perceptions of the teacher on the part of the students.

Information and Understanding

Another important motivation for communication that has direct application to the classroom is the desire to obtain information and understanding. To a major extent, the stronger this motivation is in the student, the more likely there will be effective communication between the teacher and the student. Often students will seek communication with the teacher in order to get information or to understand some point more clearly. This motivation will also stimulate interaction among students, because, as we noted previously, peers have a strong impact on student behavior. While this motivation is both normal and desirable, again, problems can occur.

One of the most basic reasons students communicate is to acquire information.

Timing can be a problem in the classroom. Normally, the teacher controls the time at which the student is to receive information and clarification. The teacher is ready, for example, at 9:10 every day. But the student may not be ready at the same time the teacher is. Thus, the student may be turning off the teacher when the teacher is ready; or, the student may be turned off by the teacher when the student is ready. This is a problem that has been increasingly recognized in education over the past few years and has led to instructional systems that provide students with greater flexibility and more options concerning when they will learn. But most classrooms still are relatively rigid. The teacher must take great care to be sensitive to when a student wants to learn, and, if possible, respond to the student at that time rather than suggesting an alternate period.

Another problem that can occur in classroom communication results from students' preference for obtaining information and understanding from a peer rather than from the teacher. This is certainly normal, because peer relationships are the strongest communication relationships that exist. When a student wishes to ask another student a question about an assignment or about what something means, this is often interpreted by the teacher as disruptive behavior, and, indeed, it may be disruptive. The teacher must take care not to stifle the students' interest in obtaining information and understanding simply because it appears to occur in the wrong place at the wrong time.

A final problem that may arise from the motivation to seek information and understanding has to do somewhat with timing but primarily with topic. A student may want to learn at the same time what the teacher wants to teach, but what the student wants to learn may not be what the teacher wants to teach at that given time. This can cause the student considerable frustration and lead to a poor relationship between the student and teacher. Recall the instance of the little boy in Chapter 3 who said that the book on penguins told him more than he needed to know. While the student may want to learn, the teacher may want to provide more information to the student than the student desires. In the ideal classroom communication environment, the student would be able to regulate not only the time, but the depth of learning. Unfortunately, few classroom environments exist where this type of freedom is possible.

Influence

A very important outcome in all of human communication is influence. It is no less important in communication in the classroom. Students often seek communication in order to influence others or to be influenced themselves. They may seek to communicate with the teacher in order to change the teacher's mind about a policy in the classroom. They may seek to communicate with their peers in order to modify their behavior. Similarly, they may seek to talk with their peers in order to determine what the peer norms are so that they can conform their behavior to those norms. Since both teacher and students are seeking to influence one another, the expected outcome would seem to be increased communication. But, problems do occur.

When the teacher and the student are not seeking the same change, communication is likely to be ineffective. Although they are interacting with one another and are both being motivated by influence motivations, each is trying to modify the other's behavior in different ways. It is likely that both will fail.

Similarly, a problem can occur when the teacher and the student's peers are both exerting influence, but not in the same direction. When this occurs, the teacher will usually lose.

Since students are usually in a low-power position, they quickly learn that they can more effectively influence their peers than they can their teacher. Consequently, they tend to reduce their communication with the teacher, because they do not see it as productive of the influence outcomes desired. This again presents a problem. They will turn more and more to interaction with their peers, where greater success is possible.

Decision Making

Students often must make decisions concerning their academic or social lives. Frequently, they are not sure what decision is correct, and thus they will seek information from others in order to obtain needed data or advice. Often students want other people's opinions before making their own private decisions. In other cases, they engage in communication with teachers or with other students so that they may jointly reach a decision. Again, the student may encounter problems as a result of this communication motivation.

Most students, even in the upper grades, lack knowledge about the decision-making process. Even if they have the necessary information and opinions, they don't know how to put it together. Teachers are often insensitive to this problem. Almost as often as not, the student seeks communication with the teacher for help in the decision-making *process*, not simply to obtain information or the teacher's opinion. Teachers are usually willing to give information and opinion, but they are not as ready to work with the student to reach the actual decisions required. A student must be given some freedom in decision making in order to develop decision-making skills, but the school atmosphere very often works against this. Prescriptive approaches to education implant decisions in students, but do not plant decision-making *processes* in students. If the student has been in this type of prescriptive educational system for a long time, the motivation to engage in decision making may be considerably reduced.

Confirmation

Some decisions are made very firmly; others are more tentative. In either case, after a decision is made, it is common for students to seek communication with other people to be certain that their decisions were correct. Remember that when a person chooses from a variety of alternatives, particularly when more than one of those alternatives is attractive, they are often disturbed by having to reject one desirable alternative in order to accept another. To reduce this psychological stress, people communicate with others in order to confirm that other people would have made similar choices had they been in the same position.

Students will very frequently turn to teachers for confirmation of their private decisions. Often they will suggest to the teacher that they are "thinking about doing such and such." They have really decided to do such and such, but they are not sure enough of themselves to be publicly committed to that course of action. They will then gauge the teacher's response to that projected behavior to see whether or not it conforms with adult expectations. The teacher should recognize the tentativeness of this kind of a decision and be very careful in responding. If the behavior the student suggests appears to be inappropriate, the teacher is very likely to be able to modify that decision if the student is approached tactfully. However, if the teacher reacts very negatively and then attempts to influence the student, it is likely the student will rebel against the influence attempt and carry through with the inappropriate behavior.

One of the more important needs for confirmation in the classroom is a confirmation that the student has actually learned the material in the class. The teacher may perceive that testing does give that confirmation to the student; however, the student is much more likely to obtain confirmation through oral interaction with teacher and peers than as a result of a score on an examination. The teacher who does not take the time to permit students this kind of interaction denies them a very important reinforcement for their learning behavior. If this occurs over time, this student may indeed learn much less.

In summary, the normal motivations to communicate focus on five major outcomes of communication. The student needs affinity, needs information and understanding, needs to influence and be influenced, needs to make decisions, and needs confirmation. Both students and teachers communicate with one another in order to fulfill these needs. But not all students communicate to the same degree or are motivated by these outcomes to the same degree. Thus, it is important that we consider the competing motivations that may interfere with the types of communication we have described above.

WHY STUDENTS DO NOT COMMUNICATE IN THE CLASSROOM

While it is normal to seek communication with others in order to achieve the outcomes discussed above, it is also normal to avoid communication under some circumstances. Let us consider some of those circumstances.

The Desire to Be Left Alone

Everyone has a bad day once in a while, including teachers and students. The student may not feel well, may have had a disturbing emotional experience, or may just be temporarily out of sorts. Under such circumstances, it is very normal for the student not to want to communicate, particularly with the teacher. The teacher must be sensitive to this desire. When a student with whom the teacher has had a particularly good communication relationship previously does not seem to be responsive on a given day, the teacher should leave the student alone and try again on another day. Would that it were possible for students to do the same with teachers!

Avoidance of Disclosure and Exposure

Many times students do not wish to communicate with a teacher because to do so would disclose information they would prefer to conceal. It may expose the fact that the student does not know the information or has not done the assignment. This motivation not to communicate is particularly severe in the high-threat environment that exists in many classrooms. If the teacher perceives that many students in her or his classroom usually seem not to want to communicate, the teacher should consider what has happened in that classroom in the past when students have communicated. If students have been punished because they have disclosed their lack of knowledge, it should certainly come as no surprise that they want to avoid communication with that teacher now.

Alienation

While the two previous reasons for noncommunication are very normal, a lack of desire for communication may also be abnormally caused. Alienation may account for a student's reticence. The student that is alienated hates school and is often a social isolate. Such students need special attention and special help, which the typical classroom teacher is in no position to provide. In fact, attempts to reach the alienated student by the typical classroom teacher will probably only alienate him or her even further, and establish a bad relationship between the teacher and the student. The appropriate behavior for the classroom teacher is to leave this kind of student alone, because to do otherwise would probably make the situation worse. The student should be brought to the attention of the school counselor, if there is one, so that the student can obtain needed help.

The School Atmosphere

Very often the atmosphere in the school serves to motivate students not to communicate in the classroom. At least three circumstances in the school can contribute to this. The first is when the school or the individual classroom operates as a highly authoritarian system. Power is the essence of such a system, and only the dullest student will fail to learn that one can best avoid unpleasant consequences by keeping quiet rather than by talking. The authors recently visited a senior high school whose principal we will refer to here as "Adolph Eichmann." The school's approach is strictly authoritarian; the principal exerts power on the teachers and the teachers are forced to exert similar authoritarian power on the students. There is almost no communication in the classrooms in that school. Students put in their time and keep their mouths shut. Violators of this rule are in continual trouble. It is unfortunate that such atmospheres still exist, but they do. One should certainly not be surprised, however, that in such an educational environment students are not motivated to communicate with their teachers.

Insensitive teachers are another cause of a lack of motivation for communication. Some teachers provide almost no feedback for the communication in which students engage, or, even worse, provide only negative feedback. In the absence of feedback, students do not know how they are doing when they are communicating. This causes them considerable psychological stress, which they learn to avoid by not communicating. Similarly, if the only kind of feedback they get for communication is negative, they soon realize that few, if any, desired outcomes will result from their attempts at communication. Thus, their natural motivation to communicate is rapidly squelched.

Students also lose their desire to communicate in the classroom in school systems where a strong cultural bias works against the student. When one cultural grouping is predominate in the school, students who are in the minority tend to become alienated from the system. This is true whether the minority be black, female, Presbyterian, or what have you. If the communication within that school system is strongly tied to one cultural orientation, students who do not share that orientation will tend to withdraw from communication that seems, for the most part, to exclude them.

Communication Apprehension

While all of the above are explanations of why, under some circumstances, students are not motivated to communicate in the classroom, all of them combined are still less powerful in blocking communication than is communication apprehension. For the student suffering from communication apprehension, apprehension about participating in communication outweighs the student's perception of gain from communicating in any given situation. Such people are motivated to communicate by the same elements that motivate any other human being, but are blocked from acting on that motivation by an apprehension about communication itself. The communication-apprehensive student anticipates negative feelings and outcomes from communication and thus either avoids communication, if that is possible, or suffers from a variety of anxiety-type feelings while communicating. Because of the prevalence of this characteristic within our society and its major impact on communication in the classroom, we will consider communication apprehension in more detail in the following chapter.

SELECTED REFERENCES

Burgoon, J.K., and M. Burgoon.   "Unwillingness to Communicate, Anomia-Alienation and Communication Apprehension as Predictors of Small Group Communication." *Journal of Psychology* 88 (1974): 31–38.

McCroskey, J.C., and L.R. Wheeless.   *Introduction to Human Communication.* Boston: Allyn and Bacon, 1976.

Thoreson, C.E.   "Oral Non-Participation in College Students: A Survey of Characteristics." *American Educational Research Journal* 8 (1966): 199.

Communication Apprehension

After reading this chapter, you should be able to do the following.

1. Distinguish between communication apprehension and
   a. general anxiety
   b. stage fright
2. Identify five typical behaviors of highly communication-apprehensive students.
3. Explain the relationship between communication apprehension and academic achievement.
4. Identify the estimated percentage of school children who are high communication apprehensives.
5. Explain the most probable cause of high communication apprehension.
6. Distinguish between effective and ineffective means of helping high communication apprehensives.

Communication apprehension has to do *only* with apprehension about communicating, either orally or in writing. It should not be confused with a generally anxious personality. A person can be very normal in all other respects, but be highly apprehensive about communication. On the other hand, a person could be highly neurotic, afraid of his own shadow, and still not be a communication apprehensive.

We also need to distinguish between the person who is afraid to communicate generally and the person who is affected by bad days, a threat, environment, or alienation. In many cases, the behavioral outcome is the same—lack of communication—but the cause is quite different. We are talking here about an abnormal fear of communicating. The student who is a communication apprehensive will not only be fearful of communicating with the teacher, but will also be fearful of communicating with peers, parents, or anyone else. We are not talking simply about formal communication, like giving a speech before the class, for almost everyone feels some anxiety in such a situation. The communication apprehensive, however, would feel extreme anxiety in a public setting, but would also be apprehensive in a discussion among peers, or even talking to another single individual, whether it be a teacher or a peer.

You may be asking yourself at this point, "Why should I be concerned about communication apprehension? I won't have very many students with this problem." To begin with, chances are that you will have *many* students with this problem. In fact, approximately one student out of every five is a high communication apprehensive. Extensive research has indicated that between 10 and 20 percent of all college students and adults suffer from extreme communication apprehension, and the percentages may be somewhat higher in secondary and elementary schools. Communication apprehension disrupts every aspect of a person's life. It affects an individual's communication behavior both as a source and as a receiver. As a result, communication apprehensives tend to be very ineffective in their communication with teachers and peers. In order to understand the pervasiveness of this problem and the impact it has on students, now and after they become adults, we will turn our attention to several specific problems that occur.

SOME MAJOR EFFECTS OF COMMUNICATION APPREHENSION

Withdrawal Behavior

The main behavioral response to communication apprehension is the desire to withdraw from communication and interaction with other people. Adult apprehensives will go so far as to choose housing that provides them maximum isolation from other individuals in their environment. Similarly, when communication apprehensives are forced to interact in a small group, research has indicated they will select a seat that permits them to engage in the least interaction possible. In the classroom, the communication apprehensive seems to

Communication apprehension often results in social isolation and withdrawal.

be able to determine intuitively the seats that will draw high interaction from the teacher, and the student avoids those seats if at all possible. Generally, communication apprehensives will be at the periphery of the room rather than in the front or the center. Outside of the classroom communication-apprehensive students will seek to avoid contact with teachers or with other students. They will not join clubs or other extracurricular activities, and they will not enter areas in which social interaction is highly likely, unless they have no other choice. If they must enter such an area, they will tend to sit on the periphery and avoid contact with the other people. In short, the first major effect of communication apprehension is the avoidance of communication. This, however, leads to many other effects.

Occupational Choice

Research has indicated that students make their decisions about the occupations they will pursue in accordance with their level of communication apprehension. Highly apprehensive students will choose to pursue occupations that require little human interaction. On the other hand, students with low communication apprehension seek occupations that require a great deal of communication with other people. On its face, this would not seem to be a problem. Both types of students are seeking the kinds of jobs in which they would be happiest. But the problem arises because of the nature of our society. The overwhelming majority of the high-status and high-income occupations in our society require a great deal of communication. Consequently, the student who is highly apprehensive self-selects herself or himself into a lower status, lower income role in the society.

Communication Behavior

No matter what lengths they go to, communication-apprehensive students can never completely avoid communicating. When they are forced into a situation where they must communicate, several things happen. First of all, they simply talk less than other students. In fact, they will not talk at all unless strongly prompted to by someone else. When they do talk, what they say differs from typical students who are not apprehensive. Their comments in a small group interaction, for example, tend to be much less relevant to the topic being discussed than are the comments of other participants. They seem to recognize that if they say something that is relevant, they are likely to prompt a reaction from another participant which will force them to communicate again. Thus, they contribute very little to the interactions and wind up having little if any influence in the decision of the group, a decision that will in many cases have a major impact on their own well-being. This tendency to avoid risk of communication also tends to make apprehensive students disclose less about themselves. As a result, it is very difficult to get to know the communication-apprehensive student. They do not want to talk about themselves, because they have a generally low self-esteem, and besides that they really don't want to talk about *anything*.

Effects on the Student Who Is Apprehensive

Several negative effects result from the communication behaviors in which the communication-apprehensive student engages (or, more accurately, doesn't engage). To begin with, communication-apprehensive students are perceived to be less attractive than others by their classmates. As a consequence, they usually have very few, if any, friends. Research has indicated that communication apprehensives are not even liked by other communication apprehensives! Similarly, the apprehensive students are perceived as less credible by both their peers and their teachers. As if all of this were not enough, communication apprehensives, because of their lack of communication, are seldom in positions of leadership. They are the perennial followers; no one turns to them for advice; they are simply not leaders. Although the communication apprehensive may have much to offer the other students in the classroom or in any other environment, what they have to offer is lost.

When communication apprehensives, become adults they tend to be much less satisfied with their jobs than are nonapprehensives. While in school, the student communication apprehensive is much less satisfied with school, doesn't like it, and wants to get out. Since the school environment is a communication-demanding environment, it should not be surprising that the communication apprehensive generally does not like school. But this also shows up in how well the student does in school. The overall academic achievement of communication apprehensives is lower by the time they complete high school than is the achievement of nonapprehensives. This occurs in spite of the fact that there is no relationship between intelligence and level of communication apprehension.

As we noted previously, the extent of the communication-apprehension problem in the classroom is severe. Somewhere around one out of every five students is a communication apprehensive. But beyond this, another 20 percent of the students are somewhat affected by communication apprehension. There are more severe communication apprehensives in the schools than there are students *with all other handicaps combined*. It is a severe problem which plagues the student all through his or her life.

We have gone to great lengths to stress the importance of being aware of communication apprehension, because most teachers are simply not conscious of the problem and only a small handful of schools in the nation are prepared to cope with it. Unfortunately, when the teacher is not aware of the problem, he or she may severely aggravate its seriousness rather than help to overcome it. In order to develop a better understanding of communication apprehension, we need to look at both the causes and some suggested solutions.

COMMUNICATION APPREHENSION: CAUSES AND SOLUTIONS

The primary causes of communication apprehension are not yet fully known. However, we do know two things for certain. First, communication apprehension is in no way related to intelligence. Secondly, communication apprehension is not hereditary—no student is born with communication apprehension, but many develop it later. The best explanation to date about how communication apprehension develops is based on the theory of reinforcement. Let's examine that theory in greater detail and discuss how communication apprehension can be initiated in the home.

Communication Apprehension
and Differences within the Family Environment

Recent research has pointed toward family size as a major contributor to differences among children. In a massive study of nearly 400,000 nineteen year olds, it was found that intelligence and family size were highly associated. Children from small families tend to have higher intelligence than children from larger families. In addition, within any given family size, the first-born children are generally more intelligent than the children born later.

Although there has been no meaningful relationship observed between intelligence and communication apprehension, the theory that family size and spacing impact intelligence development suggests an analog for the development of communication apprehension. The essence of the theory is that the IQ of a child is a function of the average intellectual-stimulation level available in the family environment of the child. Since children have lower intellectual capacities than adults (when not corrected for age), the more children in a child's environment, the lower the average of that child's intellectual stimulation.

We have used this same assumption to advance a theory of how family size and spacing cause different levels of communication apprehension to develop in children. The essential components of this theory are:

1. Reinforcement for communication in childhood results in increased confidence in the child about her or his communication; lack of reinforcement and/or aversive response to communication attempts results in reduced confidence ergo increased communication apprehension.

2. A child who develops and exhibits skill in communication early will receive more reinforcement than other children.

3. With biological maturation held constant, the acquisition of language and communication skills is a function of the child's interaction with communication models in the child's environment and the amount and quality of reinforcement the child receives from that interaction.

4. On average, the best available models for a child are the child's parents, but the more children present in the family, the lower the percentage of the total interaction of the child with the parents.

5. In the typical family, the models that will provide the most discriminating reinforcement for the child's developing communication skills will be the parents (other children are more likely to provide indiscriminant reinforcement according to their own needs or to ignore communication attempts of younger children). But the more children present in the family, the lower the percentages of the total interaction of the child with the parent.

This theory argues, therefore, that, as family size increases, the communication skill of the children in the family decreases and the amount of positive reinforcement of communication will decrease correspondingly. While we suspect that there is a negative impact for all children in large families, the impact on later-born children is expected to be stronger, since early-born children will have a comparatively larger amount of interaction with parents during their formative years.

Two elements must be added to this general model. It should be expected that spacing between children could exaggerate or reduce the impact of family size on the child's communication development. For example, if children are spaced very closely (or multiple births occur), the impact should be greater, but if older children are approaching adulthood when the new child is born, the impact on family size should be reduced or even eliminated. The second element we must add involves the number of parents present in the family unit. In fatherless or motherless homes with more than one child, the impact of family size should be heightened, since the available interaction time with parents is reduced by half.

Children are reinforced for communicating while they are young. Therefore, they learn to value communication and engage in communication behavior more and more frequently, and learn to adapt their communication to their environment. But some home situations do not provide the necessary positive reinforcement for communication. The old saying, "Children are to be seen but not heard," is exemplary of the problem. Some parents do not reward their children for communicating; rather, they punish them for communicating. If this pattern is extensive, it is very likely to result in a communication-apprehensive child. Most kindergarten teachers are familiar with the child who would rather sit under the desk than at the desk. Thus, we cannot blame the school for being the primary cause of communication apprehension. However, the school can be a contributor to the problem.

Classroom Causes of Communication Apprehension

In most schools, certain expectations and standards work to enhance communication apprehension rather than overcome it. If the typical teacher is asked to describe a "well behaved" child, he or she will usually describe a child who is quiet and nondisruptive! Indeed, from kindergarten on, students who verbalize a great deal, particularly at inopportune moments, are punished, while the quiet child is rewarded. At the lowest levels, the quiet child is often fondled and loved more than the outgoing, aggressive child. The child who is already prone toward communication apprehension is strongly reinforced for her or his behavior in such an environment. Thus, instead of the school helping to overcome the problem that began in the home, the school continues to reinforce the negative adaptation of the child.

A second explanation for the enhancement of communication apprehension in the school is the presence of the apprehensive teacher. It is well known that students tend to model their teacher's behavior, particularly at the lower grade levels. A large number of communication-apprehensive individuals become teachers, particularly elementary teachers. These individuals tend to set negative examples for the younger people in their classes. They do not want interaction themselves, and thus cut the child off from interacting with them.

Many solutions have been suggested for overcoming communication apprehension. Unfortunately, the most frequently employed "solution" is not a solution at all—i.e., to require the student to communicate more. This varies from required public-speaking classes in the high school to required recitation in the middle grades to show-and-tell at the lowest level. All of these situations are terrifying to the communication-apprehensive child or young person.

Whether the teacher believes the young person has done well or not will make little difference, because the high communication apprehensive will feel that he or she has failed, because of his or her own internal responses. Forced communication does not overcome communication apprehension; it merely reinforces it and causes the individual to seek other forms of withdrawal behavior. Some of these are manifested in behaviors at school, like fake sickness and answers of "I don't know" when the student really does know.

A second "solution" which is seldom verbally recommended, but is often practiced by teachers, is chastisement. The child who exhibits communication-apprehensive behavior is scorned by the teacher. Such a "solution" flies in the face of almost everything we know about learning. Negative reinforcement and punishment do not have much of a positive effect on extinguishing student behavior. The only effect these types of teacher behaviors should be expected to have is to force the child to withdraw even further.

What then can be done to help overcome the problem of communication apprehension? One of the best methods is to provide the child with positive reinforcement for communication in the early years in the classroom. Communication-apprehensive children need to be rewarded for communicating, whether they are giving the right answers, whether they are disrupting the class, or whatever the outcome of their communication is. Their problem is a fear of communication. If they are rewarded often enough for communication, that problem can be overcome. But the teacher should not expect overnight miracles. A problem that has been developing for five or six years in the home is not going to be overcome in six weeks in school.

A second partial solution is to provide positive models for the communication-apprehensive child. In most classrooms, the child observes negative models: children who talk a lot are punished. The communication apprehensive quickly learns that communicating in the classroom is a bad thing, although that is certainly not what the teacher is trying to communicate to the class. Consequently, not only should the communication-apprehensive student be rewarded for communicating, but other students should be rewarded as well in the presence of the communication apprehensive. *Communication behavior should never be an object of punishment in the classroom.*

While the above solutions can have a major impact on overcoming communication apprehension in the lower grades, teachers of the middle and upper grades will still have many communication-apprehensive students, as will college teachers. Fortunately, a behavior therapy has been developed which has been found to be highly successful in helping students overcome their communication apprehension. This technique is referred to as "systematic desensitization." It is a behavior therapy that any teacher can learn to administer and does not require the presence of a trained clinician. We will only stress here that the teacher who is truly interested in improving communication in the classroom should strive to be very sensitive to the needs of the communication apprehensive and, if at all possible, should provide the means by which the communication-apprehensive child can overcome a problem that otherwise could seriously affect an entire lifetime.

Students are just like any other people. They have needs and limitations. They are motivated to communicate and motivated not to communicate. But students differ drastically from one another and cannot be put into a uniform mold. Methods that will enhance communication between the teacher and one student may directly interfere with the communication of the teacher and another student. When teachers fail to recognize this, their expectations may

This instrument is composed of twenty statements concerning feelings about communicating with other people. Indicate the degree to which the statements apply to you by marking whether you (1) strongly agree, (2) agree, (3) are undecided, (4) disagree, or (5) strongly disagree with each statement. Work quickly; just record your first impression.

*1. While participating in a conversation with a new acquaintance I feel very nervous. _____
2. I have no fear of facing an audience. _____
3. I look forward to expressing my opinion at meetings. _____
4. I look forward to an opportunity to speak in public. _____
5. I find the prospect of speaking mildly pleasant. _____
*6. When communicating, my posture feels strained and unnatural. _____
*7. I am tense and nervous while participating in group discussions. _____
*8. Although I talk fluently with friends, I am at a loss for words on a platform. _____
*9. My hands tremble when I try to handle objects on the platform. _____
*10. I always avoid speaking in public if possible. _____
11. I feel that I am more fluent when talking to people than most other people are. _____
*12. I am fearful and tense all the while I am speaking before a group of people. _____
*13. My thoughts become confused and jumbled when I speak before an audience. _____
14. Although I am nervous just before getting up, I soon forget my fears and enjoy the experience. _____
*15. Conversing with people who hold positions of authority causes me to be fearful and tense. _____
*16. I dislike to use my body and voice expressively. _____
17. I feel relaxed and comfortable while speaking. _____
*18. I feel self-conscious when I am called upon to answer a question or give an opinion in class. _____
19. I face the prospect of making a speech with complete confidence. _____
20. I would enjoy presenting a speech on a local television show. _____

Scoring Procedure

1. Add scores for items with asterisk.
2. Add scores for items without asterisk.
3. Complete the following formula: PRCA Score = 66 − Total 1 + Total 2.

Interpretation

Students with scores above 72 are probably highly communication apprehensive. Students with scores between 61 and 72 are moderately apprehensive.

Fig. 9.1 Personal report of communication apprehension—adult version.

seriously disrupt effective teaching and communication in their classrooms. We will consider this problem in the following chapter.

In Fig. 9.1, we have included a twenty-item adult version of a scale designed to measure communication apprehension. It may be used successfully with high-school students as well. Please complete the questionnaire for yourself. Instructions for scoring your own responses are presented in the table. It may be one of the most important tests you will ever take.

SELECTED REFERENCES

Barker, L. L., D. J. Cegala, R. J. Kibler, and K. J. Wahlers.   Hypnosis and the Reduction of Speech Anxiety." *Central States Speech Journal* **23** (1972): 28–35.

Barnes, R. E.   "Interpersonal Communication Approaches to Reducing Speech Anxiety." Paper presented to the Central States Speech Association Convention, Chicago, 1976.

Barrick, J. E.   "A Cautionary Note on the Use of Systematic Desensitization." *Speech Teacher* **20** (1971): 280–281.

Bashore, D. N.   "Relationships among Speech Anxiety, IQ, and High School Achievement." M.S. thesis, Illinois State University, 1971.

Behnke, R. R., and L. W. Carlile.   "Heart Rate as an Index of Speech Anxiety." *Speech Monographs* **38** (1971): 65–69.

Belmont, L., and F. A. Marolla.   "Birth Order, Family Size, and Intelligence." *Science,* **182** (1973): 1096–1101.

Breland, H. M.   "Birth Order, Family Configuration, and Verbal Achievement." Paper presented to the Midwestern Psychological Association Annual Meeting, Chicago, 1973.

Brooks, W. D., and S. M. Platz.   "The Effects of Speech Training upon Self-Concept as a Communicator." *Speech Teacher* **17** (1968): 44–49.

Bruskin Associates.   "What Are Americans Afraid of?" *The Bruskin Report*, 1973, no. 53.

Bugelski, B. R.   *The Psychology of Learning Applied to Teaching.* Indianapolis: Bobbs-Merrill, 1964.

Burgoon, J. K.   "The Unwillingness-to-Communicate Scale: Development and Validation." *Communication Monographs* **43** (1976): 60–69.

Clevenger, T., Jr.   "A Synthesis of Experimental Research in Stage Fright." *Quarterly Journal of Speech* **45** (1959): 134–145.

Daly, J. A., and J. C. McCroskey.   "Occupational Choice and Desirability as a Function of Communication Apprehension." *Journal of Counseling Psychology* **22** (1975): 309–313.

Daly, J. A., and M. D. Miller.   "The Empirical Development of an Instrument to Measure Writing Apprehension." *Research in the Teaching of English* **9** (1975): 242–249.

Daly, J. A., and M. D. Miller. "Further Studies on Writing Apprehension: SAT Scores, Success Expectations, Willingness to Take Advanced Courses, and Sex Differences." *Research in the Teaching of English* 9 (1975): 250–256.

Daly, J. A., and S. Leth. "Communication Apprehension and the Personnel Selection Decision." Paper presented to the International Communication Association Convention, Portland, Oregon, 1976.

Daly, J. A., J. C. McCroskey, and V. P. Richmond. "The Relationships between Vocal Activity and Perception of Communicators in Small Group Interaction." *Western Speech Communication,* in press.

Dymacek, D. A. "Effects of Number of Classroom Speeches on Anxiety Reduction and Performance Improvement." Paper presented to the Speech Communication Association Convention, San Francisco, 1971.

Ertle, C. D. "A Study of the Effect of Homogeneous Grouping on Systematic Desensitization for the Reduction of Interpersonal Communication Apprehension." Ph.D. dissertation, Michigan State University, 1969.

Falcione, R. L., J. C. McCroskey, and J. A. Daly. "Job Satisfaction as a Function of Employees' Communication Apprehension, Self-Esteem, and Perceptions of Their Immediate Supervisor." Monograph, University of Maryland, 1976.

Fenton, R. J., T. S. Hopf, and D. Beck. "The Use of EMG Biofeedback Assisted Relaxation Training to Reduce Communication Apprehension." Paper presented to the Western Speech Communication Association Convention, Seattle, 1975.

Freimuth, V. S. "The Effects of Communication Apprehension on Communication Effectiveness." *Human Communication Research* 2 (1976): 289–298.

Fremouw, W. J., and M. G. Harmatz. "A Helper Model for Behavioral Treatment of Speech Anxiety." *Journal of Consulting and Clinical Psychology* 43 (1975): 652–660.

Fremouw, W. J., and R. E. Zitter. "A Comparison of Skills Training and Cognitive Restructuring-Relaxation for the Treatment of Speech Anxiety." Monograph, Department of Psychology, West Virginia University, 1976.

Garrison, K. R., and J. P. Garrison. "Measurement of Talking Apprehension in the Elementary School." Monograph, University of Nebraska—Lincoln, 1976.

Giffin, K., and K. Bradley. *An Exploratory Study of Group Counseling for Speech Anxiety.* Research Monograph 12. Lawrence, Kansas: Communication Research Center, University of Kansas, 1967.

Giffin, K., and K. Bradley. "Group Counseling for Speech Anxiety: An Approach and a Rationale." *Journal of Communication* 19 (1969): 22–29.

Giffin, K., and G. Friedrich. *The Development of a Baseline for Studies of Speech Anxiety.* Research Report 20. Lawrence, Kansas: Communication Research Center, University of Kansas, 1968.

Gilkinson, H. "Social Fears as Reported by Students in College Speech Classes." *Speech Monographs* 9 (1942): 141–160.

Grutzeck, L. F. A Search for Invariant Characteristics of Reticent Elementary School Children." M.A. thesis, Pennsylvania State University, 1970.

Hamilton, P. R.   "The Effect of Risk Proneness of Small Group Interaction, Communication Apprehension, and Self-Disclosure." M.S. thesis, Illinois State University, 1972.

Hamilton, P. K.   "An Experimental Investigation of the Relation between Internal-External Locus of Control of Reinforcement and the Systematic Desensitization of Communication Anxiety." Paper presented to the Central States Speech Communication Association Convention, Chicago, 1976.

Heald, G. R.   "A Comparison of Systematic Desensitization and Conditioned Relaxation in Reducing Speech Anxiety." Paper presented to the International Communication Association Convention, Portland, Oregon, 1976.

Henning, J. H.   "A Study of Stage Fright through the Comparison of Student Reactions and Instructor Observations during the Speech Situation." M.A. thesis, Northwestern University, 1935.

Huntley, J. R.   "An Investigation of the Relationships between Personality and Types of Instructor Criticism in the Beginning Speech-Communication Course." Ph.D. dissertation, Michigan State University, 1969.

Hurt, H. T., and K. Joseph.   "The Impact of Communication Apprehension in the Process of Social Change." Paper presented to the Eastern Communication Association Convention, New York, 1975.

Hurt, H. T., R. Preiss, and B. Davis.   "The Effects of Communication Apprehension of Middle-School Children on Sociometric Choice, Affective, and Cognitive Learning." Paper presented to the International Communication Association Convention, Portland, 1976.

Ickes, W. K.   "A Classical Conditioning Model for 'Reticence.' " *Western Speech* **35** (1971): 48–55.

Knutson, P. K., and W. B. Lashbrook.   "Communication Apprehension as an Antecedent to Social Style." Paper presented to the Speech Communication Association Convention, San Francisco, 1976.

Lamb, D. H.   "Speech Anxiety: Towards a Theoretical Conceptualization and Preliminary Scale Development." *Speech Monographs* **39** (1972): 62–67.

Lehman, G.   "Family Composition and Its Influence on the Language Development of the 18–34 Month-Old Child in the American Lower and Middle Class Family." *Journal of Behavioral Science* **1** (1971): 125–130.

Lohr, J. W., and M. L. McManus.   "The Development of an Audio-Taped Treatment for Systematic Desensitization of Speech Anxiety." *Central States Speech Journal* **26** (1975): 215–220.

Lomas, C. W.   "A Study of Stage Fright as Measured by Student Reactions to the Speaking Situation.' M.A. thesis, Northwestern University, 1934.

Lustig, M. W.   "Verbal Reticence: A Reconceptualization and Preliminary Scale Development." Paper presented to the Speech Communication Association Convention, Chicago, 1974.

McCroskey, J. C.   "Measures of Communication-Bound Anxiety." *Speech Monographs* **37** (1970): 269–277.

McCroskey, J. C.   "The Implementation of a Large Scale Program of Systematic Desensitization for Communication Apprehension." *Speech Teacher* 21 (1972): 255–264.

McCroskey, J. C.   "Validity of the PRCA as an Index of Oral Communication Apprehension." Paper presented to the Speech Communication Association Convention, Houston, 1975.

McCroskey, J. C.   "Alternate Measures of Communication Apprehension." Monograph, West Virginia University, 1976.

McCroskey, J. C.   "Communication Apprehension in University and Community College Environments." Monograph, West Virginia University, 1976.

McCroskey, J. C.   "The Effects of Communication Apprehension on Nonverbal Behavior." *Communication Quarterly* 24 (1976): 39–44.

McCroskey, J. C.   "Normative Levels of Communication Apprehension among Elementary and Secondary School Students." Monograph, West Virginia University, 1976.

McCroskey, J. C.   "The Problems of Communication Apprehension in the Classroom." Paper presented to the Communication Association of the Pacific Convention, Kobe, Japan, 1976.

McCroskey, J. C.   "Classroom Consequences of Communication Apprehension." *Communication Education*, in press.

McCroskey, J. C., and J. F. Andersen.   "The Relationship between Communication Apprehension and Academic Achievement among College Students." *Human Communication Research,* in press.

McCroskey, J. C., and J. A. Daly.   "Teachers' Expectations of the Communication Apprehensive Child in the Elementary School." *Human Communication Research,* in press.

McCroskey, J. C., J. A. Daly, V. P. Richmond, and B. G. Cox.   "The Effects of Communication Apprehension on Interpersonal Attraction." *Human Communication Research* 2 (1975): 51–65.

McCroskey, J. C., J. A. Daly, and G. A. Sorensen.   "Personality Correlates of Communication Apprehension." *Human Communication Research,* in press.

McCroskey, J. C., P. R. Hamilton, and A. N. Weiner.   "The Effect of Interaction Behavior on Source Credibility, Homophily, and Interpersonal Attraction." *Human Communication Research* 1 (1974): 42–52.

McCroskey, J. C., and T. Leppard.   "The Effects of Communication Apprehension on Nonverbal Behavior." Paper presented to the Eastern Communication Association Convention, New York, 1975.

McCroskey, J. C., D. C. Ralph, and J. E. Barrick.   "The Effect of Systematic Desensitization on Speech Anxiety." *Speech Teacher* 19 (1970): 32–36.

McCroskey, J. C., and V. P. Richmond.   "Self-Credibility as an Index of Self-Esteem." Paper presented to the Speech Communication Association Convention, Houston, 1975.

McCroskey, J. C., and V. P. Richmond.   "The Effects of Communication Apprehension on the Perception of Peers." *Western Speech Communication* 40 (1976): 14–21.

McCroskey, J. C., and V. P. Richmond. "Communication Apprehension as a Predictor of Self-Disclosure." *Communication Quarterly,* in press.

McCroskey, J. C., and M. E. Sheahan. "Communication Apprehension, Social Preference and Social Behavior in a College Environment." Monograph, Department of Speech Communication, West Virginia University, 1976.

McCroskey, J. C., and M. E. Sheahan. "Seating Position and Participation: An Alternative Theoretical Explanation." Paper presented to the International Communication Association Convention, Portland, Oregon, 1976.

Merrill, D. *Reference Survey Profile.* Denver: Personal Predictions and Research, Inc., 1974.

Moore, D. L. "The Effects of Systematic Desensitization on Communication Apprehension in an Aged Population." M.S. thesis, Illinois State University, 1972.

Motley, M. T. "Stage Fright Reduction by (False) Heart Rate Feedback." Paper presented to the Western Speech Communication Association Convention, Newport Beach, California, 1974.

Mulac, A., and A. R. Sherman. "Behavioral Assessment of Speech Anxiety." *Quarterly Journal of Speech* **60** (1974): 134–143.

Mulac, A., and A. R. Sherman. "Relationships among Four Parameters of Speaker Evaluation: Speech Skill, Source Credibility, Subjective Speech Anxiety, and Behavioral Speech Anxiety." *Speech Monographs* **42** (1975): 302–310.

Nichols, J. G. "An Investigation of the Effects of Varied Rates of Training on Systematic Desensitization for Interpersonal Communication Apprehension." Ph.D dissertation, Michigan State University, 1969.

Paul, G. L. *Insight vs. Desensitization in Psychotherapy.* Stanford: Stanford University Press, 1966.

Phillips, G. M. "The Problem of Reticence." *Pennsylvania Speech Annual* **22** (1965): 22–38.

Phillips, G. M. "Reticence: Pathology of the Normal Speaker." *Speech Monographs* **35** (1968): 39–49.

Phillips, G. R., and D. Butt. "Reticence Re-Visited." *Pennsylvania Speech Annual* **23** (1966): 40–57.

Phillips, G. M., and N. J. Metzger. "The Reticent Syndrome: Some Theoretical Considerations about Etiology and Treatment." *Speech Monographs* **40** (1973): 220–230.

Porter, D. T. "Self-Report Scales of Communication Apprehension and Autonomic Arousal (Heart Rate): A Test of Construct Validity." *Speech Monographs* **41** (1974): 267–276.

Quiggins, J. G. "The Effects of High and Low Communication Apprehension on Small Group Member Credibility, Interpersonal Attraction, and Interaction." Paper presented to the Speech Communication Association Convention, Chicago, 1972.

Randolph, F. L., and J. C. McCroskey. "Oral Communication Apprehension as a Function of Family Size: A Preliminary Investigation." Monograph, Department of Speech Communication, West Virginia University, 1976.

Redding, C. W. "The Psychogalvanometer as a Laboratory Instrument in the Basic Course in Speech." M. A. thesis, University of Denver, 1936.

Rosenfeld, L. B., and T. G. Plax. "Personality Discriminants of Reticence." *Western Speech Communication* **40** (1976): 22–31.

Richmond, V. P. "Communication Apprehension and Success in the Job Applicant Screening Process." Monograph, West Virginia Northern Community College, 1976.

Richmond, V. P., and D. Robertson. "Communication Apprehension as a Function of Being Raised in an Urban or Rural Environment." Monograph, West Virginia Northern Community College, 1976.

Sohwalb, G. "Police-Specific Communication Training: A Practice Approach to Family Crises Mediation." Ph.D. dissertation, University of California at Los Angeles, 1976.

Scott, M. D., J. C. McCroskey, and M. E. Sheahan. "The Development of a Self-Report Measure of Communication Apprehension in Organizational Settings." *Journal of Communication,* in press.

Scott, M. D., and L. R. Wheeless. "An Exploratory Investigation of Three Types of Communication Apprehension on Student Achievement." Paper presented to the Speech Communication Association Convention, San Francisco, 1976.

Scott, M. D., M. Yates, and L. R. Wheeless. "An Exploratory Investigation of the Effects of Communication Apprehension in Alternative Systems of Instruction." Paper presented to the International Communication Association Convention, Chicago, 1975.

Sheahan, M. E. "Communication Apprehension and Electoral Participation." M.A. thesis, West Virginia University, 1976.

Sheahan, A. M. "The Effects of Systematic Desensitization and Communication Exposure on Speech Anxious Students." M.S. thesis, Illinois State University, 1971.

Sorensen, G. A., and J. C. McCroskey. "The Prediction of Interaction Behavior in Small Groups." *Communication Monographs,* in press.

Spielberger, C. D., ed. *Anxiety and Behavior.* New York: Academic Press, 1966.

Taylor, S. A., and P. K. Hamilton. "The Effects of the Basic Speech Course on Anxiety, Dogmatism, Cognitive Ability, and Communicative Ability." Paper presented to the International Communication Associated Convention, New Oreleans, 1974.

Weiner, A. N. "Machiavellianism as a Predictor of Group Interaction and Cohesion." M.A. thesis, West Virginia University, 1973.

Wells, J. "A Study of the Effects of Systematic Desensitization on the Communicative Anxiety of Individuals in Small Groups. M.A. thesis, San Jose State College, 1970.

Wenzlaff, V. J. "The Prediction of Leadership: A Consideration of Selected Communication Variables." M.S. thesis, Illinois State University, 1972.

Wheeless, L. R. "Communication Apprehension in the Elementary School." *Speech Teacher* **20** (1971): 297–299.

Wheeless, L. R., K. Nesser, and J. C. McCroskey. "Relationships among Self-Disclosure, Disclosiveness, and Communication Apprehension." Monograph, West Virginia University, 1976.

Witteman, H. R. "The Relationship of Communication Apprehension to Opinion Leadership and Innovativeness." M.A. thesis, West Virginia University, 1976.

Zajonc, R. B. "Birth Order and Intelligence: Dumber by the Dozen." *Psychology Today* 8 (January 1975): 37–43.

Zajonc, R. B., and G. B. Markus. "Birth Order and Intellectual Development." *Psychological Review* 82 (1975): 74–88.

Expectancies in the Classroom

After reading this chapter, you should be able to do the following.

1. Describe the psychological origins of human expectancies.
2. Define and describe what is meant by the phrase self-fulfilling prophecy.
3. Describe and/or discuss how nonverbal communication can be a source of student and teacher expectancies.
4. Describe and/or discuss how verbal and written communication can be a source of student and teacher expectancies.
5. Define and distinguish between teacher biases and teacher expectancies.
6. Summarize the effects of teacher bias on communication and self-concept.
7. Summarize the relationship between teacher expectancies and student achievement.

A few summers back we had an interesting experience while working with a group of primary and secondary educators in a course entitled, "Communication in the Classroom." During a discussion of how individual psychologies impact on communication in the classroom environment, one teacher asked us whether we were opposed to or in favor of a teacher having access to a future student's records; that is, a student with whom the teacher had no prior contact. The question must have been highly topical because, moments later, a number of the class members asked us in chorus whether we were opposed to or in favor of a teacher seeking out the opinion of another in the attempt to learn about a future student.

Since we were in a somewhat nondirective mood on that particular day, we asked the class as a whole to explore both questions. While the responses were highly varied, that of one particular teacher bothered us a great deal. She said that throughout her fifteen-year-long career, she had always consulted a student's records or with another teacher. In a rather matter-of-fact manner, to actually meeting the student on the first day of class. She continued by saying that, as a function of engaging in both practices, she had been able to predict with uncanny accuracy how a student would perform in her class— again, without ever meeting the student in a face-to-face situation. We asked this teacher about the kind of information she looked for when consulting a student's records or with another teacher. In the same matter-of-fact manner, she said that she first looked for information about a student's family—things like whether the family was highly transient, whether the student's father was employed, whether the student's mother worked or was in the home, whether the student's parents were well educated, etc. After reviewing this type of information, she pointed out that it was much easier to understand a student's academic history. For example, she had found that good students typically came from well-established homes and were the children of college-educated parents, whereas students with a poor history of academic achievement had very often attended a number of schools and were almost always the children of parents with a high-school education or less. We then asked this teacher what she perceived to be the major benefit of possessing this kind of information. Looking rather astonished at our naiveté, she replied that such information placed her in the enviable position of *knowing what to expect* from a particular student even before the first day of class.

SELF-FULFILLING PROPHECIES

Our purpose in relating this episode to you is rather straightforward. The preceding teacher's behavior is illustrative of what is commonly referred to as a self-fulfilling prophecy, or the expectancy effect. That is, a prophecy or expectancy which comes true because one simply expects it to come true. For example, in the preceding instance, the teacher prophesied, or in her words, predicted, how a student would perform in her class as a result of consulting the student's records as well as other teachers who had experience with the student. In effect, she developed a set of expectancies concerning how well the student would perform in her class. If one adheres to the premise of the self-fulfilling prophecy, then it would follow that the student would achieve exactly as this teacher expected—regardless of the student's intellectual capabilities. If this sounds far-fetched, let us assure you it is not. As the following discussion demonstrates, the phenomenon of the self-fulfilling prophecy, or the expectancy effect, is a pervasive one.

The Psychological Roots of the Expectancy Effect

Human beings learn at an early age that certain behaviors will consistently elicit a specific response from the environment. As children, for example, we quickly learn that certain behaviors on our part will consistently elicit the affection of our parents, the praise of our teachers, or the admiration of our peers. Since these kinds of responses are rewarding, we engage in these behaviors more frequently than others and attempt to generalize them to new and unique situations. We do so, however, with the expectancy that these behaviors will elicit responses identical or similar to the positive ones they have met with in the past. When this expectancy is upheld, we experience psychological well-being; when this expectancy is not upheld, we experience psychological discomfort. Since we are conditioned to minimize the probability of psychological discomfort, we sometimes go out of our way to increase the probability of the preceding kinds of expectancies being upheld—even to the point of distorting reality. Stated even more directly, we sometimes go out of our way to insure that our prophecies about our own behaviors and the responses they will elicit will come true.

Just as we develop a set of expectancies concerning our own behaviors, we also develop a set of expectancies about the behaviors of other people. Furthermore, these expectancies are very often based on stereotypes we have acquired from other people. Males, for example, have traditionally expected females to behave in a manner that is consistent with what Betty Friedan called the "feminine mystique." Some women might justifiably contend that males have gone to great lengths (i.e., committed certain behaviors) to insure that this expectation continues to be confirmed—including the denial of women's equal rights under the Constitution of the United States. Of course, women are not the only ones who have been negatively affected by the expectancies of people. So have Blacks, Chicanos, Indians, Orientals, senior citizens, and, as you will soon learn, the students in our classrooms. In any event, you should attempt to keep in mind two important points as we continue with our discussion of the self-fulfilling prophecy or expectancy effect. First, our expectancies about our own behaviors, as well as the behaviors of others, are psychologically rooted in our learning experiences. Second, since we have been conditioned to avoid psychological discomfort, we more often than not engage in behaviors designed to increase the likelihood of our expectancies being supported—even at the expense of other people.

Human Expectancies Outside the Classroom

As you might well imagine, there are innumerable examples of the expectancy effect outside the classroom environment. And, for purely arbitrary reasons, we prefer to discuss some of these examples prior to discussing the factors that give rise to teacher-student expectancies and the potential consequences of such expectancies.

A number of the best examples come from medical practice and research. For example, Greenblatt recorded an interesting case about a patient suffering from terminal cancer. Evidently, while hospitalized, this patient was exposed to information about Krebiozen, a promising new drug with important implications for the treatment of cancer. The drug was administered to this patient and, as you might well suspect, he dramatically improved. So much so, in fact, that he was discharged from the hospital. At some later date, however, this same patient was inadvertently exposed to contradictory information about the efficacy of this new "wonder drug." Suffering from a relapse, he was readmitted to the hospital. Thinking that he was once again receiving Krebiozen, he again began to recover and was subsequently discharged. The truth of the matter, though, is that he was simply receiving saline injections—a harmless mixture of water and salt that couldn't possibly affect his illness. As reported by Greenblatt, the patient finally learned that the American Medical Association had decided that Krebiozen had no measurable impact whatsoever as a cancer-fighting agent. He was admitted to the hospital for the final time and died forty-eight hours later.

In a similar account, Gordon Allport, the distinguished social psychologist, described a man who was dying of an undetermined illness. Rather matter-of-factly, the physicians responsible for this patient told him that his recovery was in question because they simply were not able to diagnose the nature of his illness. And, as a last resort, they had asked a noted diagnostician to examine him. The diagnostician examined the patient and simply said, "moribundus." As Allport tells it, some years later the same patient, who obviously didn't die, visited the diagnostician and thanked him for saving his life. Moreover, he told the diagnostician that prior to his examination the other physicians had informed him that his illness could only be abated if it were properly diagnosed. As a result, he knew his recovery was imminent once the diagnostician had informed the doctors that he was suffering from moribundus.

Although there are a number of cases almost identical to the preceding ones, probably the most startling examples of the expectancy effect have been provided by researchers employing some kind of placebo as a means of medical treatment. A placebo is an inert or innocuous substance, without any medicinal qualities whatsoever. It is typically used as a control when administering another substance in experimental research. The fact that it does not have any medicinal value, however, should not be construed to mean that it seldom impacts on an individual's condition. As a case in point, Gregory Pincus conducted several experiments focusing on the "side effects" normally associated with oral contraception. In one of these experiments, women were grouped into the following three conditions:

1. given the oral contraceptive and warned of possible side effects;
2. given a placebo rather than the oral contraceptive, but also warned of possible side effects;
3. given the oral contraceptive, but not the warning of possible side effects.

Pincus found that approximately 6 percent of the women grouped in condition three experienced nausea, vomiting, vertigo, and gastralgia—in other words, some of the side effects normally associated with oral contraception. Interestingly enough, however, the preceding maladies occurred approximately three times as much in conditions one and two, where the women had been cautioned about the possibility of side effects. Moreover, the women who received the placebo reported experiencing amenorrhea (absence of menstruation) three times as much as women in the conditions where the oral contraceptive was actually administered.

As a final case, consider an entire hospital staff that was told a new tranquilizer as well as a new energizing drug were being introduced into the hospital pharmacy. While both the drugs were really placebos, the staff reported them to be effective in about 70 percent of the cases where they had been introduced. When the staff was told to more closely observe the effects of the two drugs, the bogus energizer appeared to no longer benefit patients. In the case of the bogus tranquilizer, however, the staff continued to assess it as having significant medicinal value.

Given the preceding examples, we would hope that you have concluded, as we have, that human expectancies are potent influences on human behaviors—both from a psychological and physiological standpoint. We ask that you keep these examples in mind as we now turn to what, in our opinion, is the major source of human expectancies in the classroom.

SOURCES OF TEACHER-STUDENT EXPECTANCIES

In spite of what we might like to think about them, teachers are just as susceptible to things like racism or sexism as the next person. Moreover, teachers are not superhuman, not capable of stripping themselves of these kinds of social maladies outside the classroom at the beginning of each new day. The importance of this fact cannot be minimized. If a teacher is a racist, or sexist, or an elitist outside of class, the teacher will at least in part be a racist, sexist, or an elitist inside the classroom—complete with a set of expectancies that correspond to their particular prejudice.

Of course, a teacher doesn't just walk into a class and automatically assume the posture of a bigot or a chauvinist. Nor does a teacher simply walk into a class and, knowing nothing about a particular student, expect that student to achieve or behave in a specific manner. Needless to say, there must be something that the teacher perceives or knows about a particular student if the teacher's prejudice and corresponding set of expectancies are to be triggered. In our estimation, that something happens to be the verbal and nonverbal cues communicated to the teacher by students themselves.

Nonverbal Cues as a Source of Teacher Expectancies

As we pointed out earlier, initial student perceptions of a teacher are largely a function of what the teacher looks like. We think that teachers engage in the same process. Even more specifically, we think that teachers make inferences about a student's background, intellectual capacity, and motivation to achieve on the basis of the nonverbal cues they derive from the student's appearance. As a case in point, consider the differential perceptions and inferences a teacher might have and draw about two first graders attending a largely middle-class school. The first child smiles and readily acknowledges the fact that the teacher is directly looking at him. He is dressed in a new pair of slacks, wearing a starched and pressed white shirt, and sporting a new pair of loafers. In short, he is clean and neatly dressed. The second child stares down at his desk, purposely avoiding the teacher's gaze. He is wearing a wrinkled and threadbare T-shirt that is in need of washing, a pair of soiled jeans, and a tattered pair of tennis shoes, minus the laces. More bothersome than his clothing, however, is the state of his personal hygiene. His hair is matted in spots—obviously in need of washing. His fingernails look as if they have never been cleaned and his hands are streaked where water has washed away the dirt. His teeth are in an advanced state of decay.

Given these descriptions, how do you think our hypothetical teacher would perceive these two students? Better yet, what kinds of inferences do you think the teacher might make as a function of attending to the preceding nonverbal cues? No doubt the teacher would perceive that the two students come from decidedly different backgrounds: one distinctly middle class, the other distinctly lower class. But such a perception is, in and of itself, harmless. And, if the teacher were to stop here there would be no problem. It is more likely, however, that the teacher would begin to develop a set of expectancies about both children, based not only on these nonverbal cues, but also on the prior experiences (direct or vicarious) that the teacher has had with similar-appearing children. For example, if the teacher was familiar with the literature focusing on achievement among disadvantaged children, he or she might develop a set of expectancies consistent with the conclusions drawn in the literature. In other words, the teacher might expect that the child perceived as lower class would be less intelligent, achieve at a lower level, and would be less motivated to learn than the middle-class child. Along the same lines, the teacher might develop a set of expectancies based on past experience with a similar-appearing child who was a constant source of behavioral problems in class. In either event, however, the initial source of the teacher's expectancies would be the nonverbal cues picked up by the teacher from the students' appearances.

Nonverbal Cues as a Source of Student Expectancies
Of course, the process described in the preceding example is not one way. At the same time the teacher is sizing up the two students, the students themselves are attempting to learn what they can expect from the teacher on the basis of the teacher's nonverbal communication. For example, the well-dressed child might conclude as a function of the way the teacher looks at him that the teacher will behave positively toward him. By contrast, the unkempt child, unable to avoid looking at the teacher any longer, might sense or think that the look on the teacher's face is one of disgust and associate it with his appearance. Regardless of what the students infer from the teacher's nonverbal communication, however, they will develop an initial set of expectancies that are consistent with what they infer and gauge their behaviors by these sets of expectancies.

Verbal Cues as a Source of Teacher Expectancies
There is some empirical evidence which suggests that what one teacher says about a student may negatively predispose another teacher toward that student. Interestingly enough, we have found in our experiences with primary and secondary teachers that this is very often the case. Teachers have told us, for example, that so-called problem students are a frequent topic among teachers, as are the so-called ideal students. In effect, this means that most teachers usually have information about certain students prior to any direct contact with these students. Rather than concentrate on this obvious source of teacher bias, however, we would like to focus on a true source of teacher expectancies: the amount of verbal behavior that a student engages in.

Teachers normally place a high premium on the oral communication behaviors that their students exhibit. Under constructive circumstances, moreover, we think we can safely say that teachers are quicker to recognize and reward those students who are high verbalizers than those students who are reticent. More importantly, though, the research literature also suggests that teachers develop a differential set of expectancies about how a student will achieve in a specific subject matter on the basis of the student's verbal behaviors. In a series of studies, a number of elementary and secondary teachers were asked to read the following descriptions of two students, and were then asked to evaluate the two students' probable performance in English, arithmetic, social studies, reading, science, art, and deportment.

> Description A: Jimmy is a student at Emerson Junior High. His parents own and operate a middle-sized dry cleaners and both are college educated. When asked about Jimmy, his current teachers, as well as those who had him in elementary school, said pretty much the same thing. Jimmy is an outgoing, gregarious young man. He enjoys making presentations in front of the class, often assumes the role of leader in small-group discussions, and seems to enjoy being called on when a question is asked.

> Description B: Billy is also a student at Emerson Junior High School. His parents are teachers at the University in a neighboring community. When asked about Billy, his current teachers, as well as those who had him in elementary school, said pretty much the same thing. Billy is a shy, quiet young man. He seems to feel uncomfortable when placed in positions where he is required to orally communicate—for example, when called on to answer a question or asked to participate in small-group discussions. While he never causes trouble in class, he seems to be absent on days when oral presentations are to be made.

In spite of the fact that only scant information was given to the teachers in this series of studies about Jimmy and Billy, each felt that they had sufficient information to evaluate the two students—a finding that was interesting in and of itself. But what is most significant to the present discussion is that with the exception of science and deportment, each of the teachers concluded that Jimmy's chances of succeeding were far greater than Billy's. The question is: On what basis did they make these evaluations? They were not provided with information about the two students' intelligence, their grade-point averages, their motivation to achieve, or any other relevant criterion that we can think of. Thus, we are forced to conclude that the differential set of expectancies that these teachers developed was attributable to Billy's reticence—that is, his apprehension about oral communication. Since we have dealt with this subject (i.e., communication apprehension) at greater length in Chapter 9, suffice it to say that both the presence and absence of verbal cues on a student's part can be sources of teacher expectancies toward students.

Verbal Cues as Sources of Student Expectancies

There is some reason to believe that a student's expectancies about his or her own capabilities in a specific subject matter are very often a function of teacher evaluations. For example, a student who is consistently rewarded by a teacher for his or her performance in a given subject matter soon develops a positive set of expectancies about his or her abilities in the subject matter, and this motivates the student to further achieve. By contrast, a student who is consistently punished by a teacher for his or her performance in a subject matter soon develops a set of negative expectancies about his or her abilities in the subject matter, and this serves to impede the student's desire to achieve.

While most teachers realize that their written evaluations of a student's performance can lead to such expectancies, few teachers seem to be cognizant of the fact that their verbal evaluations of a student's performance can also lead to such expectancies. Similarly, few teachers seem to realize that they engage in many more verbal evaluations of their students than written evaluations, and that these verbal evaluations may have far greater potential as positive and negative reinforcers. As a case in point, think about written and verbal evaluations containing exactly the same content. Which do you think would contain the most information and meaning for the student? If you recall what we said about the vocalic elements of a message in our chapter on nonverbal communication, then the answer should be obvious. The verbal message would contain more information and be richer in meaning, because it would carry with it the emotions and desired emphasis the teacher has in mind, something that even the most accomplished men and women of letters have difficulty in conveying to a reader. Important as it is that a teacher remain mindful of the expectancies that can be elicited by written evaluations, it is even more important that the teacher remain cognizant of the implications of his or her verbal evaluations and the clues that such messages contain for the student.

SOME CONSEQUENCES OF EXPECTANCIES IN THE CLASSROOM

Basically, empirical studies focusing on the classroom impact of expectancies fall into two general categories: *teacher bias* and "true" *teacher expectancies*. In addition, the research has been largely one-sided in that it has been directed toward the impact of teacher expectancies rather than the impact of student expectancies.

Teacher Bias

Teacher bias is distinct from teacher expectancies. Teacher bias is the result of someone or some agent outside the classroom supplying the teacher with information about his or her students. Teacher expectancies are expectations teachers themselves formulate on the basis of their interactions with students.

Research focusing on teacher bias has yielded equivocal results regarding student achievement. In their now-classic *Pygmalion in the Classroom,* for example, Rosenthal and Jacobson report a number of studies where the expectancy effect worked to the student's advantage. As a case in point, in one study teachers were led to believe that some students were "late bloomers" and that they would achieve at an accelerated pace sometime after the begin-

Sometimes this kind of advance information can do the student more harm than it does the teacher good.

ning of the school year. In reality, however, the so-called "late bloomers" were simply students of average to below-average intelligence who had been randomly selected from the school's population. Nevertheless, these students "bloomed," just as their teachers had been told they would. In fact, first and second graders bloomed at a remarkable rate when you consider that 79 percent of them demonstrated an IQ gain of 10 points, 47 percent an IQ gain of 20 points, 21 percent an IQ gain of 30 points. While students in the upper grades bloomed in less staggering quantities, they nevertheless gained in IQ significantly more than students who had been randomly assigned to control groups. But what is even more surprising, supplementary analyses revealed that the students in the late-bloomer groups were assessed by their teachers to exhibit more intellectual curiosity and less of a need for social approval than students in the control groups.

With the exception of one study concerning a small sample of institutionalized females, however, the blooming effect reported by Rosenthal and Jacobson has not proved replicable. In fact, no less than five studies concerned with the late-bloomer effect either failed to replicate Rosenthal and Jacobson's results or reported contradictory findings. To date, then, we cannot make any firm statements about the extent to which teacher bias impacts on a student's academic achievement.

In contrast, there is considerable evidence suggesting that teacher bias has a significant impact on teaching styles, communication between teachers and students, and student self-concepts. For example, the research suggests that teachers who believe they are working with bright students expose their students to more information, allow their students to verbalize more, and engage in more praise than teachers who are led to believe they are working with students who are slow. And these effects are compounded even further if race is an experimental issue. Rubovits and Maehr report a study in which white tutors gave white students significantly more attention than black students, even when the tutors were led to believe black and white students were equal in intelligence. Finally, the research suggests that students who believe their teacher perceives them positively develop more positive self-concepts than students who hold an opposite perception.

We can't help but think that the preceding effects of teacher bias would ultimately influence student achievement in the classroom. It stands to reason, for example, that students who receive less praise, are exposed to less information, and suffer from poorer self-concepts than other students should not achieve at the same rate. Until our thinking is supported by research, however, we are reluctant to be prescriptive in this regard. We can only recommend that you remain cautious in making judgments about a student on the basis of information supplied outside the classroom.

Teacher Expectancies

While the research is somewhat inconclusive about the effects of teacher bias, it is quite clear about the relationship between true teacher expectancies and student achievement. Among other things, the research suggests that teacher expectancies are functionally related to: (1) how much pressure a teacher puts on his or her students, (2) how well students perform on the Stanford Achievement Test, and (3) how well students perform on objective measures of achievement designed by individual teachers. It is important to note, though, that the research only suggests a *functional* relationship between teacher expectancies and student achievement, which is not the same as a cause-and-effect relationship. Thus, we cannot say that a teacher's expectancies about a student will *cause* the student to achieve at a certain level. We can only say that the two are meaningfully related.

The preceding does not discount what we said earlier in this chapter. That is to say, it does not contradict the conclusion that teacher expectancies have an impact on the classroom. Instead, it suggests that the impact of teacher expectancies is yet to be clearly and totally understood. For example, it very well could be that a student's own expectancies about his or her capabilities is what causes the student to achieve at a level above, below, or equal to his or her real potential. Of course, a student's own expectations cannot help but be influenced by what a teacher communicates to the student.

SELECTED REFERENCES

Alpert, J. "Teacher Behavior Across Ability Groups: A Consideration of the Mediation of Pygmalion Effects," *Journal of Educational Psychology* 66 (1974): 348-353.

Anderson, D. F., and R. Rosenthal. "Some Effects of Interpersonal Expectancy and Social Interaction on Institutionalized Retarded Children." *Proceedings of the 76th Annual Convention of the American Psychological Association* 3 (1968): 479-480.

Baker, J. P., and J. L. Crist. "Teacher Expectancies: A Review of the Literature." In J. D. Elashoff and R. E. Snow, eds. *Pygmalion Reconsidered.* Worthington, Ohio: Charles A. Jones, 1971, 48-64.

Barber, X., and M. Silver. "Fact, Fiction and the Experimenter Bias Effect." *Psychological Bulletin Monograph Supplement* 70 (1968): 1-29.

Barber, X., and M. Silver. "Pitfalls in Data Analysis and Interpretation: A Reply to Rosenthal." *Psychological Bulletin Monograph Supplement* 70 (1968): 48-62.

Beez, W. V. "Influence of Biased Psychological Reports on Teacher Behavior and Pupil Performance." *Proceedings of the 76th Annual Convention of the American Psychological Association* 3 (1968): 605-606.

Brophy, J. E., and T. L. Good. "Teachers' Communication of Differential Expectations for Children's Classroom Performance: Some Behavioral Data." *Journal of Educational Psychology* 61 (1970): 365-374.

Brophy, J. E., and T. L. Good. *Teacher-Student Relationships: Causes and Consequences.* New York: Holt, Rinehart & Winston, 1974.

Cain, L., S. Levine, and F. Elzey. *Manual for the Cain-Levine Social Competency Scale.* Palo Alto, Cal.: Consulting Psychologists Press, 1963.

Carter, R. M. "Locus of Control and Teacher Expectancy as Related to Achievement in Young School Children." Ph.D dissertation, Indiana University, 1969.

Claiborn, W. L. "Expectancy Effects in the Classroom: A Failure to Replicate." *Journal of Educational Psychology* 60 (1969): 377-383.

Clark, K. B. "Educational Stimulation of Racially Disadvantaged Children." In A. H. Passow, ed., *Education in Depressed Areas.* New York: Bureau of Publications, Teachers College, Columbia University, 1963, pp. 142-162.

Conn, L., C. Edwards, R. Rosenthal, and D. Crowne. "Perception of Emotion and Response to Teachers' Expectancy by Elementary School Children." *Psychological Reports* 22 (1968): 27-34.

Davidson, D. C. "Perceived Reward Value of Teacher Reinforcement and Attitude Toward Teacher: An Application of Newcomb's Balance Theory." *Journal of Educational Psychology* 63 (1972): 418-422.

Davidson, H., and G. Lang. "Children's Perception of Their Teacher's Feelings Toward Them Related to Self-Perception, School Achievement, and Behavior." *Journal of Experimental Education* 29 (1969): 107-118.

Dusek, J. B. "Experimenter Bias in Performance of Children at a Simple Motor Task." *Developmental Psychology* 4 (1971): 55-62.

Dusek, J. B. "Experimenter-Bias Effects on the Simple Motor Task Performance of Low- and High-Test Anxious Boys and Girls." *Psychological Reports* **30** (1972): 107–114.

Dusek, J. B. "Do Teachers Bias Student Learning?" *Review of Educational Research* **15** (1975): 661–684.

Dusek, J. B., and E. J. O'Connell. "Teacher Expectancy Effects on the Achievement Test Performance of Elementary School Children." *Journal of Educational Psychology* **65** (1973): 371–377.

Elashoff, J. D., and R. E. Snow, eds. *Pygmalion Reconsidered.* Worthington, Ohio: Charles A. Jones, 1971.

Evans, J., and R. Rosenthal. "Interpersonal Self-Fulfilling Prophecies: Further Extrapolations From the Laboratory to the Classroom." *Proceedings of the 77th Annual Convention of the American Psychological Association* **4** (1969): 371–372.

Finn, J. D. "Expectations and the Educational Environment." *Review of Educational Research* **42** (1972): 387–410.

Flanagan, J. C. *Test of General Ability: Technical Report.* Chicago: Science Research Associates, 1960.

Fleming, E. S., and R. G. Anttonen. "Teacher Expectancy as Related to the Academic and Personal Growth of Primary-Age Children." *Monographs of the Society for Research in Child Development* **36**, no. 50 (1971), Serial No. 145.

Flowers, D. E. "Effects of an Arbitrary Accelerated Group Placement on the Tested Academic Achievement of Educationally Disadvantaged Students." Ph.D. dissertation, Teachers College, Columbia University, 1966.

Friedman, N. *The Social Nature of Psychological Research: The Psychological Experiment as a Social Interaction.* New York: Basic Books, 1967.

Good, T. L., and J. E. Brophy. "Teacher-Child Dyadic Interactions: A New Method of Classroom Observation." *Journal of School Psychology* **8** (1970): 131–138.

Good, T. L., and J. E. Brophy. "Behavioral Expression of Teacher Attitudes," *Journal of Education Psychology* **63** (1972): 617–624.

Good, T. L., and J. E. Brophy. "Changing Teacher and Student Behavior: An Empirical Investigation." *Journal of Educational Psychology* **66** (1974): 390–405.

Good, T. L., N. Sikes, and J. E. Brophy. "Effects of Teacher Sex and Student Sex on Classroom Interaction." *Journal of Educational Psychology* **65** (1973): 74–87.

Harari, H., and J. W. McDavid. "Name Stereotypes and Teacher Expectancies." *Journal of Educational Psychology* **65** (1973): 222–225.

Jensen, A. R. "How Much Can We Boost IQ and Scholastic Achievement?" *Harvard Educational Review* **39** (1969): 1–123.

José, J., and J. Cody. "Teacher-Pupil Interaction as It Relates to Attempted Changes in Teacher Expectancy of Academic Ability and Achievement." *American Educational Research Journal* **8** (1971): 39–49.

Long, B. H., and E. H. Henderson.   "Certain Determinants of Academic Expectancies Among Southern and Non-Southern Teachers," *American Educational Research Journal* **11** (1974): 137–147.

Meichenbaum, D., K. Bowers, and R. Ross.   "A Behavioral Analysis of Teacher Expectancy Effect." *Journal of Personality and Social Psychology* **13** (1969): 306–316.

Mendels, G. E., and J. P. Flanders.   "Teachers' Expectations and Pupil Performance." *American Educational Research Journal* **10** (1973): 203–211.

Meyer, W. J., and G. G. Thompson.   "Sex Differences in the Distribution of Teacher Approval and Disapproval among Sixth-Grade Children." *Journal of Educational Psychology* **47** (1956): 385–397.

O'Connell, E., J. Dusek, and R. Wheeler.   "A Follow-Up Study of Teacher Expectancy Effects." *Journal of Educational Psychology* **66** (1974): 325–328.

Pellegrini, R. J., and R. A. Hicks.   "Prophecy Effects and Tutorial Instruction for the Disadvantaged Child." *American Educational Research Journal* **9** (1972): 413–418.

Pitt, C. C. V.   "An Experimental Study of the Effects of Teachers' Knowledge or Incorrect Knowledge of Pupil IQs on Teachers' Attitudes and Practices and Pupils' Attitudes and Achievement." Ph.D. dissertation, Columbia University, 1956.

Rist, R. G.   "Student Social Class and Teacher Expectations: The Self-Fulfilling Prophecy in Ghetto Education." *Harvard Educational Review* **40** (1970): 411–451.

Rosenthal, R.   *Experimenter Effects in Behavioral Research.* New York: Appleton-Century-Crofts, 1966.

Rosenthal, R.   "Experimenter Expectancy and the Reassuring Nature of the Null Hypothesis Decision Procedure." *Psychological Bulletin Monograph Supplement* **70** (1968): 30–47.

Rosenthal, R.   "Empirical vs. Decreed Validation of Clocks and Tests." *American Educational Research Journal* **6** (1969): 689–691.

Rosenthal, R.   "Interpersonal Expectations: Effects of the Experimenter's Hypothesis." In R. Rosenthal and R. Rosnow, eds., *Artifact in Behavioral Research.* New York: Academic Press, 1969, pp. 182–277.

Rosenthal, R., and L. Jacobson.   *Pygmalion in the Classroom.* New York: Holt, 1968.

Rosenthal, R., and D. B. Rubin.   "Pygmalion Reaffirmed." In J. D. Elashoff and R. E. Snow, eds. *Pygmalion Reconsidered.* Worthington, Ohio: Charles A. Jones. 1971, pp. 139–155.

Rosenthal, R., S. S. Baratz, and C. M. Hall.   "Teacher Behavior, Teacher Expectations, and Gains in Pupils' Rated Creativity." *The Journal of Genetic Psychology* **124** (1974): 115–121.

Rothbart, M., S. Dalfen, and R. Barrett.   "Effects of Teacher's Expectancy on Student-Teacher Interaction." *Journal of Educational Psychology* **62** (1971): 49–54.

Rubovits, P., and M. Maehr.   "Pygmalion Analyzed: Toward an Explanation of the Rosenthal-Jacobson Findings." *Journal of Personality and Social Psychology* **19** (1971): 197–203.

Rubovits, P. C., and M. L. Maehr. "Pygmalion Black and White." *Journal of Personality and Social Psychology* **25** (1973): 210–218.

Schwebel, A., and D. Cherlin. "Physical and Social Distancing in Teacher-Pupil Relationships." *Journal of Educational Psychology* **63** (1972): 543–550.

Seaver, W. B. "Effects of Naturally Induced Teacher Expectancies on the Academic Performance of Pupils in Primary Grades." Ph.D. dissertation, University of Illinois, 1971.

Snow, R. "Unfinished Pygmalion." *Contemporary Psychology* **14** (1969): 197–199.

Staines, J. W. "The Self-Picture as a Factor in the Classroom." *British Journal of Education* **28** (1958): 97–111.

Thorndike, R. L. "Review of Pygmalion in the Classroom." *American Educational Research Journal* **5** (1968): 708–711.

Thorndike, R. L. "You Have to Know How to Tell Time." *American Educational Research Journal* **6** (1969): 692.

Willis, S., and J. E. Brophy. "Origins of Teachers' Attitudes Toward Young Children." *Journal of Educational Psychology* **66** (1974): 520–529.

Yunker, B. The Power of Positive Teaching." *Family Circle,* May 1970, pp. 34, 95–96, 98.

11

Communication, Interpersonal Solidarity, and Student Needs

After reading this chapter, you should be able to do the following.

1. Identify and describe three interpersonal needs students experience.

2. Describe patterns of behaviors which are likely to result when these interpersonal needs are left unsatisfied.

3. Describe the relationship between interpersonal needs and academic needs.

4. Explain the major advantage of the democratic style of leadership over the authoritarian style of leadership.

5. Describe no less than five classroom benefits which may occur when teachers decrease the psychological distance separating them from their students.

As we have implied throughout this book, our ability to accurately interpret and appropriately respond to another person's communication behaviors largely depends on what we know about that person. Generally speaking, the accuracy of our interpretations, as well as the appropriateness of our responses, will be proportionate to the amount of information we possess about a person. Thus, we are more likely to accurately interpret and appropriately respond to the communication behaviors of someone we know quite well than of someone we know only casually. No doubt you've long been aware of the fact that you seem to communicate at an optimum level with the people you are closest to.

We wonder, however, how many teachers ever come to really know their students—that is, know their students as unique identities with a corresponding set of intellectual and interpersonal needs. Probably fewer than we would like to think. Teachers simply are not in the habit of consciously attempting to decrease the psychological distance that normally separates teacher and student. Some, in fact, may believe that such attempts are well beyond their responsibilities as teachers. But are they really?

It seems to us that the fundamental responsibility of any teacher is to create a classroom environment where students can satisfy both their intellectual and interpersonal needs. It also seems to us, however, that this responsibility can't possibly be met unless teachers are willing to try and reduce the psychological distance separating them from their students. Of course, this is neither an easy nor risk-free task. It is not easy, because teachers are, by definition of their role, psychologically distant from their students. It is not risk-free because, in the attempt to reduce this distance, teachers may have to violate their defined role.

In this chapter, we would like to talk about how teachers can improve their communication with students and promote interpersonal solidarity in the classroom, by decreasing the psychological distance between themselves and students. This will entail a discussion of some of the more important needs students experience; how teachers can create a classroom environment that will assist students in satisfying these needs; and how, by creating such an environment, teachers can reduce the psychological distance separating them from their students.

STUDENT NEEDS

All too often, teachers assume that they are responsible for only one set of a student's needs—those specifically related to the acquisition of academic skills. Teachers of this genre tend to believe that if a student exits the classroom in the possession of an academic skill that he or she was previously lacking, they have met their pedagogical responsibilities part and parcel.

While a student's academic needs are of primary concern in the class-room, teachers should recognize that students experience personal and inter-personal needs as well. These needs play a major role in the classroom environment. Left unsatisfied, for example, they not only will have a negative impact on the interpersonal dynamics of the classroom, they will also diminish the probability of students satisfying their academic needs as well. Let's take a look at three interpersonal needs representative of those experienced by students, and examine some of the ways these needs can interfere with the acquisition of academic skills.

The Need for Social Inclusion

Few of the needs experienced in the educational setting are as potent as the need for social inclusion. Basically, this interpersonal need concerns the degree to which a student is successful in associating and interacting with other students. When a student is able to readily satisfy the need for social inclusion, there is no problem. However, students who are unsuccessful in their attempts to associate and interact with other students are likely to engage in behaviors that will hinder the satisfaction of their academic needs as well. Students who have consistently failed to satisfy their need for social inclusion are likely to adopt one of two patterns of behavior: undersocial behavior or oversocial behavior.

Students who engage in undersocial behavior are likely to remain aloof from other students and act as if they're totally independent. In effect, they say to themselves, "Since no one gives a damn about me, why should I give a damn about them?" Of course, this attitude represents an attempt to compensate for an inability to associate and interact successfully with other students. In other words, it is a facade.

As you would imagine, little good can result from undersocial behavior. For one thing, other students are not likely to try to initiate or sustain inter-action with a student who engages in undersocial behavior. Thus, that student's need for inclusion will continue to go unsatisfied. In addition, students who cut themselves off from other students also cut themselves off from an important learning resource. Much of what we do in the classroom requires working cooperatively. If a student denies himself or herself access to other students, this kind of cooperation is not likely to result. Consequently, those who engage in undersocial behavior also may experience difficulties in satisfying academic needs.

Students who engage in oversocial behavior suffer from the same perception as those who engage in undersocial behavior. Instead of becoming self-indulgent, though, the overly social tend to manifest attention-getting behaviors. For example, in the classroom, a student who has consistently failed to satisfy the need for inclusion is likely to interact at inappropriate times or try to dominate interaction at times when the teacher deems it appropriate. Outside the classroom, such students may try to attract attention to themselves by engaging in behaviors that violate accepted social practices. Regardless of the actual behaviors the overly social student engages in, they are not likely to serve any useful purpose. Instead, they are more likely to elicit less-than-favorable responses from other students. These responses, moreover, are bound to interfere with the overly social student's ability to satisfy his or her academic needs.

As you can see, then, failure to satisfy the need for social inclusion can influence more than the interpersonal dynamics of a class—it can seriously detract from a student's academic performance. We should point out also that when a student's behaviors disrupt a class, as is often the case with students who are overly social, the academic needs of other students may suffer.

The Need for Behavior Control

In addition to the need for social inclusion, students also need to feel that they are capable of making decisions that will influence their peers. At the same time, students need to realize that they can't make *all* of the decisions that have some impact on the classroom. On an individual level, the need for behavior control is a student's need to feel that others regard him or her as competent and responsible when it comes to decision making; on an interpersonal level, it concerns how comfortable students are with the degree of control they exert over each other.

The need for behavior control is present at almost all levels of education. In the elementary school, for example, teachers sometimes reward a student by allowing him or her to make a decision that will affect the class. While the teacher may not think that such opportunities are all that special to students, let us assure you that students do. In fact, students at the primary level often will compete in the effort to make a decision regarded as inconsequential by the teacher.

Be that as it may, failure to satisfy this need on a consistent basis may cause real problems for a student. Students who fail to satisfy the need for behavior control may come to believe that both teachers and students perceive them as incompetent and irresponsible. Obviously, such a perception is not conducive to a healthy self-concept. And this is reflected in the first pattern of behaviors such students are likely to exhibit: submission.

Students who truly believe that others regard them as incompetent and irresponsible may begin to shirk responsibilities that are rightfully theirs, try to pass on assigned responsibilities to others, or gravitate toward positions that are wholly subordinate. This submissive posture is hardly consistent with the educational goals most teachers set for their students. From an academic standpoint, it is absolutely essential that students learn and feel comfortable about making decisions. From an interpersonal standpoint, it is just as essential that students learn to share responsibilities which are required by assigned decision-making activities. Thus, if a student becomes submissive as a function of his or her failure to satisfy the need for behavior control, the student is not likely to acquire necessary intellectual and interpersonal skills.

Failure to satisfy the need for behavior control, however, does not guarantee that a student will become submissive. To the contrary, some students will assume an "I'll show them" posture and attempt to monopolize, rather than share, decision-making responsibilities. Like the student who becomes submissive, the student who becomes autocratic will experience both interpersonal and academic difficulties. At a minimum, other students are likely to resent an autocratic student's attempt to dictate policy in matters involving the entire class. And, if this resentment becomes great enough, students may try to ostracize socially the student who has assumed the role of autocrat. Aside from the fact that the autocratic student may become an interpersonal thorn in the side of the class, s(he) also may begin to experience academic problems. These problems, moreover, probably can be attributed to the student's inability to function cooperatively in the classroom.

Left unsatisfied, consequently, the need for behavior control can have a serious and negative impact on a student's self-concept. This impact may manifest itself in one of two ways: submissive or autocratic behavior. In either case, the effects will be the same: severe interpersonal difficulties and disruption of the student's academic performance.

The Need for Affinity
Earlier in the book, we said that one of the primary motivations for communicating is to establish affinity. We also said that students have an inner need for warm relationships with other people, including teachers.

Generally speaking, the need for affinity is a student's need to feel that (s)he is capable of both giving and receiving affection. Failure to consistently satisfy this need is likely to yield one of two patterns of behavior: underpersonal behavior or overpersonal behavior. Both patterns of behavior are predicated on the student's perception that (s)he is perceived by others as cold or unfeeling.

Students who are underpersonal are capable of interacting and associating with other people. The problem is not so much their ability to affiliate, however, as it is the level of affiliation. Underpersonal students try to avoid becoming psychologically close to other people; they are reluctant to reveal more than superficial information about themselves to students and teachers. Two problems are likely to result from this reluctance. First, the underpersonal student's reluctance to disclose probably will perpetuate the perception that he or she is cold or unfeeling. Second, the student's reluctance to reveal information to the teacher will increase the probability of the teacher inaccurately interpreting and inappropriately responding to the student's communication behaviors. In the long run, therefore, the overly cautious behavior of the underpersonal student will have a definite impact on his or her interpersonal relationships with other students, and may have a very real impact on academic achievement.

Whereas students who are underpersonal are excessively cautious about their relationships with other people, overly personal students throw caution to the wind. Such students are quick to reveal even the most intimate information about themselves to students and teachers, are likely to try to rush the progression of their relationships with other students, and are prone to ignore their academic needs as they try to satisfy their need for affinity. Mutual affinity, of course, does not evolve overnight. Along the same lines, people do not expect mere acquaintances to reveal intimate information about themselves. Rather than satisfying the need for affinity, consequently, the preceding behaviors probably will be met with suspicion and distrust, which can only serve to compound any academic problems the overly personal student has already experienced.

Before moving on, we should point out that *all students* may engage in underpersonal and overpersonal behavior at one time or another. This also holds true for the patterns of behavior we described when discussing the need for behavior control and the need for social inclusion. The preceding labels, therefore, should not be used as a convenient means by which to pigeonhole students having problems. Rather, our intent is to alert teachers to some of the more important interpersonal needs students experience and to some of the behaviors that may result when these needs are left unsatisfied. Please keep this in mind as we begin to discuss the impact of the classroom environment on the satisfaction of these various needs.

CLIMATE MAKING IN THE CLASSROOM ENVIRONMENT

Realistically, no single classroom agent can guarantee the satisfaction of a student's intellectual and interpersonal needs. Whether students are successful in satisfying their needs will depend on their individual behaviors, on the behaviors of other students, and, most importantly, on the behaviors of the teacher.

Leadership Style of the Teacher

There are no cookbook strategies that teachers can turn to in the attempt to assist their students in satisfying intellectual and academic needs. In the effort to create a classroom environment that maximizes the probability of students satisfying these needs, however, a teacher cannot overlook his or her style of leadership.

Surprisingly enough, the research suggests that there is no singularly superior style of leadership when it comes to student achievement. Students seem to achieve as well under an authoritarian style of leadership, for example,

This is an example of democratic leadership. Students and teacher are equally involved in the decision-making process.

as they do under a democratic style of leadership. The research also suggests, however, that students appear to be better adjusted and hold more favorable attitudes toward the total learning environment when the leadership style is democratic. Thus, while the autocratic style may serve to satisfy the *academic* needs of students, the democratic leadership style appears to assist students in satisfying their *interpersonal* needs as well.

Of course, it is next to impossible for most teachers to assume a completely democratic style of leadership—that is, a style of leadership which invites student participation at all levels of decision making and in the sharing of all responsibilities. Even so, we believe that teachers can go a long way toward making their classrooms more democratic by simply inviting their students whenever and wherever possible to participate in decision making and the sharing of responsibilities. Toward that end, however, teachers must realize that, in the classroom: they are not the center of the universe; a student is not helpless without their assistance; students are not incapable of learning on their own; students can sometimes teach a student when the teacher can't; and students, regardless of age, are perfectly capable of making at least some decisions or of taking on at least some responsibility. In other words, teachers must realize that they do not have to do all of the things that they are currently doing for fear of student anarchy. Such a realization is, in fact, essential if students are to personally and interpersonally grow.

In the effort to become a more democratic leader in the classroom, teachers sometimes find themselves in the position of needing to know more about their students than their cultural heritage (which may be obvious) or their current reference group (which also may be obvious). In other words, teachers sometimes need to communicate with students on a psychological rather than cultural or sociological dimension. Needless to say, many teachers find this uncomfortable, because it is either contrary to their normal behavior as a teacher or simply contrary to what they believe is the proper role for a teacher to assume when communicating with a student.

If teachers are to become sensitive to their students' personal and interpersonal needs, however, communication on the psychological dimension appears to be unavoidable. For one thing, as a teacher begins to "loosen up," students will very often volunteer psychological information about themselves. How, then, can teachers insure that such exchanges will always be constructive?

While we would be like to offer an easy answer to this question, there simply isn't one. Communicating with students on a psychological dimension as well as allowing students to participate in some of the decisions that affect them involves risk. In light of the impact such commitments can have on a student's intellectual, personal, and interpersonal growth, though, the risk is well worth taking.

Aside from the fact that the democratic style of teaching provides students with a vehicle for personal and interpersonal growth, it can lead to a highly productive learning environment. More specifically, it can lead to heightened productivity, originality, and creativity, because the democratic style is sensitive to the needs of both the individual and the group and, as a result, very often facilitates the individual and group achieving at a maximum level.

Supportive Communication

Teachers can also facilitate the satisfaction of student needs by engaging in supportive communication behaviors and by encouraging their students to do likewise. A teacher's communication behavior, as well as the communication experiences that he or she designs for the classroom, have a tremendous impact on a student's self-esteem. Positive personal and interpersonal growth demands that a student have some positive perception of himself or herself in terms of characteristics and abilities, his or her relationship to others, and his or her relationship to the larger environment. It is crucial, then, that teachers communicate with their students as supportively as possible—regardless of whether their students are performing at a standard that is less than ideal. By the same token, it is crucial that teachers attempt to creat an environment where students also engage in these behaviors, supporting their classmates or communicating their criticisms in a supportive manner.

Dependence and Centrality

Finally, teachers can promote the kind of environment we've been talking about by stressing two notions: dependency and centrality. Personal, as well as interpersonal, growth requires that students come to grips with the fact that, while they are individuals, they are also members of a group and are, to some extent, dependent on members of the group. As a result, teachers should attempt to communicate to students that one's allegiances must go beyond self. To this end, teachers should structure at least some activities where the success of the individual is tied to the success of the group.

While recognition of group membership is important, it is even more important to personal and interpersonal development for students to have a positive image of themselves in relationship to the group. Too often, when teachers attempt to democratize their classrooms, they neglect the role of the individual within the group. Adopting a democratic style of leadership or promoting better interpersonal relationships does not require sacrificing individuality in favor of groupness. Rather, it means that students and teachers become sensitive to the fact that the classroom experience is most rewarding when individuals work as a cohesive unit toward some common goal.

COMMUNICATION AND INTERPERSONAL SOLIDARITY

While the preceding suggestions will not eliminate each and every problem a teacher faces, they can go a long way towards improving communication in the classroom and promoting interpersonal solidarity amongst teachers and students.

Communication

When a teacher assumes a democratic role and makes the decision to communicate with students on a psychological dimension, the psychological distance separating teacher and student will begin to diminish. As this distance continues to decrease, the teacher will begin to learn more and more about the identities of his or her students. As we pointed out in the opening of this chapter, this information will assist the teacher in better interpreting, and in more appropriately responding to, the individual communication behaviors of each student.

By the same token, as the psychological distance between teachers and students decreases, the students themselves will learn new and important information about their teacher. As a result, they also will be in a position to better interpret, and respond more appropriately to, the communication behaviors of their teacher. Thus, the fidelity of the communication transactions occurring in the classroom will be improved for both teacher and student.

Interpersonal Solidarity

When a group of students realizes that in working together they can satisfy their personal as well as interpersonal needs and yet not sacrifice their individuality, benefits beyond more effective communication are likely to accrue.

For example, in many classrooms, students are led to believe that learning is a competitive game in which some must win and others must lose. And, while they may be told that they are not to compete against one another, that is exactly what they end up doing. Such a classroom environment inevitably generates distrust among students and encourages them to become guarded and uncommunicative—lest they divulge something that may enhance their fellow opponents chances of winning. In a classroom where students have learned that by working together they can maximum both individual and group rewards, however, this does not occur. Students realize that by sharing skills and by being open and communicative with one another, they will increase the likelihood of the group achieving its goal and thereby increase the likelihood of each group member achieving his or her individual goals.

Moreover, when students work together in the effort to satisfy their personal and interpersonal needs, there need not be any losers. For example, imagine that a group of twelve students of varying intelligence and skills is assigned a group project. As a function of their varying levels of intelligence and varying skills they may produce a superior project—each contributing to the superior project and each, along with the group, receiving some measure of praise. But what if the assignment had been made to twelve individuals? The result, no doubt, would have been twelve projects ranging from superior to mediocre. As a result, some students would receive the teacher's praise, while others would be ignored or perceive that their efforts were being punished. Obviously, the more rewarding, and therefore enjoyable, a student perceives a learning experience, the more probable it is that he or she will associate the experience with positive attitudes and values.

Finally, there is a good reason to believe that knowledge or skill acquisition under healthy interpersonal circumstances may be internalized by students—that is, incorporated with their day-to-day behavior. This conclusion is based on the fact that when the aversive properties of the classroom are minimized—e.g., competition, negative criticism, excessive evaluations of the individual, etc.—and an interpersonal climate that is conducive to both personal and interpersonal need satisfaction is introduced, the probability of a student's learning experiences being pleasant are increased.

In closing, we would like to reemphasize the fact that students' needs go beyond the acquisition of academic skills. Long after forgetting what happened on a particular date in history, or how to conjugate a French verb, or how to solve an algebraic equation, students will continue to experience the needs we have talked about. Thus, we accomplish a number of things when we try to reduce the distance between ourselves and our students and thereby assist them in satisfying these needs. At the very minimum, we may thwart the possibility of interpersonal needs interfering with the satisfaction of academic needs, improve communication, and promote interpersonal solidarity. At the same time, we also may be assisting our students in satisfying interpersonal needs when classrooms, for them, have long been a thing of the past.

SELECTED REFERENCES

Alschuler, A., D. Tabor, and J. McIntyre.   *Ten Thoughts.* An element of the *Achievement Motivation Series.* Middletown, Ct.: Education Ventures, 1970.

Bellack, A., J. Davitz, H. Kliebard, and R. Hyman.   *The Classroom Game: The Language of the Classroom: Meanings Communicated in High School Teaching.* Cooperative Research Project No. 1497, New York Institute of Psychological Research, Teachers College, Columbia, 1961.

Berlyne, D. E.   "Notes on Intrinsic Motivation and Intrinsic Reward in Relation to Instruction." In J. Bruner, ed., *Learning About Learning: A Conference Report.* Washington, D.C.: U.S. Department of Health, Education and Welfare, Office of Education, 1966.

Biehler, P. F.   *Psychology Applied to Teaching.* Boston: Houghton Mifflin, 1974.

Boy, A. and G. Pine.   *Expanding the Self: Personal Growth for Teachers.* Dubuque: William C. Brown, 1971.

Fox, R., M. B. Luski, and R. Schmuck.   *Diagnosing Classroom Learning Environments.* Chicago: Science Research Associates, 1966.

Getzels, J. W., and H. A. Thelan.   "The Classroom Group as a Unique Social System." In *The Dynamics of Instructional Groups, 49th Yearbook of the National Society for the Study of Education.* Part II. Chicago: University of Chicago Press, 1960, Chapter 4.

Horwitz, M.   "Hostility and Its Management in Classroom Groups." In W. W. Charters and N. L. Gage, eds., *Readings in the Social Psychology of Education.* Boston: Allyn and Bacon, 1963.

James, M., and D. Jongeward.   *Born to Win: Transactional Analysis with Gestalt Experiments.* Reading, Mass.: Addison-Wesley, 1971.

Kagan, J.   "Motivational and Attitudinal Factors in Receptivity to Learning." In J. Bruner, ed., *Learning about Learning: A Conference.* Washington, D.C.: U.S. Department of Health, Education and Welfare, Office of Education, 1966, Superintendent of Documents Catalogue Number FS 5.212: 12019.

Maslow, A. H.   *Motivation and Personality.* New York: Harper & Row, 1954.

Rogers, C. R.   *Freedom to Learn.* Columbus: Merrill, 1969.

Smith, M. D.   *Learning and Its Classroom Applications.* Boston: Allyn and Bacon, 1975.

Walberg, H. J.   "Predicting Class Learning: An Approach to the Class as a Social System." *American Educational Research Journal* 4 (November 1969a): 529–542.

Walberg, H. J. "Teacher Personality and Classroom Climate." *Psychology in the Schools* 5 (April 1969b): 163–169.

Walberg, H. J., and G. J. Anderson. "Classroom Climate and Individual Learning." *Journal of Educational Psychology* 59 (1968): 414–419.

Conflict in the Classroom

After reading this chapter, you should be able to do the following.

1. Define and give examples of conflict.

2. Identify and describe the three major types of conflict confronting teachers and students.

3. Identify and describe the major sources of dysfunctional conflict in the classroom.

4. Discuss the four major methods by which dysfunctional conflict can be reduced.

5. Describe at least three potential effects of creative differences or constructive conflict.

Social conflict is as much a part of the American scene as Monday Night Football. It is a part of life that many have come to accept as inevitable. Pervasive as conflict is, however, few people seem to understand much about it. Teachers we have worked with, for example, almost universally believe that conflict in the classroom is to be avoided; that it is always dysfunctional; that little, if any, good can result from it. We suspect, moreover, that these teachers have tried to pass this philosophy along to their students.

While it is quite true that conflict is very often dysfunctional, it is also true that, when properly managed, conflict can be a constructive social enterprise. Yet this constructive side of conflict is seldom understood, much less taught. And this bothers us a great deal, because we believe that teachers and students who know little about conflict are more susceptible to its ugly side. Thus, in this chapter, we would like to confront head-on the nature and origins of conflict in the classroom. Specifically, we will discuss: (1) the conceptual elements of conflict, (2) the types of conflict commonly faced in the classroom, (3) the classroom sources of dysfunctional conflict, (4) the resolution of dysfunctional conflict, and (5) creative differences in the classroom.

CONFLICT CONCEPTUALIZED

Conflict Defined

Quite candidly, there is no universally accepted definition of conflict. Some profess that conflict exists when one individual behaves in such a way that she or he can maximize gains and minimize losses at the expense of another person. Others argue that conflict involves promises and threats designed to improve a person's chances of obtaining something she or he dearly wants.

For our purposes, we will say that *conflict exists when people are committed to incompatible courses of action designed to achieve some goal.* The emphasis we wish to make here is on the incompatible courses of action rather than the desired goal. This is because we believe that conflict can occur between people who want to achieve goals that are not necessarily incompatible. A teacher and a set of parents, for example, may desire to reach an identical goal with respect to the parents' child. That is to say, both the teacher and set of parents may want the child to demonstrate significant improvement in a particular academic subject. At the same time, however, the child's teacher and parents may disagree about the course of action they should take in order to facilitate improvement. The teacher may believe that improvement depends on the child completing assigned homework, whereas the child's parents may believe that improvement depends on how much time the teacher is willing to spend with the child on an individual basis.

Of course, conflict also may involve both incompatible courses of action and incompatible goals. Parents may demand that a teacher spend more time with their child in order to improve the child's chances of attending college. In contrast, the teacher may take exception to this course of action on the grounds that the child would be better off attending a vocational school. Thus, in this case, both the course of action and the desired goal would define the conflict existing between the child's teacher and the child's parents.

The Psychological Nature of Conflict

As the preceding examples might lead you to suspect, conflict is largely a perceived phenomenon. This is not to say that instances of "true" conflict do not exist, but that conflict—true or otherwise—is mediated by our perceptions. Since our perceptions reflect our attitudes, beliefs, and values, people may perceive the sources of conflict in quite different ways. These differential perceptions, moreover, may be fuel for the fire under conditions of intense, dysfunctional conflict.

Boston, Massachusetts and Kanawah County, West Virginia immediately come to mind in this regard. It's hard not to recall the angry white faces of parents in South Boston as they hurtled convenient missiles at black children being bussed to formerly all-white schools. Similarly, we can vividly recall the protestations of hooded Klansmen outside the Kanawah County Courthouse, as well as the homemade bombs police found inside neighboring schools.

The differential perceptions of the factions in Boston and Kanawah County served to intensify rather than alleviate the extant conflicts over bussing and textbooks. In Boston, whites perceived that desegregation through bussing would lead to the destruction of their neighborhoods. Blacks perceived the resistance of whites as evidence of the continued presence of racism in America. In Kanawah County, the antitextbook faction perceived that the content of certain books would serve to undermine religious and fundamentalist principles taught in the home. Those in favor of the textbooks, however, perceived that the content of the same books would serve to enrich the student population's educational experience.

The point we wish to make is that it is impossible to talk about conflict without also talking about the psychological process of perception. Morton Deutsch, the noted scholar on conflict, points out: " . . . Even the classical example of pure conflict—two starving men on a lifeboat with only enough food for the survival of one—loses its purity if one or both of the men have social or religious values which can become more dominant psychologically than the hunger need or the desire for survival" (1969, p. 10).

TYPES OF CONFLICT

Basically, three types of conflict commonly confront teachers and students. *Procedural conflict* is characterized by disagreement over the course of action that should be taken in order to reach some goal. Procedural conflict was exemplified, in part, by the disagreement between the teacher and set of parents in our earlier example. You'll recall that the teacher and parents shared in identical goal, but disagreed about how that goal might be best achieved. Procedural conflict is pervasive in most educational settings. Teachers and administrators, for instance, frequently disagree about the means by which some academic goal might be attained. Likewise, teachers within a specific academic unit (e.g., language arts) commonly disagree about which classroom procedures are most likely to yield the desired set of learning behaviors from their students.

Closely linked to procedural conflict is *substantive conflict*. This second type of conflict, however, is most concerned with incompatible goals. Substantive conflict occurs in a full range of academic contexts. As was the case with procedural conflict, substantive conflict frequently exists between teachers and administrators, as well as between teachers within a specific academic unit. Going a step further, substantive conflict also commonly occurs between teachers and students. In middle schools or junior high schools, the achievement of certain social goals may be more important to a student than the achievement of academic goals. For instance, a student may spend the majority of his or her time trying to gain entrance to a peer group held in high esteem. Seeing this, a teacher may take the student aside and try to persuade him or her that gaining entrance to the peer group is not as important as academic achievement. While the teacher's intentions are laudable in this instance, the teacher should recognize that she or he is also inviting substantive conflict. Obviously, we are not recommending that the teacher avoid the student. Instead, we are simply trying to make you cognizant of the fact that taking a student aside in the preceding manner may increase the potential for conflict. As we later point out, though, such conflict may be healthy and constructive.

If substantive conflict is not managed, it may give rise to *interpersonal conflict*. Of the three types of conflict that confront teachers and students, interpersonal conflict is potentially the most dysfunctional. It exists when people are committed to incompatible attitudes, beliefs, or values. Usually, imcompatible attitudes, beliefs, or values lead to disliking.

When a student dislikes a teacher, she or he is much more likely to challenge, refuse to cooperate, or simply turn off the teacher. If the student intensely dislikes the teacher, moreover, manifestations of his or her dislike will be more observable—for example, the student will probably vocalize this dislike both implicitly and explicitly. Such public behavior may have a tremendously negative impact on the total classroom environment.

It would be naive to assume that teachers treat all students equitably. Teachers can't help but like some students more than others. If a student *perceives* that a teacher dislikes him or her, or if, in fact, a teacher *does* dislike a student, interpersonal conflict is inevitable. As we have pointed out from time to time, teachers cannot hide their psychological self from their students. It is foolish, consequently, to think that interpersonal conflict with students can consistently be avoided.

Interpersonal conflict also has a negative impact on learning. Student dislike for a teacher will affect the way in which the student processes messages, the student's exposure to information, the student's susceptibility to the teacher's influence, and the degree to which the student will learn from the teacher. Furthermore, each of these effects will be in a negative direction.

It goes without saying that a teacher's dislike for a student will produce similar effects. A teacher who dislikes a particular student will probably avoid close contact with the student, develop a negative set of expectancies about the student's capabilities, and resist influence attempts on the part of the student.

The above-mentioned types of conflict do not represent all of the types of conflict that may confront students and teachers. It seems to us, however, that procedural, substantive, and interpersonal conflict are the most pervasive in the educational environment. We also need to make mention of the fact that, if properly managed, these three types of conflict need not be wholly dysfunctional.

SOURCES OF DYSFUNCTIONAL CONFLICT

At this point, we would like to turn your attention to what we believe are the major sources of dysfunctional conflict in the classroom. While each of these sources may operate independently of one another, they are more likely to operate interdependently.

Competition

Competition and conflict often are treated synonymously. In competitive situations, though, only one person can "win" in the lay sense of the word. As we have defined conflict, one person need not win as a function of another person losing.

Be that as it may, there is perhaps no greater single source of conflict in the classroom than competition. Like some learned Vince Lombardi, teachers seem to be operating under the misconception that competition always will bring out the best in their students. As a result, they unwittingly encourage students to compete and create artificial situations designed to induce competition.

Consider something as deceptively innocent as displaying "outstanding" student work on a prominent bulletin board in an elementary-school classroom. Certainly outstanding work should be rewarded. But what do you think the display communicates to students whose work seldom, if ever, appears on display? Do you think it communicates to such students that they need to work harder? More likely, it serves as a reminder of the fact that their work was evaluated as less than outstanding.

The real danger of excessive competition, however, is that it induces less than desirable interpersonal behaviors. Research focusing on competitive situations suggests at least three negative effects in this regard. First, the research indicates that communication between people in competition is untrustworthy and restrictive. In effect, this means that people who compete will communicate the inverse of their intentions to one another. Once the parties are sensitized to this, they also will begin to communicate less frequently or will break off verbal communication altogether. As one writer has pointed out, this lack of communication will serve to intensify competition, as well as increase the likelihood of outright conflict.

A second effect of competition is that it fosters the belief that there is only one way to resolve conflict when it does, in fact, occur. More often than not, this misperception leads the competitive parties to believe that the conflict can be resolved only if one party yields to the demands of the other. In reality, then, conflict resolution becomes a win-lose proposition.

Finally, excessive competition will cause students to become suspicious or openly hostile toward one another. It is not uncommon to find that students who habitually compete harbor intense mutual dislike. As we have already pointed out, intense dislike or interpersonal conflict can be a highly destructive influence in the classroom. Dislike also tends to be contagious—that is, one student's dislike for another may carry over to the student's friends.

As you can readily see, an excessive emphasis on competition in the classroom is to be avoided. This is not to say that competition is to be avoided altogether; rather, there are limits to its value. When competition becomes excessive, its values will diminish or even disappear.

Inaccurate Perceptions

The way in which we perceive an event provides us with a second source of dysfunctional conflict in the classroom. Returning to our examples of Boston and Kanawah County, you'll recall that we said that the differential perceptions of the various factions served to intensify the conflicts over bussing and textbooks. Just as differential perceptions can lead to conflict, so can inaccurate perceptions.

Perception concerns how you see an event, as well as the context in which the event occurred. If we are familiar with an event (e.g., a student's customary way of behaving), as well as the context in which the event occurs (e.g., the athletic field), we tend to generalize the event and context to less familiar ones. Thus, if you were used to seeing a student bully other students in a gym class, you might generalize the student's bullying behavior to contexts with which you are less familiar. And this is exactly where the problem lies. There is no guarantee that what you perceive to happen frequently in gym class frequently happens elsewhere. Failure to realize this, moroeover, increases the probability of an event being perceived inaccurately.

Both teachers and students tend to indiscriminately generalize their perceptions of each other to new and unfamiliar contexts. Teachers, for example, frequently expect a student's behavior in a particular class to generalize to other classes. Students also expect teachers to behave outside of class as they behave inside the class. If these perceptual generalizations prove inaccurate, they may become an agent of conflict.

Individual Differences

Failure to recognize and respect individual differences in the classroom is the final source of conflict we shall discuss. By individual differences, we mean things like attitudes, beliefs, and values; intelligence and demonstrated abilities; and even personal appearance.

Every individual is, in one way or another unique. While these individual differences often work to a teacher's advantage, they also can be sources of trouble, particularly when the differences between students and teachers are extreme. As a case in point, consider what may happen when a teacher who comes from a highly traditional WASP background takes a job in an urban ghetto. This hypothetical teacher is likely to differ from his or her students on a number of dimensions. For one, the teacher's use of the language probably will deviate quite noticeably from student usage. For another, the teacher's background probably will be totally dissimilar to that of his or her students—a fact that will be reflected in almost all behaviors.

In this example, conflict can be encouraged from one of two possible directions. If the teacher fails to realize and respect the fact that his or her students are not like him or her, the teacher may engage in behaviors that will prove offensive to the students. For instance, she or he may use words, phrases, or examples that, in the students' culture, have an entirely different connotation than the teacher intended. Consequently, the students may judge the teacher a bigot, elitist, or even worse.

Of course, the students themselves also may not recognize or respect the difficulties the teacher is experiencing as a function of his or her dissimilar background. Rather than attempting to help the teacher overcome these difficulties, the students may engage in behaviors that will invite dysfunctional conflict.

It should by now be clear that individual differences, whether real or perceived, can lead to dysfunctional conflict in the classroom. Remember, as we said in Chapter 5, it is not enough simply to recognize that students may be different. In addition, one must also *respect* the fact that they are different and demonstrate this respect in one's classroom behavior.

RESOLVING DYSFUNCTIONAL CONFLICT

Now that we've explored the nature and sources of dysfunctional conflict, we need to focus on the way in which it can be resolved. The preceding discussion suggests that we can manage the potential sources of dysfunctional conflict by

Not all conflict need be dysfunctional. Teachers must learn to manage conflict in constructive ways.

deemphasizing competition, by being careful in our perceptual generalizations, and by recognizing and respecting individual differences. The question now is: How can we resolve dysfunctional conflict once it occurs?

Interpersonal Rewards

Too often, dysfunctional conflict in the classroom is a by-product of the reward system. And this is tied to what we said earlier about excessive competition. When students are forced to compete strenuously for the available rewards in the classroom (e.g., grades, recognition, responsibilities), they tend to view each other as adversaries. In the extreme, they may even lose sight of the fact that their relationships with each other can be a tremendous source of reward. So what happens when dysfunctional conflict is introduced in the highly competitive classroom? Most likely, the students will generalize their adversary relationships to the conflict at hand. This will serve to intensify the conflict, as well as make it more difficult to resolve.

In contrast, when students hold their relationships with one another in high esteem, the rewards associated with the relationships will carry over to their dysfunctional conflicts. The value they attach to their relationships, moreover, will work against the escalation of the conflict. What this suggests is that the students themselves will manage and attempt to resolve the conflict,

because the issue in conflict will have less reward power than their relationships.

The probability of students developing this kind of affinity largely depends on the teacher. At a minimum, she or he must be willing to commit time
and effort to teaching the value of interpersonal relationships in the classroom. Even more importantly, the teacher must be willing to create a classroom environment where grades are secondary rather than primary reinforcers. By and large, excessive competition is the result of grades being
treated as primary reinforcers. Once students learn from their teacher that this
is not the case, they will begin to manage their own conflict as a function of
interpersonal rewards.

The Restoration of Trust

Even students who have had a long and rewarding association with each other
may find themselves in situations of intense, dysfunctional conflict. Remind-
ing them of the reward power of their relationship, of course, is one way to
assist them in resolving their differences. Under conditions of intense conflict,
however, even the best of friends may become suspicious and distrustful of
each other. Thus, in this kind of situation, the teacher may need to assist the
students in confronting and dealing with the behaviors that are generating
their distrust.

One way the teacher can assist the students in restoring mutual trust is to
make sure that they communicate their intentions to each other. This will obvi-
ate the possibility of further violations of trust. Such an approach also may
help the students to understand the reasons for their actions, an insight that
may lead eventually to a resolution of the conflict, as well as restore the relationship to its former state.

This kind of openness and candor also will tend to restore trust between a
teacher and student experiencing conflict. Too often, both parties mistakenly
assume that openness and candor is tantamount to admitting responsibility for
the conflict. As a result, both may avoid rather than initiate communication.
Obviously, verbal reticence is likely to fuel suspicion and distrust.

Before moving on, we need to point out that a teacher will not always be
able to restore trust between students, or between teacher and student. In extreme cases, a teacher's efforts to do so may aggravate the conflict instead of
leading to its resolve. When this happens, the teacher should immediately seek
out the assistance of a third party who is held in high esteem by both of the
conflicting parties.

Reinstating Communication

Whatever the strategy for resolving conflict, communication will be involved.
Conflict resolution demands that the parties communicate with each other.
Yet, some caution must be exercised in this regard. If communication is to be
effective, the conflicting parties must follow certain guidelines.

First, the parties should strive to make sure that their communication is nonthreatening. If, for example, one party's communication style elicits a defensive stance from the other party, conflict may escalate. Second, each party in the conflict should attempt to positively reinforce the other parties through communication. Negative communication behaviors will beget negative communication behaviors. Third, communication should focus on strategies designed to maximize the gains and minimize the losses of all parties involved. If one party communicates in such a way that s(he) still appears intent on winning, a similar pattern of communication is likely to be elicited from other parties. Finally, all of the parties should steer away from communicating about deep-seated interpersonal feelings. There will be plenty of time to explore such problems once the conflict (i.e., the immediate problem) is reduced to manageable terms.

Communication is essential to the resolution of conflict. But remember what we said in the very first chapter of this book. Communication is not some twentieth century panacea for each and every problem we confront. Communication, particularly with respect to conflict, is a "double-edged sword." While it is the primary medium by which conflict is resolved, it is also the primary medium by which conflict is introduced. Thus, communication must be carefully managed if it is to be an effective agent of conflict resolution.

Negotiation and Compromise

Many times students engaged in conflict will perceive that they have only one of two outs—winning or losing. As we have repeatedly emphasized, however, conflicts are not necessarily zero-sum games. One person doesn't necessarily have to lose, nor does one person necessarily have to win.

Assuming some measure of trust has been restored and communication has been reintroduced and managed, the students can be directed toward negotiation and compromise. Basically, negotiation involves a search for common goals, mutually acceptable alternatives, or strategies for sharing rewards. Once students have been induced to negotiate, they usually find that they both can win if they are willing to yield ever so slightly. They can negotiate to the degree to which they are willing to yield, moreover, in their search for some mutually acceptable compromise.

Once again, though, we need to stress that the process of negotiation and compromise must be carefully managed. If this process fails to produce early results, the students will be prone to readopt the attitude that they are involved in a win-lose situation. If this does, in fact, become the case, they may revert to threatening or hostile patterns of communicating.

Although we have considered each of the methods of conflict resolution separately, it would be to your advantage to use them in conjunction with one another. After all, conflict resolution is a process, and the process includes stages where each of the methods we have discussed may, or may not, prove effective.

CREATIVE DIFFERENCES IN THE CLASSROOM

We suggested at the outset of this chapter that conflict, when properly managed, can be a constructive social enterprise. What we mean by this is that, generally, disagreements over procedures, over substantive issues, or over interpersonal behaviors can be constructive forces within the classroom.

Motivation

When properly managed, for example, disagreements among students can be a potent motivational source. Nothing is quite as frustrating as total pacifism in the classroom. Most teachers expect their students to question, challenge, and explore the subject matter at hand. Of course, this is not always the case. There is no guarantee that what a teacher perceives to be stimulating or motivational will be similarly perceived by his or her students. A teacher may talk until "blue-in-the-face" and still fail to excite or motivate students.

If conflict can be introduced and controlled, however, students may feel compelled, as a function of the challenge, to express themselves—to articulate their opinions and feelings. As long as the teacher controls the climate by inducing his or her students to avoid threats or deception, such conflicts can be wholly beneficial. Furthermore, the teacher who is a skillful conflict manager can also control the level of intensity of the conflict and thereby thwart the possibility of the conflict becoming dysfunctional.

Creativity

Motivation and creativity are closely linked. For example, when a student's ideas are challenged by other students, the student may be motivated to reexamine and reevaluate the validity of his or her ideas. This process of re-examination and reevaluation may lead the student to develop even more creative ideas.

The difficulty here, of course, is that students sometimes attack rather than challenge a student's ideas. Under attack, the student is likely to become defensive and mount a counterattack. In such situations, creativity will be stifled, because the student will feel compelled to defend his or her ideas even if they are indefensible.

Thus, if conflict is to be used as a means for inducing creativity, the conflict must be managed and controlled. Legitimate challenges or differences of opinion should be encouraged. At the same time, the teacher must make sure that these challenges or differences of opinion do not take the form of threats. To reiterate, threatening communication behaviors will elicit defensiveness rather than induce creativity.

Understanding

In order to control or manage some phenomenon, a person must know something about that phenomenon. Too often conflicts become dysfunctional because the parties in conflict with each other know little about the nature of conflict, the sources of conflict, or the methods by which it can be resolved.

If conflict is altogether avoided in the classroom, students will never come to know how it can be constructively managed and reduced. On the other hand, if students are exposed to the nature and sources of conflict, as well as instructed in the management and resolution of conflict, they may learn to generalize this knowledge to situations outside the classroom. It seems to us, then, that controlled conflict in the classroom may facilitate the understanding of conflict, including both its dysfunctional and constructive side. Since conflict is an unavoidable dimension of all our lives, the advantages of such an understanding should be obvious.

Conflict in the classroom is inevitable. Simply because conflict is inevitable, however, does not necessarily mean that it has to be dysfunctional. In closing, we would like to point out that you, the teacher—not the student—have primary control over the sources of conflict in the classroom. Control and manage them well.

SELECTED REFERENCES

Bixenstine, V. E., N. Chamber, H. Potash, and B. V. Wilson. "Effects of Asymmetry in Payoff on Behavior in a Two-Person Non-Zero-Sum Game." *Journal of Conflict Resolution* 8, no. 2 (1964): 151–159.

Bonacich, P. "Norms and Cohesion as Adaptive Responses to Potential Conflict." *Sociometry* 35, no. 3 (1972): 357–375.

Borah, L. A., Jr. "The Effects of Threat in Bargaining: Critical and Experimental Analysis." *Journal of Abnormal and Social Psychology* 66, (1963): 37–44.

Boulding, K. *Conflict and Defense.* New York: Harper & Row, 1962.

Bovard, E. W. "The Effects of Social Stimuli on the Response to Stress." *Psychological Review* 66 (1959): 267–277.

Brown, J. S. "Principles of Interpersonal Conflict." *Journal of Conflict Resolution* 1, no. 2 (1957): 135–153.

Broxton, J. A. "A Test of Interpersonal Attraction Predictions Derived from Balance Theory." *Journal of Abnormal and Social Psychology* 63, (1963): 394–397.

Caplow, T. "A Theory of Coalitions in the Triad." *American Sociological Review* 21, (1956): 489–493.

Deutsch, M. "A Theory of Cooperation and Competition." *Human Relations* 2 (1949): 129–152.

Deutsch, M. "An Experimental Study of the Effects of Cooperation and Competition Upon Group Processes." *Human Relations* 2 (1949): 199–231.

Deutsch, M. "Conflicts: Productive and Destructive." *The Journal of Social Issues* 25 (1969): 7–41.

Deutsch, M. "Trust and Suspicion." *Journal of Conflict Resolution* 2 (1958): 265–279.

Deutsch, M., and R. M. Krauss. "Studies of Interpersonal Bargaining." *Journal of Conflict Resolution* 6 (1962): 52–76.

Ellis, J. G., and V. Sermat. "Motivational Determinants of Choice in Chicken and Prisoner's Dilemma." *Journal of Conflict Resolution* (1968): 374–380.

Festinger, L. *A Theory of Cognitive Dissonance.* Stanford: Stanford University Press, 1957.

Fisher, R. J. "Third Party Consultation: A Method for the Study and Resolution of Conflict." *Journal of Conflict Resolution* 16, no. 1 (1972): 67–94.

French, J. R., Jr., and D. H. Raven. "The Bases of Social Power." In *Studies in Social Power*, D. P. Cartwright, ed. Ann Arbor: University of Michigan Press, 1959, pp. 118–149.

Gallo, P. S., and C. G. McClintock. "Cooperative and Competitive Behavior in Mixed-Motive Games." *Journal of Conflict Resolution* 9, no. 1 (1965): 68–78.

Gibb, J. R. "Defensive Communication." *Journal of Communication* 2 (1961): 141–148.

Greseluk, J., and H. H. Kelly. "Conflict Between Individual and Common Interest in a Personal Relationship." *Journal of Personality and Social Psychology* 21, no. 2 (1972): 190–197.

Grinker, R., and J. Spiegal. *Men under Stress.* Philadelphia: Blakiston, 1945.

Heider, F. "Attitudes and Cognitive Organization." *Journal of Psychology* 21 (1946): 107–112.

Heider, F. *The Psychology of Interpersonal Relations.* New York: Wiley, 1958.

Jandt, F. E. *Conflict Resolution through Communication.* New York: Harper & Row, 1973.

Janis, I. L. "Decisional Conflict: A Theoretical Analysis." *Journal of Conflict Resolution* 3 (1959): 6–27.

Janis, I. L., and D. Katz. "The Reduction of Intergroup Hostility: Research Problems and Hypotheses." *Journal of Conflict Resolution* 3, no. 1 (1959): 85–100.

Kahn, R. L., and E. Boulding, eds. *Powers and Conflict in Organizations.* New York: Basic Books, 1964.

Kee, H. W., and R. F. Knox. "Conceptual and Methodological Considerations in the Study of Trust and Suspicion." *Journal of Conflict Resolution* 14, no. 3 (1970): 357–366.

Krauss, R., and M. Deutsch. "Communication in Interpersonal Bargaining." *Journal of Personality and Social Psychology* 4 (1966): 572–577.

Levinger, G. "Kurt Lewin's Approach to Conflict and Its Resolution: A Review with Some Extensions." *Journal of Conflict Resolution* 1, no. 4 (1957): 329–339.

Lewin, K. *Resolving Social Conflict.* New York: Harper & Row, 1948.

Loomis, J. L. "Communication, the Development of Trust and Cooperative Behavior." *Human Relations* 12 (1959): 305–315.

Mazur, A. "A Nonrational Approach to Theories of Conflict and Coalitions." *Journal of Conflict Resolution* 12, no. 2 (1968): 196–205.

Miller, G. R., and H. W. Simons, eds. *Perspectives on Communication in Social Conflict*. Englewood Cliffs, N. J.: Prentice-Hall, 1974.

Newcomb, T. M. "An Approach to the Study of Communicative Acts." *Psychological Review* 60 (1953): 393–404.

Pepitone, A., and R. Kleiner. "The Effects of Threat and Frustration on Group Cohesiveness." *Journal of Abnormal and Social Psychology* 54 (1957): 192–199.

Phillips, B. R., and M. V. DeVault. "Evaluation of Research on Cooperation and Competition." *Psychological* 3 (1957): 389–392.

Phipps, T. E., Jr. "Resolving Hopeless Conflicts." *Journal of Conflict Resolution* 5, no. 3 (1961): 274–278.

Pruitt, D. G. "Indirect Communication and the Search for Agreement in Negotiation." *Journal of Applied Social Psychology* (1971): 205–239.

Rapoport, A. *Fights, Games, and Debates*. Ann Arbor: University of Michigan Press, 1960.

Sarnoff, I., and P. G. Zimbardo. "Anxiety, Fear, and Social Affiliation." *Journal of Abnormal and Social Psychology* 62 (1961): 356–363.

Schelling, T. C. *The Strategy of Conflict*. Cambridge, Mass.: Harvard University Press, 1960.

Sherif, M. *In Common Predicament: Social Psychology of Intergroup Conflict and Cooperation*. Boston: Houghton-Mifflin, 1966.

Sherif, M. "Supraordinate Goals in the Reduction of Intergroup Conflict." *American Journal of Sociology* 58 (1958): 349–356.

Sherif, M., O. J. Harvey, B. J. White, W. R. Hood, and C. W. Sherif. *Intergroup Conflict and Cooperation: The Robbers Cave Experiment*. Norman: University of Oklahoma Press, 1961.

Solomon, L. "The Influence of Some Types of Power Relationships and Game Strategies on the Development of Interpersonal Trust." *Journal of Abnormal and Social Psychology* 61 (1960): 223–230.

Summers, D. A. "Conflict, Compromise, and Belief Change in a Decision-Making Task." *Journal of Conflict Resolution* (1968): 215–221.

Stagner, R. *The Dimension of Human Conflict*. Detroit: Wayne State University Press, 1967.

Tedeschi, J. T., J. Powell, S. Lindskold and J. P. Galragan. "The Patterning of 'Honored' Promises and Sex Differences in Social Conflicts." *Journal of Social Psychology* 78 (1969): 297–298.

Tedeschi, J. T., B. R. Schlenker, and T. V. Bonoma. *Conflict, Power, and Games*. Chicago: Aldine, 1973.

Thibaut, J. W., and J. Coules. "The Role of Communication in the Reduction of Interpersonal Hostility." *Journal of Abnormal and Social Psychology* 47 (1952): 770–777.

By Way of Summary . . .

You have now come to the end of *our* exploration of the relationship between communication and learning. We hope, of course, that this will not be the end of *yours*. We would like to believe that throughout the remainder of your professional career, you will continually adapt and modify your communication behavior to the learning needs of your students. In fact, we encourage you to send us examples of your uses of the variables discussed in this book. Let us know what you were trying to do, what you did, and what learning outcomes you accomplished.

Once again, let us stress that effective communication is the single most important prerequisite to effective learning. The better you are able to manipulate the communication process, the better you will be in helping students to achieve to their maximum potential. And this is what makes teaching such a rewarding and *important* profession. No other profession affects so many lives in so many ways. The ways in which you communicate with students not only helps them to develop specific concepts about classroom content, it also helps to shape their attitudes, beliefs, and values about the "real world" and the people in it. You create attitudes in them about politics and religion, social groups and individuals. You provide them with a model of how to get along with a wide variety of people. And, perhaps most important of all, you help to shape their values about learning and intellectual development. Thus, even though instructional aids and media teaching devices are useful, there is no substitute for the human contact you provide through communication. Because we believe this so strongly, we have written this book. We congratulate you for your choice of a career. Whether you are a "new boot" or an "old hand," we wish you an exciting and rewarding professional life and hope that we have contributed to your understanding of the communication process.

ndex

AUTHOR INDEX